THE CIVILIAN IN WAR

EXETER STUDIES IN HISTORY
General Editor: Jonathan Barry

Other titles in this series include:

THE CIVILIAN IN WAR

The Home Front in Europe, Japan and the USA
in World War II

Edited by

JEREMY NOAKES

Exeter Studies in History No. 32
University of Exeter Press

First Published in 1992 by
University of Exeter Press
Reed Hall
Streatham Drive
Exeter EX4 4QR
UK

British Library Cataloguing in Publication Data

A catalogue record of this book is available from the British Library

ISBN 0 85989 357 X

Typeset in Times by Nigel Code, University of Exeter
Printed in the UK by BPCC Wheatons, Exeter

Contents

Contributors

Dr. Tobias Abse is a Lecturer in Modern European History at the University of Leeds and the author of *Sovversivi e fascisti a Livorno: Lotta politica e sociale (1918-1922)* (Milan, 1991). He is currently engaged on a history of the Italian Communist Party between 1943 and 1991.

Hilary Footitt is Head of Languages at the Polytechnic of Central London. With John Simmonds she has published *France 1943-45* (Leicester, 1988) in the 'Politics of Liberation' series published by Leicester University Press. She is currently working on a political history of post-war France.

Joanna Hanson completed her PhD at the School of Slavonic and East European Studies, University of London. She is the author of *The Civilian Population and the Warsaw Uprising of 1944* (1982). At present she is preparing a study of the history of Poland between 1944 and 1947 and writing on current Polish problems.

Mark Harrison is Senior Lecturer in Economics at the University of Warwick. He is author of *Soviet Planning in Peace and War, 1938-1945* (Cambridge, 1985) and (with John Barber) *The Soviet Home Front 1941-1945: A Social and Economic History of the USSR in World War II* (Harlow, 1991). He is currently engaged in research on Soviet wartime national accounts and defence burdens

Bob Moore is Senior Lecturer in European and International History at Bristol Polytechnic. His publications include *Refugees from Nazi Germany in the Netherlands, 1933-1940* (1986) and he is currently preparing a book on the persecution of the Jews in the Netherlands during the Second World War.

Ian Nish was in Japan as an interpreter with the British Commonwealth Occupation Forces (BCOF) in the immediate post-war years. He has taught at the University of Sydney and (since 1962) at the London School of Economics, becoming professor of international history there in 1980. He has written a number of works, mainly in the field of Japan's foreign relations, most recently *The Origins of the Russo-Japanese War* (London, 1985)

Jeremy Noakes is Professor of History at Exeter University. He is the author of *The Nazi Party in Lower Saxony 1921-1933* (1971), (with Geoffrey Pridham) *Nazism 1919-1945* 3 vols (Exeter, 1983-1989) and a number of articles on various aspects of Nazi Germany. He is currently completing the fourth and final volume of *Nazism 1919-1945* on the German Home Front in World War II.

John Simmonds is Principal Lecturer in European History at Anglia Polytechnic. With Hilary Footitt he has published *France 1943-45* (Leicester, 1988) in the 'Politics of Liberation' series published by Leicester University Press and articles on the French Communist Party in the war and post-war period. He is currently working on a political history of post-war France.

Andrew Thorpe is Lecturer in History at Exeter University. He has published *The British General Election of 1931* (Oxford, 1991), *Britain in the 1930s* (Oxford, 1992) and edited *The Failure of Political Extremism in Inter-War Britain* (Exeter, 1991) in the Exeter Studies in History series. He is currently working on a Longman Handbook, *Britain in the Era of the World Wars*.

Neil Wynn is Principal Lecturer and Head of History at the Polytechnic of Wales. Formerly editor of the British Association for American Studies' *Newsletter*, he has published articles and reviews on twentieth-century American history, black American history, and war and social change. He is the author of *The Afro-American and the Second World War (1976)* and *From Progressivism to Prosperity* (1986) and co-editor of *America's Century: perspectives on twentieth-century America* (1991).

1

Introduction

This book is based on a series of lectures held at the University of Exeter in the Michaelmas term of 1989 to mark the fiftieth anniversary of the outbreak of the Second World War. The theme of the series was 'The Civilian in War: the Home Front in World War II' and the intention was to bring the results of recent research to a wider audience. The countries covered were chosen to reflect the broad range of experience undergone by the civilian populations during the war as citizens either of belligerent or occupied states or – in the case of France and Italy – both in succession. The Soviet Union was simultaneously a belligerent and an occupied power and, in this case, it was decided to concentrate on the issues raised by her conduct of the war rather than by the German occupation.

The main current focus of research on the Second World War is the question of how far the war influenced social change in the various countries which were affected by it. This is clearly a crucial issue and one which has already generated much fruitful research and controversy.[1] However, the focus of these lectures was intended to be rather different. First, as far as the major belligerents were concerned, the aim was to examine how successful they were at mobilising the civilian population for the war effort at home and what effects this process of mobilisation had on the civilian population. Above all, how far and in what ways were they able to sustain the morale of the civilian population under the unprecedented pressures generated by the Second World War ?

In this connection, the experience of the First World War as the first 'total war' is particularly illuminating. By 1916, the size of the military forces committed to battle and their enormous consumption of *matériel* forced the belligerent states to impose unprecedented controls over their economies and societies in order to mobilise the necessary resources. However, some of the governments failed to carry their populations with them and the last two years of the war saw increasing social unrest as a number of the belligerent states buckled under the strain of war. The Tsarist regime in Russia was overthrown by revolution in February 1917, while its successor, the Provisional Government, failed to consolidate its power and was replaced by the Bolshevik dictatorship in October. Historians are unanimous on the crucial role played by the war in the Russian revolutions of 1917, even though they may disagree about the relative significance of that role. Germany was wracked by strike action in 1917 and, above all, in January 1918, while impending defeat on the battlefield in the early autumn of 1918 was immediately followed by a revolution which overthrew the Second Reich. Austria-Hungary was riven by ethnic tensions which had been exacerbated rather than healed by the war and which led to the disintegration of the Habsburg empire in the process of defeat. Even the western democracies, France and Britain, suffered severe social stresses which tested their polities and societies to the limit.

Yet the Second World War involved the civilian populations of the belligerent powers to an even greater extent than had the first. This is reflected in the casualty figures. Whereas in the First World War the vast bulk of the casualties were suffered by the military, in the Second World War the position was reversed. However, the Second World War did not provoke revolution and civil unrest was minimal in all the countries involved. Why was this ?

The experience of the First World War certainly formed an important part of the background planning of the Second. The 1920s and 1930s had seen the publication of an extensive literature on 'total war', drawing lessons from the experience of the First World War on the need for the effective mobilization of national resources and to sustain popular support for war. This climate of opinion was reinforced by the fact that both the German and the British governments exaggerated the role of social unrest in Germany's defeat in 1918. The 'stab in the back ' myth was believed by both sides. All this contributed towards ensuring that the morale of the civilian population was given a much higher priority in the Second World War than it had received in the First.

What then do the contributions in this volume tell us about the relative success of the various belligerents in coping with the challenge which the war posed for their societies both in terms of mobilising their civilian populations for war and at the same time sustaining their morale in the process ?

All the belligerent states were faced with the problem of the finite human resources available to them and the difficulty of competing demands from the armed forces on the one hand and the economy on the other and the need to achieve a balance between the two. As Mark Harrison shows, this problem was particularly acute in the Soviet Union where the initial concentration on the requirements of the armed forces both in terms of military recruitment and the defence industries threatened a collapse in the civilian economy during 1942. However, all the states succeeded in increasing employment.[2] Some of this increase came from demographic growth in the numbers coming on to the labour market. In the United States, for example, an average of 900,000 people per year joined the labour market between 1939 and 1944. In the United Kingdom half a million extra people came on to the labour market between 1939 and 1943. However, the main sources of increase were the absorption of the pre-war unemployed, the employment of women, the old, the young, and foreigners.

Whereas Germany and the Soviet Union had entered the war with full employment, indeed, in the case of Germany with serious labour shortages in key areas such as agriculture, Britain and the United States benefitted from the fact that their economies had been operating below maximum capacity during the pre-war period and, therefore, there was spare labour available to be mobilised for the war effort. By 1943, unemployment in the United States had been reduced by 7.4 million since 1939 and in Britain by 1.2 million since 1940. Some additional labour supplies could be mobilised from the employment of younger and older people. In Russia, for example, by 1942 those under 18 formed 15 per cent and those over 50 twelve per cent of the labour force compared with 6 and 9 per cent respectively in 1939. In Britain, it has been estimated that up to one million people may have worked beyond their retirement age.

It was, however, women who provided the most obvious extra source of labour. In Britain women who had not hitherto been employed or had been housewives formed 80 per cent of the total addition to the work force between 1939 and 1943. The American female labour force increased by 32 per cent from 1941 to 1945 and in 1944 they formed 35.4 per cent of the civilian labour force.[3] In the Soviet Union women made up 38 per cent of the labour force in 1940 and 53 per cent in 1942.[4] In Italy, as Dr. Abse shows, the Fascist regime was obliged to repeal legislation designed to exclude women from the labour market and they became of vital importance not only to the industrial but above all to the agricultural sector. In Germany the significance of female labour has tended to be underestimated because of a failure to make allowances for the numbers of non-waged women employed in family enterprises such as farms and small businesses.[5] Moreover, by 1944, women made up 41 per cent of the civilian labour force, including foreign workers, and 51.1 per cent of the German civilian labour force so there can be no question of German women not playing a major role in the war effort as labour, quite apart from their contribution as housewives and parents bearing the brunt of the civilian burdens of war. Nevertheless, as I suggest in my contribution, there does appear to have been a relative failure to mobilize German women into the directly war-related industries by comparison with most of the other main belligerents. A crucial factor enabling the German authorities to avoid having to conscript women into war industries – at least until a late stage – was the availability of foreign labour.

Foreign labour was a key resource for two of the main belligerents – Germany and Japan. In the case of Germany foreign workers had become indispensable to her war effort by 1942 at the latest when she employed 4.1 million, forming 11.7 per cent of her work force.[6] By 1944, the number had increased to 7.1 million, forming 19.7 per cent of the work force and 29.3 per cent of that employed in industry. By July 1945 Japan was employing 1.4 million Koreans.[7]

Although the labour shortage varied from state to state, with Britain suffering most and the United States least acutely, all states suffered from shortages of labour in certain spheres, of certain kinds (skilled), and at certain junctures. However, the opportunities for workers to exploit these shortages by insisting upon improvements in wages and working conditions was limited not simply by the increased coercive powers of governments as a result of the war but also by the self-discipline of the workers themselves who were aware of the danger of undermining the war effort. Labour relations within the two democracies of Britain and the United States maintained a delicate balance. Strikes were banned in both countries and yet there were more strikes during the war than in the 1930s. Governments, however, proceeded cautiously in pursuing strikers. In Britain labour was controlled by the Secretary of the Transport and General Workers Union, Ernest Bevin, as Minister of Labour, while in the United States the government lent on employers to fulfill the obligations contained in the labour legislation of the 1930s by threatening to withhold war contracts if they failed to do so.

Among the non-democratic belligerent powers, governments were less squeamish about enforcing labour discipline. However, even here wages and earnings rose significantly above pre-war levels with the single exception of Germany. And in Germany this was compensated for by the fact that prices were held down more effectively than anywhere else. Taking 1936 as 100, the wholesale prices in the United States in 1944 were 129, the retail prices 127; in Japan 325 and 390; in Britain 176 and 137; and in Germany 113 and 113.[8] Moreover, governments could also to some extent counteract the inflationary tendencies inherent in wage increases by steering consumption through holding down prices on rationed goods while allowing the prices of unrationed goods to rise - in Britain, for example, alcohol and tobacco – or else, as in Germany, by encouraging savings schemes (e.g. the so-called 'iron savings scheme'). The figures for civilian consumption reflect the extent of the sacrifices made by the populations of the various belligerent powers. Compared with the pre-war period, civilian consumption went up 16 per cent in the United States, but went down by 16 per cent in Britain, by 24 per cent in Germany, and by 31 per cent in Japan.[9]

The issue of civilian consumption raises the question of morale. How far was morale influenced or even determined by material factors – the supply of consumer goods and, above all, foodstuffs? Historians are agreed that the combination of inflation and food shortages played a crucial role in the deterioration of Russian and German morale during the First World War which culminated in revolution. And this fact had not been lost on those involved in organising the home front in the Second World War. For example, plans for rationing food and other commodities had already been drawn up and were implemented in Germany at the outbreak of war. Systems of rationing were introduced in the other states during the first phase of the war.

The evidence from the contributions to this volume suggests that material factors did indeed have a significant impact on morale. We have seen that wages increased in all the belligerent states with the exception of Germany during the second half of the war. But just as, or even more important, was the availability of goods. The Security Service (SD) reports on German popular opinion show the discontent aroused by shortages of fuel and certain commodities such as shoes in the winter of 1939-40 and, above all, the major impact made by the cut in food rations in the spring of 1942. Mark Harrison points out that in the Soviet Union 'giving extra rations to war workers was a powerful incentive to participate and perform reliably' and the same was true of German miners.[10] Andrew Thorpe shows how the British government rejected proposals for a limited (basal) diet and emphasized the importance for morale of a more varied diet and of non-essentials such as beer and tobacco. By contrast, the inadequacy of food supplies in Italy in 1942, combined with the extensive black market, almost certainly contributed to the outbreak of mass strikes in March 1943 in rather the same way as the food shortages and discontent over the unfairness of the distribution of the burdens of war had resulted in the outbreak of strikes in Germany in 1917 and January 1918.

Nevertheless, as Dr. Harrison points out, the experience of Leningrad, whose citizens continued to resist the German siege despite over a year of virtual starvation, shows that there was not an invariable direct link between food supplies and morale. It is also significant that in Germany complaints about shortages were much more vigorous in the winter of 1939-40 than they were in 1943, when the population had much more to worry about as a result of bombing and the deteriorating military situation.

What other factors influenced morale? In the first place, the evidence for both Britain and Germany suggests that, as one would expect, morale tended to respond to the course of the war but not always in the most obvious way. Thus, the high point of German morale came in June 1940 after the surprisingly easy defeat of Germany's old enemy, France, although the mood of euphoria owed as much or more to the belief that the war would soon be over as to the victory itself. Nevertheless, morale was not necessarily related to military success or failure. German morale was lower in the early summer of 1943 than it was in the early summer of 1944, although her military situation had markedly deteriorated in the meantime.[11] Similarly, as Dr. Thorpe shows, the lowest point in British morale came during the phoney war of 1939-40 before any significant military action had taken place. This period also saw the lowest point in German morale before the reverse in front of Moscow in December 1941. It was a period when nothing seemed to be happening and people's fear of the unknown took the form of a general irritability. In contrast, by the summer of 1940, when Britain's fortunes were apparently at their lowest, morale had greatly improved. The situation was clear cut: the people faced a challenge and knew what was expected of them.

The impact of propaganda is one of the most difficult aspects of morale to assess. Propaganda and indoctrination were most pervasive in the totalitarian states. In Japan, for example, according to Professor Nish, 'morale was kept up by blatant suppression of the truth'. But, even in the democracies governments exercised extensive control over the media. There does seem to have been widespread scepticism about official propaganda. The demand in Britain for 'less exhortation and more news', noted by Dr. Thorpe, was echoed in Germany. There, as the official media became discredited, so people tended to rely more on alternative channels of information such as relatives home on leave from the front. Nevertheless, it would be dangerous to dismiss the role of propaganda in sustaining morale altogether. Marlies Steinert, for example, in her very thorough study of the development of German popular opinion between 1939 and 1945 attributes some at least of the short-term improvement in German morale between 1943 and 1944 to the regime's propaganda efforts, notably the *Vergeltung* myth promising the deployment of ultimate weapons of revenge, although other factors were also at work.[12]

Where propaganda failed to convince, the totalitarian regimes resorted to terror. Indeed, in Nazi Germany the use of terror increased during the course of the war in proportion to the failure of other mechanisms for sustaining morale. But Germany was not alone. The contributions on Japan and the Soviet Union indicate the importance of harsh repressive measures in keeping their populations in line. Although the First World War also saw the repression of opposition - the imprisonment of Karl Liebknecht and Rosa Luxemburg in Germany and the enforced exile of Lenin from Russia are merely the most obvious examples - nevertheless the actions of Nazi Germany and the Soviet Union between 1939 and 1945 were on a difficult plane altogether. How far they contributed to sustaining the war effort is extremely difficult to assess. However, the reports of popular opinion in Nazi Germany in the winter of 1943 suggest that the growing use of terror at that time helped to stop an increasingly overt wave of criticism of the government which was threatening to get out of hand.[13] In Britain and the United States individuals such as Oswald Mosley, whose previous record suggested that they might be a threat, were imprisoned and whole groups such as German immigrants or Japanese Americans whose loyalty appeared suspect were interned, but no attempt was made to use terror systematically.

If terror represented a negative element in sustaining morale by preventing the emergence and organisation of opposition, leadership was an important positive force. Again, its relative importance is difficult to assess. But it is surely significant that every belligerent state saw the emergence of a war leader whose role gained an added dimension by comparison with peacetime. This was, in part of course, the result of the exigencies of war leadership which required a greater concentration of power, but it also represented a qualitatively different relationship between the population and its leader under the stresses of war. In other words, in a period of extreme crisis people wanted to put their trust in a leader to a greater extent than in peacetime. There was of course a limit to the extent that a leader's prestige could survive setbacks. Thus, Hitler's prestige was on the wane from the beginning of 1943 and by the end of 1944 disillusionment with the Führer was widespread. As Dr. Abse shows, the same process occurred somewhat earlier in the case of Mussolini. But it is clear from the various reports on German popular opinion how important belief in Hitler had been in sustaining morale for much of the war.[14] Andrew Thorpe shows that *mutatis mutandis* the same was true of Churchill in Britain.

Morale was also inevitably affected by the degree to which there was a sense of social solidarity. War does not inevitably create social solidarity; indeed, the First World War had demonstrated just how socially divisive it could be. Tensions can develop through an accentuation of 'in-group' feelings with the result that minorities are exposed to increased hostility and discrimination. This occurred in the United States where, as Neil Wynn shows, Japanese Americans and Blacks suffered from this phenomenon, but also in the Soviet Union where the regime deported ethnic minorities such as the Crimean Tartars and the Volga Germans for alleged disloyalty. Nazi Germany also exploited this psychological mechanism in its policy towards the Jews and its attempt to establish a *Herrenmensch-Untermensch* relationship between the German population and foreign workers in Germany.

Social tension can also be created by the disruptive effects of war. The contributions on Germany, Britain, and the United States show how both the evacuation of
large numbers of city dwellers to the countryside to avoid, or as a result of, the
effects of bombing, and the migration of large numbers of rural workers to the cities
or new towns created tensions between the newcomers and the indigenous inhabitants as a result of differences in manners and *mores*. In Italy too the war resulted
in a growing gap between city and country in this case as a result of conflicts over
food supply.

Finally, social tensions can develop from a sense that the burdens of war are being
distributed unfairly. This was the case in Germany and Russia between 1914 and
1918, for example. Partly, at least, as a result of this experience, governments were
particularly sensitive to this problem during the Second World War. While the war
by no means removed all social privileges and, in the case of Germany, created new
ones for those who staffed the various bureaucracies running the Nazi empire,
nevertheless, the existence of reasonably efficient rationing and the introduction of
conscription, both military and civil, helped to ensure that the burdens of war were
more evenly spread than ever before. Similarly, the effects of bombing, being
socially indiscriminate, could help to generate a sense of community. As Dr. Abse
shows, however, this was not invariably the case. For, whereas in Britain and
Germany the adverse effects on morale of bombing tended to be localised and
temporary, in Italy bombing had a much more demoralising effect. Here the obvious
incompetence of the regime at dealing with its effects compounded existing
resentment over its failure to distribute the burdens of war equitably.

How far then was patriotism a factor in sustaining morale ? This too is a difficult
issue to assess and much depends on the political traditions of the country concerned. Thus, in the case of Italy Dr. Abse shows that Fascist attempts to generate
a militant Italian nationalism had gone only skin deep and proved insufficient to
counteract the provincialism which had been the bane of Italian nationalists since
the Risorgimento. By contrast, Communist attempts to eliminate all traces of
Russian nationalism fortunately proved to have been abortive enabling the regime
to exploit national feelings by, for example, making significant concessions to the
Army and the Russian Orthodox Church. While admitting that 'the whole subject
of patriotism and collaboration has remained a large blank space in Soviet historiography', Mark Harrison concludes that 'whatever its determinants and character
Soviet national feeling was probably a big factor in the civilian war effort.' The
subject is of course complicated by the ethnic diversity of the Soviet Union. Some
of the nationalities of the Soviet Union – initially at any rate – saw their national
interest best served by collaboration with the Germans. The fact that the Nazi

leadership rejected the policy proposed by Alfred Rosenberg of favouring some ethnic groups at the expense of the Great Russians and insisted on treating all inhabitants of the Soviet Union as 'sub-human' certainly facilitated the Soviet war effort.[15]

Indeed, arguably, the most important factor determining morale was what was envisaged as the alternative to fighting. Thus what inspired the citizens of Britain in the summer of 1940 and of Leningrad between the autumn of 1941 and the winter of 1942-3 was the realization that Nazi Germany threatened to destroy their whole way of life and quite possibly their physical existence. Equally, what kept the Germans fighting until May 1945 was the realization that defeat would mean the revenge of the Allies and in particular of the 'Bolsheviks' for German actions committed over the previous five and a half years, a terrifying prospect indeed. As the Hamburg Public Prosecutor reported on 31 January 1944: 'People are becoming increasingly aware that a surrender would not bring relief but rather create a situation compared with which the worst possible terror attacks (i.e. bombing) would only represent temporary bagatelles. Everybody is gradually becoming aware that, in the event of a German defeat, even if individuals managed to survive, Germany would face endless misery and the nation would lose its identity.'[16]

The second part of this collection focuses on states which were occupied by Nazi Germany. Nazi plans for a New Order in Europe envisaged a hierarchy of nations ranging from those at the top such as the Netherlands and Norway which were considered to be racially on a par with the Germans and suitable for future absorption into the Greater German Reich, through nations such as France which were considered civilized but racially inferior to Germany, to the Slav nations which were considered to be more or less sub-human, although there was also a hierarchy within the Slavs, with the Poles and Russians at the bottom.[17] This hierarchy was reflected in the treatment of the various territories – for example, in graduated food rations and in the varying levels of education that were permitted. However, as the war progressed and the need to exploit the territories for the German war effort increased so the difference in treatment between the various territories diminished somewhat without, however, ever disappearing. For one Oradour-sur-Glane thousands of Russian and Polish villages were destroyed. The contributions in this volume cover examples of the three different categories of occupied territory and aim to assess the impact of German occupation on the civilian population.

However, before looking at examples of these categories there is the case of Italy to consider. Italy was unique in that having been a belligerent it then suffered two distinct occupations - by the Allies in the south and by the Germans in the north. Indeed, according to Harold Macmillan, who was Allied High Commissioner in southern Italy in 1944, 'Italians had the dual experience of being occupied by the Germans and liberated by the Allies... It was difficult to say which of the two processes was the more painful or unsettling.'[18] While clearly an exaggeration, this statement does draw attention to the severe hardship undergone by the civilian population in the South during 1943-5 as a result of the incompetence, indifference and, in some cases, malevolence of the occupying forces. The motto of official policy was 'keep existing administration and temper defascistization with discretion'.[19] The result was a restoration of the pre-fascist regime in the south with all the notorious corruption and social injustice traditionally associated with Southern notable-type politics. As Dr. Abse points out, most of the 'latter day anti-Facistis' in Sicily brought in to replace purged Fascists 'were in reality mafiosi with good links with the Italian-Americans who had arrived in quantity in the American army'.

In the north Mussolini's Republic of Salo had virtually no room for independent initiative, while the German occupation authorities were riven by the rivalries between the various agencies which were so typical of the Nazi regime as a whole. Significantly, the Wehrmacht was generally associated with the most harsh approach, a point which is in line with recent research on the extent of the Wehrmacht's involvement in the atrocities carried out in the Soviet Union. As far as the German occupation was concerned, Italy plunged almost overnight from the privileged status of an ally to the position of a despised renegade. In fact, the official status of ally had barely concealed the increasing contempt in which the Italians were held by the German people in general and the authorities in particular. As a result, Italy's defection unleashed a wave of resentment which reduced the Italians to a level of treatment within the Nazi hierarchy of nations comparable to that of the Poles and the Russians. This feeling contributed to fuel a repression which was also grounded in the exigencies of war and the response to partisan activity.

It was these harsh policies of conscription and terror which, as in other parts of Europe, were primarily responsible for provoking mass resistance which was then organized by Communist and other intellectuals. The armed resistance of the peasants in the mountains and the mass strikes in the cities of northern and central Italy during 1944 were the most striking manifestation of resistance to Nazi occupation in the whole of western Europe. Dr. Abse draws particular attention to the often neglected role of women in the Resistance and to an often underestimated form of Resistance, namely the extent to which Italian peasants risked their lives in sheltering escaped Allied prisoners. As far as the nature of Italian resistance was concerned, Dr. Abse provides a judicious assessment of the controversy over whether the violent events between September 1943 and April 1945 constituted a war of national liberation or a civil war, concluding that they contained elements of both as well as of a class war.

In his study of the Netherlands, which came near the top of the Nazi hierarchy of occupied nations, Dr. Moore shows the great variety of experiences and conditions which existed under German occupation and the significant impact which it had on the Dutch social structure. Despite the fact that the Netherlands were one of the most ideologically favoured occupied territories and that the occupation began 'gently', ideological, economic, and military imperatives resulted in increasing pressures on the Dutch population. These pressures were met with growing resistance which in turn produced a German response in a vicious cycle of resistance and repression. The attempts by the Germans to encourage collaboration met with very limited success and the Dutch Fascists in the NSB and other pro-Nazi organizations were despised by the rest of the population. The effects of occupation forced many Dutch people to become 'a nation of law breakers' obliged to steal and use the black market to survive. And, whereas the main effect of the occupation between 1940 and 1942 had been to reinforce the Dutch traditions of family and communal life, as communications became restricted so, after 1942, the effect of the conscription of large numbers of males to work in Germany, many of whom went undeground to avoid the draft, was to reverse this process. The worst effects of the occupation were felt in the final months when food shortages became so acute, particularly in the west of the country, that there was virtual starvation.

In France the result of the German occupation was division – not only between the supporters of Vichy and the Resistance but even within the Resistance itself. The roots of these divisions lay deep in French history and more specifically in the pre-war decade. However, in their contribution, John Simmonds and Hilary Footit show that, whatever their differences on other issues, the members of the various Resistance groups shared with each other and indeed to some extent with Vichy itself a common perspective on the role of women. Despite the crucial part played by women in the Resistance who formed 'the ground floor of the underground', the Resistance's ideas on their role in the home front were dominated by female stereotypes and tended to reinforce or sustain those roles. Even the Left, while happy to admire the active front-line role played by women in the Soviet Union, were not prepared to envisage women playing an equivalent part in France. The Resistance was unified in seeing women's role as primarily 'the guardian of the children and menfolk in the home, whereas in reality there was an equality of effort by men and women in the Resistance'.

Finally, Poland is perhaps the most interesting case since there the Nazis set about destroying a whole society. Joanna Hanson shows in graphic detail what this meant in practice for Polish citizens. However, she also deals with a topic which has often been neglected in the past, namely the Soviet occupation of eastern Poland between September 1939 and June 1941, showing that in some respects it was as ruthless and barbaric as that of the Nazis. In Poland morale was sustained by a strong sense of Polish national identity and a history of resistance against oppression. In the face of the destruction of their state and civil society the Poles responded by creating an underground state and an underground society. However, as in France, the Resistance movement reflected the previous divisions within pre-war Polish society which had been only temporarily overlaid by the Sanacja regime.[20]

The case of Poland is a remarkable tribute to the resilience of the human spirit under conditions of extreme adversity. However, resistance was bolstered by material and above all moral support from outside, from the Polish government in exile, and by the growing belief in the eventual defeat of Germany. Moreover, the costs were very high. For the impact on Poles of being forced in effect to become outlaws in their own land in order physically to survive, let alone sustain a resistance movement, weakened the whole moral order. Paradoxically, in order to oppose the immoral German occupation they were obliged to abandon many of the norms of a civil society: to lie, to steal, to work slowly and poorly. Corruption as a strategy of survival or even resistance was to have unfortunate repercussions for post-war Poland. Moreover, it would be hazardous to draw too optimistic conclusions from the Polish experience since the Nazi experiment in destruction was, mercifully, first modified by the exigencies of war and then cut short by defeat.

NOTES

1. For further references see the collection of articles edited by Arthur Marwick, *Total War and Social Change* (London, 1988) and the literature referred to in it.
2. For the following see A.S. Milward, *War, Economy and Society 1939-1945* (London, 1977), passim.
3. Cf. L. Rupp, *Mobilizing Women for War. German and American Propaganda 1939-1945* (Princeton, New Jersey, 1978), pp. 84ff.
4. Cf. Milward (above, note 2), p. 220.
5. Cf. R.Overy, 'Blitzkriegwirtschaft ? Finanzpolitik, Lebensstandard und Arbeitseinsatz in Deutschland 1939-1942' in *Vierteljahrshefte für Zeitgeschichte* 1988, pp. 425ff.
6. Cf. Milward (above, note 2), p. 223.

7. Cf. J.B. Cohen, *Japan's Economy in War and Reconstruction* (Minneapolis, 1949), p. 301.
8. Ibid., p. 97.
9. Ibid., pp. 354, 416.
10. Cf. W. Werner, *Bleib übrig! Deutsche Arbeiter in der nationalsozialistischen Kriegswirtschaft* (Düsseldorf 1983) p. 245.
11. Cf. M. Steinert, *Hitlers Krieg und die Deutschen* (Düsseldorf and Vienna, 1970), pp. 424, 447.
12. Ibid., pp. 420, 424.
13. Ibid., p. 424.
14. I. Kershaw, *The 'Hitler Myth'. Image and Reality in the Third Reich* (Oxford 1987), p. 171.
15. Cf. A. Dallin, *German Rule in Russia 1941-1945. A Study of Occupation Policies* (Boulder, Colorado, 1981), pp. 46ff.
16. Steinert (above, note 11), p. 436.
17. Cf. W. Dlugoborski, 'Faschismus, Besatzung und sozialer Wandel. Fragestellung und Typologie' in W. Dlugoborski (ed.), *Zweiter Weltkrieg und sozialer Wandel. Achsenmächte und besetzte Länder* (Göttingen, 1981), pp. 23ff.
18. Quoted in P. Ginsborg, *A History of Contemporary Italy. Society and Politics 1943-1988* (London, 1990), p. 38.
19. Ibid., p. 36.
20. J.T. Gross, *Polish Society under German Occupation* (Princeton, New Jersey, 1979), p. 304.

2

BRITAIN

Andrew Thorpe

On 12 September 1940 the M.P. and diarist Harold Nicolson dined on grouse with Guy Burgess at the Reform Club in London. As he walked home afterwards, he was caught in an air raid. Terrified, he sheltered in a shop doorway, where he found a drunken prostitute, who asked him to take care of her because she was frightened. Nicolson, needless to say, did not enjoy the challenge and was not eager to repeat it. Only the Second World War could have thrown the upper-class, homosexual man of letters and the earthy streetwalker together in this way, for both were civilians in a conflict which involved non-combatants to a hitherto unprecedented degree.[1]

Few if any historical events have excited so much research and debate as the origins, course and consequences of the Second World War, and for none of the combatants has this been more true than Britain. The orgy of publication and broadcasting which recently marked the fiftieth anniversary of the war's outbreak suggests, indeed, that had the war not existed then it would have been necessary for academics and journalists to have invented it. Yet much of the debate is more concerned with diplomacy and military strategy than with the social history of the combatants. And while the British civilian experience during the Great War of 1914-18 has, in recent years, been subjected to close analysis, there has been less on the later period.[2]

The main focus of writing on British society during the Second World War has been the question of how far the war changed that society. The official histories published during the 1950s, tended towards the view that war had a 'remarkable' impact, making possible the welfare state and managed economy which seemed to characterise post-war Britain. As myth piled upon myth, a cruder version emerged in the popular consciousness: that by singing 'Roll out the Barrel' in their millions in the air raid shelters, the British had forged a new collective spirit and consciousness. During the war this was reflected in new proposals for social legislation, and after the war, in the development of supposedly 'consensus' politics. Arthur Marwick, in a series of books and articles from the mid-sixties onwards, basically accepted the thesis of radical social change, but others, like Pelling, Calder and Smith have been far more sceptical. Much of this debate has become rather stale and self-serving, and the time is ripe to adopt a different focus on the British civilian at war. Because civilians' active support for the war effort was crucial, their morale had to remain at a reasonable level. This paper will ask how far it did so, and why, touching on aspects of mobilisation, before attempting, finally, to relate its findings to the debate about how far the war changed British society.[3]

I

Morale is notoriously difficult to define, but is taken here to mean a belief in the justice of and necessity for the war effort, reflected in a willingness to undertake and continue the fight until victory is won, even in the face of great hardship. It does not necessarily mean cheerfulness or exuberance; grumbling could be a useful safety-valve. On this basis, it can be concluded from a number of indicators that British civilian morale, while fluctuating, remained at a level compatible with the vigorous prosecution of the war effort throughout the period 1939-45.

The first such indicator was public opinion polling. Although polls showed serious fluctuations, two basic points emerge. Firstly, both Britain's wartime Prime Ministers, Neville Chamberlain (to May 1940) and Winston Churchill, had a considerable stock of goodwill. Chamberlain, whose work had crashed to ruins with the outbreak of war, nonetheless had the support of 70 per cent of those polled in November 1939, and although the decline in morale engendered by the prolongation of the 'Phoney War' period up to the spring of 1940 was reflected in a fall in his approval rating, the figure remained over 50 per cent until the eve of his demise in May 1940. Churchill, who succeeded him, had an approval rating of 88 per cent by August that year, and 87 per cent the following June. He was at his least popular after the sudden fall of Tobruk in June 1942, but even then 78 per cent supported him. A year later the figure was 93 per cent. Such approval suggested that there was considerable goodwill for the uncompromising approach offered by Churchill. His government as a whole never approached such levels of popularity. But generally the majority of the population were behind it; only at times of deep disappointment, such as the fall of Tobruk, did its approval rating fall below 50 per cent. On the whole, then, opinion polling suggested reasonably good morale throughout the war.[4]

The second direct indicator of public feeling was the somewhat impressionistic 'morale chart' compiled by the Ministry of Information on the basis of Home Intelligence weekly reports between March 1941 and December 1944. The chart shows considerable vicissitudes in morale. A low point was reached in early June 1941, with the withdrawal from Crete being followed by the heavy air raids which were, in fact, to mark the end of the 'Big Blitz'. Morale then rose considerably following the entry of the Soviet Union into the war, but sank back as the Germans pressed deep into Soviet territory. November 1941 saw a recovery, as improved Soviet resistance was accompanied by the opening of the Libyan campaign. February 1942 again saw a very low point after the fall of Singapore, but by June there was a considerable recovery, with apparent success in Libya, further Soviet resistance, and heavy air raids on Cologne. However, the chart confirms that the fall of Tobruk later that month came as a nasty surprise and severely dented British morale. By the end of the year, though, it had risen considerably, boosted by victory at El Alamein, the Soviet resistance at Stalingrad, and on the domestic front the publication of the Beveridge Report on *Social Insurance and Allied Services*, which seemed to promise a brave new world of social welfare after the war and which, unprecedentedly for an official publication, became an overnight bestseller. Morale generally rose to a peak in September 1943 with the surrender of Italy, before falling back into a rather flat period in which continuing military success was countered in the public mind by renewed heavy raids on London (the 'Little Blitz') and general war-weariness: 1943 was probably the worst year of the war for British civilians. Things only really picked up with the end of the 'Little Blitz' and the allied invasion of Normandy in the late spring of 1944. The belief now was that the war would be brought to a speedy conclusion, and so the flying bomb and rocket attacks on London, which started about this time, had less of an impact than might otherwise have been the case. Later in the year allied reverses suggested the Germans would still take some beating, and so morale waned, but early in 1945 it became clear that the end was near, although concern about the likely shape of post-war Britain – particularly insofar as war industries were being run down and unemployment was reappearing – now served to replace military worries in damping enthusiasm. On the whole, however, the 'morale chart' suggests that civilians remained firmly behind the war effort, although it is a pity that we do not have similar information about the 'Phoney War' period, for it is then that morale seems to have been at its lowest.[5]

The buoyancy of civilian morale is also suggested by the more subjective reports of Mass-Observation, the private social survey operation set up in 1937 by Tom

Harrisson and Charles Madge. For example, using these reports many years later, Harrisson assessed the impact of heavy air raids thus:

> The blitz was a terrible experience for millions, yes. But it was not terrible enough to disrupt the basic decency, loyalty..., morality and optimism of the vast majority. It was supposed to destroy 'mass morale'. Whatever it did destroy, it failed over any period of more than days appreciably to diminish the human will, or at least the capacity to endure.

M-O reports were full of grumbles, but contained little that suggested defeatism or the despair upon which it thrives. Life went on; people adapted. The overwhelming impression was that hardships would have to be borne – albeit with no lack of complaint – because any alternative to victory was unthinkable for the vast majority of people.[6]

That this was the case is also supported by what can be discerned of popular opinions of those who were seen as defeatist, pacifist, or disloyal to the war effort. Firstly, the evidence of wartime by-elections is instructive, especially on the 'Phoney War' period. On the outbreak of war Labour and the Liberals, while refusing to enter the Chamberlain government, accepted an electoral truce whereby any seat falling vacant would be filled by a nominee of the incumbent party. This meant that of 138 by-elections during the war with Germany, 65 were unopposed. In the rest, the major parties (usually the Conservatives) were challenged by independent or minor party candidates. From May 1941 onwards, these challengers were almost invariably radicals or socialists of one form or another, and while critical of the Churchill Coalition government (or at least the Conservative party) had no doubts about fighting against Nazi Germany. For example, Common Wealth, the middle-class party which captured a number of Conservative seats from 1943 onwards, couched its argument for common ownership partly in terms of its being the best way of winning the war. The period up to May 1941 is more interesting for the purposes of this paper, for in that time three parties opposed to the war – the Communist party of Great Britain (C.P.G.B.), the British Union of Fascists (B.U.F.), and the Independent Labour party (I.L.P.) – ran candidates, and some anti-war independents also stood. Not one of the fifteen candidates managed to gain a seat; most lost their deposits in straight fights, no mean achievement. The best performances came at Kettering, where in the depth of the 'Phoney War' in March 1940 an unofficial Labour candidate gained just over a quarter of the votes, and at East Renfrew in May, when the I.L.P. polled just under a fifth of the votes cast. By contrast, none of the three B.U.F. candidates polled more than three per cent of the votes cast, despite standing in areas of relative strength for the movement: Lancashire, Leeds and the East End of London. These futile challenges came to an end with the banning of the B.U.F. in May 1940, the C.P.G.B.'s change of line following the German invasion of the Soviet Union the following year, and the I.L.P.'s final collapse.[7]

These results reflected a more general public hostility. The C.P.G.B.'s not altogether unimpressive expansion of the later 1930s was wiped out once it followed Moscow's new anti-war line in September 1939, and it only revived with the switch back of policy in 1941. Opinion was similarly hostile towards the Fascists: there was no outcry when the B.U.F. was banned, and its members interned, on rather flimsy evidence in May 1940. Indeed, when its leader, Sir Oswald Mosley, was released from prison on health grounds in 1943, it unleashed a bitter public outcry, reports 'flood[ing] in of hostile public reaction throughout the country'. Similarly, although there was less of the virulence against those of foreign origin than there had been in the Great War, in July 1940 a poll suggested that nearly half the population wanted all aliens to be interned. Even in the first part of the war, then, when support for the war effort was, perhaps, at its most precarious, there was nothing really substantial upon which pacifists, defeatists or fifth columnists could build.[8]

Willingness to participate in voluntary war work, like air raid precautions (A.R.P.) and the local defence volunteers (L.D.V., or Home Guard) was another index of morale. In the case of A.R.P., though, it helps to highlight the fact that civilian morale was probably never lower than in the period up to May 1940. At the outbreak of war, A.R.P. had had 1.6 million members. A minority of them were paid, at a cost of £3 million a month. By the end of 1939 they were being criticised fiercely in the press and in parliament. There had been no air raids, so they were, it seemed, getting money for nothing. Wardens became the butt of ridicule. Many volunteers left. A.R.P. seemed on the verge of collapse and Chamberlain had to intervene, warning in January 1940 that things would get worse before long. This had some effect, and in any case there was soon more than enough for A.R.P. to do; but the episode is instructive for the low state of civilian morale during the 'Phoney War'. It was only when the war took a turn for the worse, with the German invasion of the Low Countries and France, that morale improved significantly, assisted in no small degree by the replacement of Chamberlain by the more vigorous Churchill. On 14 May a broadcast appeal to civilians to serve in the newly-formed L.D.V. resulted in 250,000 recruits within twenty-four hours. Many people were galvanised into firmer commitment to the war effort by the sense of emergency; the ignominious defeat of Dunkirk became a victory, and King George VI could write privately that with the fall of France he felt 'happier now that we have no allies to be polite to & pamper'. Yet while there was much of this spirit around, it would be rash to take recollections of it at their face value. Many people believed the war was lost, but tended not to say so: at the time, for fear of being seen as defeatist; later, because of the knowledge of ultimate victory. Even so, the willingness of Britons to undertake voluntary war duties suggests firm commitment to the war effort, except during the winter of 1939-40; and even then, the findings of opinion polls and the results of by-elections suggested that there was no serious defeatism or pacifism.[9]

Evidence from the workplace also suggests that people were behind the war effort. There was direction of labour on a scale unprecedented in Britain, and this was accepted by the unions and most workers with little question. The very fact that the Minister of Labour and National Service from May 1940, Ernest Bevin, could use persuasion rather than coercion suggested a considerable stock of working-class goodwill towards the fight against the Axis powers. The average working week rose from 46.5 hours in October 1938 to a peak of 50.0 in July 1943. When placed at the side of additional voluntary work in A.R.P., firewatching and so on, this meant a great strain. But the new conditions were accepted. True, real wages rose during the later part of the war; but it could be argued in that case that the pressure of workers indifferent to the war effort would have been to reduce hours, not to increase them, safe in the knowledge that a shorter week would not reduce their standard of living. Absenteeism could be taken as an index of disaffection with the war effort, and indeed, it sometimes reached worrying proportions, particularly in munitions factories. But much of it was explained by women workers having to shop, to queue, or to look after children, particularly since many of the women coming into the factories had not been workers before the war and were living in areas where there was less of a tradition of female employment than in, say, Lancashire, where unofficial support networks existed. Much of the absenteeism was inevitable and had nothing to do with morale; in October 1943 it was accepted by government and employers that workers would need to be absent from time to time, and so an effective scheme for requesting leave was introduced. Despite the cumulative strain between 1943 and 1945, the problem did not increase significantly in magnitude. In coalmining, things did get worse as the war wore on, but much of this was due to problems of an ageing – and thus ailing – workforce in an arduous occupation. Perhaps the best illustration of the morale of the workforce was that even after the most serious air raids people returned to work as soon as they had arranged new accommodation. After the massive raid on Coventry in November 1940, the city was 'mostly back to full industrial production within five days'. The evidence of industrial disputes, similarly, does not point to war-weariness or anti-war feeling among the workforce. There were no anti-war strikes, and Trotskyite agitators made a minimal impact. Strikes and lockouts were banned under M.L.N.S. Order 1305 (July 1940), but disputes cannot be prevented by laws, and the number of working days lost rose every year between then and 1944, when almost four times as many (3,696,000) were lost as in 1940 (941,000). Yet in many ways these figures support the view that when the peril was greatest, in 1940, workers were prepared to put up with their lot, whereas as things became easier they felt more freedom to air their grievances. Nineteen-forty remains the year with the fewest days lost through disputes since records began in 1893.[10]

The British war economy, indeed, was mobilised far more extensively far earlier than the German. This reflected a number of things. Firstly, Britain, unlike Germany, had no choice. She was fighting for her very survival, whereas Germany was dictating the pace during the early years of the war. This also accounts for the acceptance on the part of business of extensive state control. Secondly, a democracy had a better feel of what its members would take, and what they would not. This was especially the case after May 1940, with the entry into government of Labour ministers who, in many cases, retained close touch with working-class attitudes. Thirdly, it was certainly the case in the early part of the war that people accustomed to fairly high levels of unemployment early in the war were just relieved to have work. Finally, there were fewer ideological barriers to the employment of women. While Summerfield is right to point out that male policy-makers were reluctant to see any serious challenge to male hegemony and the domestic ideology, they were able to reconcile this with an increase in female employment on the grounds that such employment would be temporary. The domestic idyll might be the ideal society for such policy-makers, but the domestic idyll was not seen as an option if Germany won the war. There were priorities.[11]

Overall, then, evidence from the workplace tends to confirm the view of civilian attitudes that has been built up in this section. Broadly, morale remained healthy, although not without serious downturns after military reverses. The populace continued to support the government of the day, and when it seemed – in May 1940 – that there might have been unrest, the British system was flexible enough to permit the formation of a new government under Churchill from within the existing House of Commons. Morale was probably at its nadir, paradoxically, during the winter of 1939-40, when there was no aerial attack and little fighting but when prices were rising faster than wages. It was an enervating, irritating period of waiting for the unknown. Yet even then the point should not be carried too far; an essentially Conservative government retained the support of more than half the population, as did its ostensibly discredited leader, Chamberlain, while parties which opposed the war were regularly humiliated at the polls and no significant anti-war movement grew up. Adversity from mid-1940 onwards merely confirmed civilian support, perhaps even increased it; now people could see the enemy and did not like it. Overall, then, civilians supported the war effort, despite the hardships involved. It remains to explain why this was the case.

II

Pre-war governments had been, if not obsessed, then heavily preoccupied with the question of civilian reactions to a major war. Technological developments – particularly long-range bombers, but also poison gas and better submarines – suggested that, even more than in the Great War, the civilian would be as much in the front line as the soldier in uniform. And how would civilians react to that? The collapse of Germany in 1918 preyed on many minds. The 'stab in the back' theory – that an undefeated army had been betrayed by domestic disturbance – was one to which Britain's pre-war planners, no less than the Nazis, subscribed. For those planners, often of military background and somewhat contemptuous of anyone not in uniform, the average civilian was less the British bulldog than the pampered poodle: lacking in moral fibre, easily demoralised, neurotic under pressure and as likely to snap at its owner as at the latter's assailant.

The effect of aerial bombardment on civilian life was the greatest worry. Reading the forecasts of planners today, with the benefit of hindsight, it is difficult to avoid the conclusion that no claim could be too outlandish. Estimates of bomb capacity and likely casualties based on the experience of a few Zeppelin raids during the Great War had been revised upwards in the light of the use of Italian bombers in Abyssinia and German ones in Spain, so that by March 1939 the scenario was for at least 700, but possibly up to 3,500, tons of bombs to be dropped on the first day of the war, with 700 tons per day for some weeks thereafter. It was expected that anything up to a quarter of this tonnage would be poison gas. There would be 72 casualties per ton of bombs dropped. There was talk of 200,000 casualties in the first ten days, a third of them fatal.[12]

Against this it was thought that little could be done. There were new defences, such as radar and better fighter planes; children could be evacuated from the danger zones and passive defences could be improved by the employment of A.R.P. wardens and the construction of shelters and trenches. Gas masks were issued to the entire population. Yet the mood in Whitehall remained that of former premier Stanley Baldwin: 'the bomber will always get through'. Churchill had talked of three or four million people flooding out of London 'under the pressure of continuous air attack'. Planners felt that there would also be up to three times as many cases of neurosis, mental illness, insanity. On these projections the first fortnight of war would see over 900,000 physical casualties (over 300,000 fatal) and 3,000,000 psychological casualties. Aerial bombardment, it seemed, would mean the onset of the apocalypse.[13]

But as we now know, these estimates were far too pessimistic. There were no serious German raids until the summer of 1940, a year after the outbreak of war. It was something of a paradox, noted above, that morale seemed to improve once the bombing had begun. Now at least people felt involved, and also knew that the raids were neither so heavy nor so destructive as most had feared. In addition, sheltering facilities had been improved considerably since September 1939. This is not to trivialise the raids that took place. Most large centres in Britain were bombed at some stage during the 'Big Blitz' (September 1940-May 1941). On the night of 18-19 September 350 tons were deposited on London. The first big raid on Coventry, in November, saw over 500 tons dropped, and was so destructive that it added a new word to the German language, *Coventrieren*. Bombing continued intermittently almost until the end of the war: raids on tourist cities during April-July 1942, 'tip and run' raids on a wide range of targets from then until early 1944, the 'Little Blitz' of industrial areas January-March 1944, and V-weapon attacks (flying bombs, rockets) thereafter.[14]

This was a different pattern to that predicted by the pre-war planners, but would the result be much the same anyway? In some places, morale seemed for some time to be on the point of collapse. Mass-Observation found that in Coventry after the first big raid:

> There were more open signs of hysteria, terror, neurosis, observed than during the whole of the previous two months together in all areas. Women were seen to cry, to scream, to tremble all over, to faint in the street, to attack a fireman, and so on. ... On Friday (15th) evening, there were several signs of suppressed panic as darkness approached. ... If there had been another attack, the effects in terms of human behaviour would have been much more striking and terrible.

Many citizens felt that Coventry was finished. Meanwhile, Plymouth, which suffered six raids between November 1940 and April 1941, was another city where the predictions seemed to have been borne out; the Home Secretary, Herbert Morrison, believed that the large numbers of people trekking out of the city at night suggested that its morale had gone completely.[15]

Yet Plymouth was not finished; most of the people there who trekked out into the countryside at night as protection against further raids trekked back in the morning for work, as they did in many other areas. Similarly, Coventry was back at work within a week; and in any case, what stands out from the M-O report is the fact that the scenes of disorder witnessed were exceptional. Morale was not cracked by aerial bombardment for a number of reasons. Firstly, the raids were neither as heavy nor as concentrated as pre-war planners had anticipated. Secondly, the casualty ratio was nothing like that predicted. The 70,995 tons dropped during the war should have resulted, according to the pre-war ratio, in 5,111,640 casualties, 1,703,880 of them fatal. In fact, there were 297,610, 60,595 of them fatal. The ratio of casualties per ton was not 72 but 4; morale was, accordingly, far less affected than had been feared. Thirdly, there was protection in the form of shelters and trenches. Londoners ignored official advice, a significant minority using tube stations as deep shelters, while confounding official fears that this would lead to a 'deep shelter mentality' among an army of 'timorous trogladytes' by leaving every morning to go to work. Fourthly, the development of post-raid services also contributed to the maintenance of morale. In many places this development was rather sporadic and *ad hoc*, but as local authorities became better organised, and co-ordinated with voluntary bodies, the rest centres for the homeless became more comfortable and the dissemination of information was greatly improved. Fifthly, revenge attacks could help lift spirits, although, either for humanitarian reasons or because they feared provoking still further attacks on themselves, those in the worst-hit areas were often the least vengeful. Finally, there was a resilience about the British people which came as a surprise to most of those in authority. This is not to subscribe wholeheartedly to the 'Roll Out The Barrel' view. But people did readjust quickly to a life involving the blackout, lack of sleep and the ever-present threat of death. Often a kind of grim fatalism took over. For all these reasons, bombing did not have the catastrophic consequences predicted.[16]

On the basis of those predictions, however, pre-war governments had believed that lives could be saved by the evacuation of large numbers of people from coastal areas, ports and industrial towns into the countryside. Morale would be bolstered too, because parents could at least be sure that their loved ones were safe. So, on the outbreak of war, millions of children, some with their teachers or mothers, were sent away to be billeted with families in supposedly safer areas. In three days 1,473,000 people were moved, with their consent. (Around 2,000,000 more people evacuated themselves privately.) But many soon drifted back as the promised air raids did not materialise. Although there were further waves in late 1940 and mid-1944, evacuation remained unpopular. It broke up families; it imposed new burdens in the reception areas, not least on the families who took evacuees in. Not all cases were bad. Farmers picked strong boys who would help them on the farm. Many children and hosts got on very well. But many did not, and it was these stories that hit the headlines. Caricatures soon developed of the evacuee child as a lice-ridden, ill-clad, bed-wetting, foulmouthed horror; of the evacuee mother as a sluttish, homesick and idle layabout; of the host as a snobbish, interfering, exploitative tyrant. Of course, this was not the whole story, but government circles were worried that social divisions were being highlighted. Yet it is too simplistic to portray the division as being between middle-class hosts and working-class evacuees. It was as much a clash between rural and urban workers and their lifestyles. Among ordinary men in a Somerset pub there was 'some ill feeling ... that strange women from the cities were in the habit of coming into the tap room in the evenings and drinking half a pint, or even gin, like a man. Such a thing had never happened before in the village, and no one liked it.' The clash, as Nicolson realised, was 'not between the rich and the poor but between the urban and the rural poor'. Titmuss recorded the story of the six-year-old from Glasgow who was reprimanded by his mother in front of their hostess: 'You dirty thing, messing the lady's carpet. Go and do it in the corner.' It did not take a bourgeois to be appalled by such habits. Rather, the worst horror stories of slum evacuees – which were by no means typical – represented a challenge to notions of 'respectability' which were shared by working- and middle-class alike. Even so, the experience of the first evacuation was so traumatic for all concerned, especially in government circles, that the later waves of evacuation were far better planned and executed. Insofar as it was supposed to have boosted morale, the first wave of evacuation, at any rate, seemed to have been a dismal failure.[17]

Yet evacuation did have its benefits. It saved lives; it enabled parents, freed from family ties, to work longer hours in the war industries; and it relieved overburdened city authorities of many social welfare duties. By mixing up the population it gave a powerful impetus towards universalistic provision of welfare services, such as was later to be embodied in the post-war 'welfare state' rather than allowing the authorities to retain more selective pre-war practices. It also acted as a safety-valve: it was an option parents had if the raids got worse. That was a considerable source of reassurance to many.

Evacuation raised for government another of its bogeymen: social division. Most inter-war Conservative statesmen had been wary of 'the masses', and although Chamberlain was less fearful than Baldwin, his predecessor, there was considerable fear of how the population at large would respond to war. There had only been three elections held on the basis of universal adult suffrage, one of which (1929) had produced a Labour government and another of which (1931) was by now seen as an exceptional event. Many pointed to the Britain of the 1930s and saw it as a period of conspicuous consumption on the one hand and grinding poverty on the other. Of course, this was simplistic; but it preyed on the minds of those in power, who were relieved, after extensive bombing of the East End of London, that the West End was also attacked. Here, though, was a key to greater social cohesion: bombs did not discriminate between buildings any more than between prostitutes and men of letters, and if even Buckingham Palace could be bombed, then in a very real sense everyone was 'in it together'. This had already found political form in Churchill's Coalition government. Like the nation, it was not always unanimous. But there was a basic agreement that the war had to be seen through to the bitter end. For in fact, the British working classes were far more patriotic than the largely middle-class people in Whitehall realised: as George Orwell noted perceptively in 1941, their patriotism was 'profound, but ... unconscious'. Similarly, as Orwell pointed out, there was no substantial upper- or middle-class fifth column movement. If British society in the 1930s had exhibited some signs of cleavage, they were nowhere near as great or as significant as those which were to lead France towards ignominious surrender at the very time that Britain was preparing to stand alone against German aggression.[18]

Before the war, the government had believed that its own propaganda could play a major role in maintaining civilian morale. It was wrong. The morale-boosting campaigns of the Ministry of Information (MoI) were often ignored, sometimes irritating, and almost always ineffective. This was hardly surprising. The best antidote to air raids that an eve-of-war MoI committee could come up with was the vigorous dispensation of cups of tea to the frightened populace. The MoI's first poster campaign was a disaster. '*Your* courage, *your* cheerfulness, *your* resolution will bring *us* victory' might have seemed a stirring cry to its composers, but to most people it read as though the many were going to be fighting for the good of the few. Later campaigns were often little better. What the public wanted was less exhortation, which it saw as patronising, and more news, for the release of the latter increased a sense of responsibility and trust and also prevented the circulation of rumour. The withholding of news of the Norwegian campaign in the spring of 1940 was a major reason why the country was so taken aback when the reverses were finally revealed. It took government some time to see this, but from July 1941, when the newspaper proprietor and Churchill acolyte, Brendan Bracken, took over at the MoI, more news began to be released. The ministry also came to play a useful role in helping government to know more than ever before about ordinary people through its involvement with Mass-Observation and the Wartime Social Survey. But the exhortation stopped. Propaganda had not played the role in maintaining morale that the planners had hoped it would.[19]

In short, many of the expectations of the pre-war planners had been less than wholly fulfilled. The outbreak of war was not followed by heavy air raids. When raids began, over a year later, they were nothing like as destructive as had been anticipated. Nor did they produce a general collapse of morale or destroy social cohesion; rather the reverse. But two of their major means of lifting spirits - evacuation and propaganda - had had at best limited success in doing so. So why was morale maintained throughout the war?

III

As well as the factors mentioned above, six other considerations helped to maintain civilian morale during the Second World War. They were the nature of the enemy and the progress of the war itself; leadership; aspects relating to work; the supply, distribution and quality of food and other essentials; the availability of less strictly essential goods and entertainment; and the promise of a better future after the war.

The first of these was in some ways the fundamental one. The enemy was such that there was little doubt that victory must be had; left-wingers, who hated fascism, were as committed as anyone, something of a contrast with the Great War. Morale tended to fluctuate with Britain's fortunes in the war, as noted above, and from late 1942 onwards, it was clear that the war would be won. Thus war-weariness was countered by confidence in the success of the effort. Before that, there was still a sense of excitement which helped to buoy up morale. In addition, it was a war of movement: there was none of the trench warfare of 1914-18 which might, had it been repeated, have led to a general feeling of futility and discontent. All in all, it was during the early part of the war, when real wages were falling, nothing seemed to be happening and there was great fear of the unknown, that morale was at its lowest.

Leadership was another important factor in maintaining morale, although it is difficult here to separate myth from reality. Chamberlain was not a good wartime leader. Arguably the most formidable force in inter-war British politics, he was almost certainly suffering terminally from cancer by the time war broke out, and to this was added bitter disappointment at his failure to preserve the peace. He seemed to many to lack the will to fight. His successor never gave that impression. Always a political pugilist, Churchill was the ideal man to take office in May 1940. He made a significant positive impact on wartime morale. He inspired the country through his broadcast speeches and his bulldog spirit, and boosted morale by visiting bombed areas. Just as important, though, was the all-party nature and general air of competence of the government Churchill led. The presence of Britain's leading trade unionist, Bevin, at the M.L.N.S. reassured many workers who might otherwise have been less ready to change working practices in the interests of war production. The removal of the 'Men of Munich' during 1940 also helped gain public confidence. The leading politicians of the 1930s were soon discredited as having led Britain in irresolute and wrongheaded policies abroad and unimaginative and parsimonious policies at home. This was rather unfair, but it took hold, as the massive sales of 'Cato's' *Guilty Men* (1940) showed. The 'ins' of the 1930s – Chamberlain, Hoare, Simon, Halifax, *et al* – were thrust from meaningful office at home. This undoubtedly boosted morale during 1940.[20]

A number of factors relating to work and wages also helped to maintain civilian spirits. Firstly, unemployment was eliminated from the economy after the spring of 1940, once the economy had switched over more or less fully to a war footing. This in itself was enough to lift the spirits of the one million plus who had been unemployed until the outbreak of war, many of them for months or even years. Sober social surveys during the 1930s had come to the conclusion that many of these people would never work again. Now there was a labour shortage (see Table 1); married women were now implored to enter the factories, although, as Summerfield has shown, male poicy-makers 'searched for a compromise between the two spheres of [women's] activity, domestic and industrial, such that neither would be profoundly changed'.

Table 1. *Unemployment, 1938-45*

June	Registered Insured Unemployed
1938	1,710,000
1939	1,270,000
1940	645,000
1941	198,000
1942	87,000
1943	60,000
1944	54,000
1945	103,000

Source: *Ministry of Labour Gazette*

Secondly, wages rose, partly due to the shortage of labour. Thirdly, price controls were introduced on basic food stuffs in December 1939 on a temporary basis, and from August 1940 these subsidies were made 'permanent' in order to reduce the chances of a damaging spiral of wage-price inflation. In April 1941 the subsidies were extended further; clothing prices were controlled and the introduction of cheap 'utility' clothing and furniture later in that year eased the inflationary pressure still further. All this meant a significant increase in real wages during the war. What is perhaps most noteworthy after that is the fact that it was after more than two years of war, when war-weariness and discontent might have been expected to start taking hold, that wages really began to outstrip prices, so giving a powerful boost to morale just when it was needed (see Table 2).

Table 2 . *Cost of Living, Wage Rates and Weekly Earnings, 1938-45*

Month	Cost of Living (all items)	Weekly Wage Rates (all industries)	Weekly Earnings (manufacturing)
1938 Oct	...	...	100
1939 Sep	100	100	...
1940 Jan	112	105-6	...
Jul	120	113-14	130
1941 Jan	126	118	...
Jul	128	122	142
1942 Jan	129	127	146
Jul	129	131-2	160
1943 Jan	128	133	165
Jul	129	136-7	176
1944 Jan	128	139-40	179
Jul	130	143-4	182
1945 Jan	130	145-6	176
Jul	133½	150-1	180

Source: H.M.S.O., *Statistical Digest of the War* (London, 1951), p. 8.

Bevin's determination to use his powers at the M.L.N.S. to promote working-class standards, as with his Catering Wages Act, 1943, also helped keep labour relations harmonious, as did his preference for persuasion over coercion. There were break-downs, but good sense usually prevailed. There were no mass prosecutions of strikers. Morale was bolstered, then, by full employment, rising real wages, and a flexible government response to industrial difficulties.[21]

Morale also depended, of course, on whether there was anything on which to spend those increased wages. The most essential issue was the quantity, quality and distribution of food. In the inter-war years, British agriculture had been severely depressed, and the country had relied heavily on imports. Shipping space was obviously at a premium in wartime, as the Germans waged a fierce battle against British vessels, and food had to vie for space with essential raw materials and other commodities. In the years 1934-8 the annual average amount of food imported had been 22.5 million tons, yet in November 1940 the war cabinet was forced to recognise that only 15.5 million tons of food could be imported in the second year of the war; and as it turned out, the actual figure for 1941 was some way below that. After that, imports fell even lower, partly because of foreign exchange shortages (although American Lend-Lease, amounting to around 7 per cent of consumption per annum, helped) and partly because of the effects of submarine attacks in the Atlantic. Losses of food at sea amounted to 700,000 tons in each of 1940 and 1941, and 500,000 tons in 1942. Much less was lost following victory over the submarines in the early part of 1943. Shipping production began to show a net gain, but despite this food imports did not rise greatly (in each of the years between 1942 and 1945 inclusive, imports never exceeded 12 million tons). The country got by, though, mainly because the government had promoted domestic agriculture on an unprecedented scale. The amount of land ploughed was increased by half, there was considerable mechanisation and more use was made of fertilisers, so that domestic food production rose dramatically over 1938-9 by 36 per cent to 1941-2 and by 91 per cent to 1943-4.[22]

Throughout the war, then, the overall quantity of food available was sufficient to feed Britain, provided that it was distributed effectively. For that, rationing was the answer. In the first months of war, food distribution became a source of great social friction; few topics aroused such ire. With reluctance and characteristic nervousness, Chamberlain's war cabinet began to ration key foods like butter, bacon and sugar. Margarine, meat, cheese, soap, sweets and tea were included later. The system was not watertight, and there was a constant struggle to get a little extra. There was a black economy but its historian has concluded that there was not in any meaningful sense 'a black market' such as thrived in America and most of Europe. This was 'a tribute to the success of British rationing policy, based on a genuine sense of shared national sacrifice', and to a well-administered and equitable policy.[23]

The quality of the food available was also important. In 1940, when things looked particularly grim, a committee of scientists reported that the nation's nutritional needs could be met by a 'basal diet' comprising wholemeal bread, oatmeal, fats, milk, potatoes and vegetables. Ministers and officials were horrified: such a diet would have dire consequences on morale. Churchill, always aware of the importance of a satisfactory diet, insisted early in 1941, to the dismay of officials, that consumption should be cut as little as possible even if that meant taking up valuable shipping space with items that were not strictly essential. The government was slow to raise the wheat extraction rate for flour because of the unpopularity of brown bread in most households. Food policy overall was reflected by the advice of the Ministry of Food official 'to put the basal diet to sleep for the duration of the war'. Morale was not going to be allowed to suffer unduly because of food, and fortunately Britain's position was always strong enough to ensure this. In addition, the better allocation of resources, and enforced concentration on healthier foods, meant the diet of the average Briton actually improved during the war.[24]

It also helped morale that the supply of less strictly essential goods and of entertainment was maintained as far as possible. Once again, flexibility and humanity in government combined with British and American seapower made this possible. For all that it was lamented by sections of the population, the British civilian was highly susceptible to the appeal of beer and tobacco, and government was highly susceptible to the appeal of the tax revenues they produced. Accordingly, beer – albeit watered-down – continued to be produced in large quantities. Rationing was never introduced, although some publicans evolved their own schemes for combating the rather erratic supply system. Despite transport shortages and the bulkiness of bottled beers, 'little or nothing was done to deny [them] to any part of the country'. Overall, beer consumption rose by a quarter during the war, helped by higher wages and severe cuts in the production of spirits.[25]

Tobacco also had a vital part to play. A shortage of cigarettes after an air raid, for example, could have an effect on the nervous condition of many people, as was the case in Southampton late in 1940. Government recognised this. In March 1942 it agreed, despite the acute shipping situation, that 'in the interests of efficiency and morale', 'tobacco supplies should be maintained at the level of demand', so extra space was allocated during the coming year to prevent stocks falling to a dangerously low level. Indeed, by 1943, imports were outstripping those of the last year of peace. The importance of tobacco supplies to morale was widely recognised.[26]

The same was true of entertainments. At the outbreak of war, in anticipation of massive aerial attack, all public places of entertainment were closed down. They were soon reopened. The effect on morale of continued closure was not something to be contemplated with equanimity. In the midst of air attack people were to look for entertainment despite – or because of – their troubles. In Southampton the few places that remained open did 'a roaring trade', and M-O found that young Londoners craved diversion. Even the football pools were revived. During the height of the London blitz, cinemas remained open; by the middle of the war, nationally, up to 30,000,000 seats a week were being sold, and since many of the films shown – such as Howard's *First of the Few* or Olivier's *Henry V* – were intended to boost morale, this was no bad thing. Whereas expenditure on food, clothing and household goods fell during the war, that on beer rose by a quarter, on tobacco by a sixth, and on entertainments by over two fifths. The effect on civilian morale was considerable. Ascetics' dreams were thwarted, but the result was a far happier nation. What is 'good' is not always best.[27]

Finally, many have argued that a key factor in maintaining civilian morale was the promise of a better future after the war. While historians differ as to whether this promise was a good thing, few would dispute its existence. The inter-war decades rapidly became discredited: the 'outs' got their revenge while the inter-war leaders were hamstrung in defending their by no means execrable record by the widespread belief that they were to blame for the war. Thus there emerged a strong body of opinion to the effect that 'things must never be the same again'. This did not only cover left-wingers. The Ministry of Information soon came to the conclusion that it was the best way to inspire Britons in the war effort, although its early statements, were bland. In fact Churchill was keen to avoid precise statements before the end of the war, but he was unable to stop plans like the Beveridge report being mooted. The immense popularity of that report certainly suggested that many civilians were boosting their own morale with visions of a brighter future, and white papers on employment and health, and the Education Act of 1944, seemed to be moving in the same direction. And underneath all this was a flood of books, pamphlets, broadcasts and films all telling the same story. The MoI's own film unit came to be staffed with left-wingers who produced masses of films along the same lines, contrasting a grim picture of the inter-war years with the full employment of wartime and concluding that if only government continued to organise the nation's resources in peacetime then a prosperous future was assured. Such films generally concluded with advice to vote to ensure that there was no return to the 'bad old days', which was basically a call to vote Labour. Feature films often conveyed a similar message against the backdrop of a very partial image of inter-war Britain: thus *Love on the Dole* (1941) ended with a statement from the Labour minister A.V. Alexander that such conditions as the – fictional – film showed must never be allowed to return. If it would be going too far to say that all this talk of a better post-war world inspired the nation to victory, it did at least remove a lot of the fear that wartime gains would be snatched away once peace was restored, as was believed to have been the case after 1918. Thus it helped to boost morale, particularly since there was so little consideration given to those who might lose out under the new regime.[28]

IV

The government planners of the 1930s would have been pleasantly surprised by the resilience of the British civilian at war. They had feared that aerial attack and privations would lead to mass hysteria, massive casualties and the opening up of social divisions on an unprecedented scale. The home front might be the one on which the war was lost, as was believed to have been the case in Germany in 1918. The expedients they thought would be especially useful in combating such problems – evacuation and propaganda – turned out, in the event, to be of limited value. Instead, civilian morale was maintained by patriotic feeling for a struggle that was eventually successful; faith in the nation's leaders; rising wages and full employment; adequate supplies of good food and 'essential luxuries' like tobacco; and a hope that the post-war world would be a better one. Given these, morale never looked like cracking, particularly after the enemy came out in his true colours with the onset of the 'Big Blitz' in September 1940; even before then, while there had been confusion and some demoralisation, there had been no substantial support for the few who believed that the war was not worth fighting.

The war had revealed, above all, that British society was not as fragmented as the inter-war pessimists had believed. Similarly, it showed that that society was more malleable than they had thought to be the case. In the 1930s governments had been nervous of initiating substantial changes in legislation or practice, even though they had sometimes wanted to, for fear of letting loose movements and forces they could not control. Compelled by circumstances to make some of those changes, they found that this was not so, although it took sections of the Conservative party some years to appreciate the fact. The war helped to promote change in Britain, and that change often made a substantial difference to the lives of ordinary people. But as this paper has suggested, those changes could only be limited because, in many essentials, the British people remained the same. As they were not made into quivering jellies by the air raids, so they were not made into utopian idealists by the MoI film unit. Their social, economic and political concerns, beyond victory in the war, remained narrowly focussed. This was perfectly understandable, but its corollary was a lack of scope for governments to transform society, even if they had wanted to do so. Within those parameters there was a meaningful shift in emphasis because of the new possibilites opened up by the war, but it would not do to overstate it. The British civilian at war was in most ways the same person as before or after, but living for six years under different conditions. Harold Nicolson and the prostitute would have been as ill-at-ease with each other in a darkened doorway in 1946 as they had been in 1940.

NOTES

1. H. Nicolson, *Diaries and Letters 1939-1945* (London, 1967), p. 112, diary 12 Sept. 1940.
2. J.M. Winter, *The Great War and the British People* (Cambridge, 1986); B. Waites, *A Class Society at War: England 1914-1918* (Leamington Spa, 1987); J. Turner (ed.), *Britain and the First World War* (London, 1988).
3. R. Titmuss, *Problems of Social Policy* (London, 1950), p. 506; A. Marwick, *Britain in the Century of Total War* (London, 1968);id., 'People's War and Top People's Peace? British society and the Second World War', in A. Sked and C. Cook (ed.), *Crisis and Controversy: Essays in Honour of A.J.P. Taylor (London, 1976), pp. 148-64; id., The Home Front: the British and the Second*

World War (London, 1976), p. 11; H. Pelling, *Britain and the Second World War* (Glasgow, 1970), p. 326; A. Calder, *The People's War: Britain 1939-1945* (London, 1971), p. 20; H.L. Smith (ed.), *War and Social Change: British Society in the Second World War* (Manchester, 1986), p. x.

4. Pelling, (above, note 3), pp. 60-1, 90, 132, 155, 186.
5. I.McLaine, *Ministry of Morale: Home Front Morale and the Ministry of Information in World War II* (London, 1979), endpapers.
6. T. Harrison, *Living Through the Blitz* (London, 1976), p. 280; A. Calder and D. Sheridan, (ed.), *Speak For Yourself: a Mass-Observation Anthology, 1937-49* (London, 1984), p. 83.
7. P. Addison, 'By-elections of the Second World War', in C. Cook and J. Ramsden (ed.), *By-Elections in British Politics* (London, 1973), p. 166.
8. R. Thurlow, 'The Failure of British Fascism 1932-40', in A. Thorpe, (ed.), *The Failure of Political Extremism in Inter-War Britain* (Exeter, 1989), pp. 83-4; B. Donoughue and G.W. Jones, *Herbert Morrison: Portrait of a Politician* (London, 1973), p. 304; Calder, (above, note 3) p. 152.
9. T.H. O'Brien, *Civil Defence* (London, 1955), pp. 203-8, 298, 341-7; Calder, (above, note 3), pp. 121-2; Pelling, (above, note 3), p. 87.
10. H.M.S.O., *Statistical Digest of the War* (London, 1951), p. 204, 81; P. Inman, *Labour in the Munitions Industries* (London, 1957), pp. 277, 283; Harrison, (above, note 6), p. 141; H. Pelling, *A History of British Trade Unionism* (3rd edn., Harmondsworth, 1976), pp. 294-5.
11. P. Summerfield, *Women Workers in the Second World War: Production and Patriarchy in Conflict* (London, 1984).
12. Titmuss, (above, note 3), pp. 4-7, 10, 14.
13. Baldwin, 10 Nov. 1932, and Churchill, 28 Nov. 1934, quoted in ibid, p. 9; ibid, p. 20; cf. J.B.S. Haldane, *A.R.P.* (London, 1938).
14. O'Brien, (above, note 9), pp. 296, 390, 404-5.
15. Harrison, (above, note 6), pp. 135, 212.
16. Titmuss, (above, note 3), pp. 559, 556; Harrison, (above, note 6), pp. 151, 251, 38.
17. Titmuss, (above, note 3), pp. 101, 562; H.V. Morton, *I Saw Two Englands: the Record of a Journey Before the War, and After the Outbreak of War, in the Year 1939* (London, 1942), p. 215; Nicolson,(above, note 1), p. 33, diary14. Sept. 1939; Titmuss, (above, note 3), p. 122.
18. Nicolson, (above, note 1), pp. 114-15, diary 17 Sept. 1940; G. Orwell, *The Lion and The Unicorn: Socialism and the English Genius* (London, 1941), pp. 28-9.

19. McLaine, (above, note 5), pp. 280, 27, 31; Harrison, (above, note 6), p. 285; McLaine, (above, note 5), p. 60.
20. Harrison, (above, note 6), p. 213; Marwick, (above, note 3), p. 131.
21. Pilgrim Trust, *Men Without Work* (Cambridge, 1938), p. 220; H.M.D. Parker, *Manpower: a Study of War-Time Policy and Administration* (London, 1957), pp. 433, 438; Summerfield, (above, note 11), p. 29.
22. S. Pollard, *The Development of the British Economy, 1914-80* (London, 1983), p. 205; R.J. Hammond, *Food* (3 vols., London, 1951-62), I:392; W.K. Hancock and M.M. Gowing, *British War Economy* (London, 1949), pp. 265, 240; C.B.A. Behrens, *Merchant Shipping and the Demands of War* (London, 1955), pp. 340, 293.
23. Hancock and Gowing, (above, note 22), pp. 175-6; E. Smithies, *The Black Economy in England Since 1914* (Dublin, 1984), pp. 69, 84.
24. Hancock and Gowing, (above, note 22), pp. 425, 316; Hammond, (above, note 22), I:94-5.
25. Hancock and Gowing, (above, note 22) pp. 493, 485.
26. Ibid, p. 493; *Statistical Digest*, (above, note 10), p. 167.
27. Harrison, (above, note 6), pp. 166, 172-3, 75; Calder, (above, note 3), pp. 74, 204, 422-3; *Statistical Digest*, (above, note 10), p. 203.
28. P. Addison, *The Road to 1945: British Politics and the Second World War* (London, 1977); C. Barnett, *The Audit of War: the Illusion and Reality of Britain as a Great Nation* (London, 1986); McLaine, (above, note 5), p. 172; Nicolson, (above, note 1), p. 130, diary 3 Dec. 1940; N. Pronay, '"The land of promise": the projection of peace aims in Britain', in K.R.M. Short (ed.), *Film and Radio Propaganda in World War II* (London, 1983), p. 64.

3

GERMANY

Jeremy Noakes

On the outbreak of war in September 1939 Germans on the home front were faced with a dual task: to mobilize the nation's resources for the war effort to maximum effect, while simultaneously maintaining the morale of the civilian population in order to sustain a consensus for war. The two tasks were closely interrelated: the methods used for resource mobilization were bound to react on morale, while in turn morale would crucially influence the success of resource mobilization. However, they were also inherently contradictory: the requirement to switch resources from civilian to military needs was bound to place additional burdens on the civilian population with consequent deleterious effects on morale. Thus, the regime had to try and square a circle: to mobilize maximum resources without at the same time undermining morale. Civilian morale in war was a particularly sensitive issue for the Nazi regime. The German revolution and defeat of November 1918 had been a traumatic event for Hitler and, as he repeatedly asserted, he was determined to prevent another November 1918.[1] In this at least he and his regime were successful. There was no revolution. The Nazi regime only collapsed after total defeat and military occupation.

Hitler had been preparing for war since achieving power in January 1933 and doing so with the full support of the German elites. The pre-war years had seen the German economy more thoroughly geared to war than those of the other belligerents. Only in Japan and the USSR was the proportion of net national product devoted to personal consumption lower than in Germany during the late 1930s, and Germany had produced far more combat munitions between 1935 and 1939 than any other power and as much in real terms as her future enemies combined.[2] Between 1936 and 1939, the regime had introduced a whole battery of measures with which to direct the economy – controls over investment, raw material allocation, prices, wages, and the direction of labour. However, Germany was very far from having an economy geared to total war by 1939. There was no rationing, labour conscription was still being used sparingly, and a large amount of resources was being poured into prestige building projects to glorify the regime and its various organizations.

A consensus is now emerging among historians that the failure fully to mobilize the German economy for war by 1939 was not the product of a coherent strategy of Blitzkrieg, although there is disagreement about the regime's effectiveness in mobilizing the economy for war between 1936 and 1942.[3] However, it did not consciously intend to limit rearmament. Such limitation was rather the result of a combination of political pressures and serious flaws in the administrative structures of German economic mobilization. On 23 May 1939, Hitler informed the Commanders-in-Chief of the *Wehrmacht* and their chiefs of staff: 'All armed services and governments must try to secure a short war. However, the Government has to prepare for a war of ten or fifteen years duration.'[4] Following this line, the regime appears to have operated on the simple principle of 'producing as much and as quickly as possible'. However, the effectiveness of German rearmament was seriously undermined by a lack of coordination and coherent planning. Control was divided between the *Wehrmacht*, which was responsible for the armaments sector as such, and the Economics Ministry which was responsible for other sectors of the econonmy which were significant for rearmament. The result was damaging friction between the two. Moreover, the various branches of the *Wehrmacht* found it impossible to coordinate their demands on the economy, with each section of the armed forces going its own way under constant pressure from the Führer to expand. The result was a war of all against all.[5] Moreover, political concern about morale prevented the regime from imposing tough measures such as the closing down of parts of the consumer sector or the imposition of rationing.

The result of all this economic activity was that the economy was overloaded.[6] Already, at the start of 1939, industry reported that firms were operating at a level of between 10 and 20 per cent beyond their capacity depending on the extent to which the particular branch was involved in rearmament. The result was a repeated slipping of delivery dates, which had a knock-on effect since many firms were sub-contractors. The biggest bottle-neck was labour. By 1939, it was estimated that Germany was short of one million workers with mining and, above all, agriculture most seriously affected. This resulted in competition between employers for scarce labour which, despite wage controls, lead to an increase in wages. Given the difficulty of expanding the consumer goods sector to meet rising demand, while simultaneously increasing rearmament, this development had serious inflationary implications. Above all, the issue of labour was the one where the two issues of resource mobilization and popular morale were most intimately related and it is, therefore, the aspect of resource mobilization on which this paper will concentrate.

With the outbreak of war in September 1939, the regime hoped to be able to use the emergency as an excuse to bring the economy under control and at last gear it fully to the needs of war. This objective lay behind the War Economy Decree of 4 December 1939.[7] It was intended to impose sacrifices on the population by cutting wages and increasing taxes, measures which would be partially offset by a reduction in prices. The decree abolished all bonuses for overtime, night shift and Sunday working, ordered the fixing of maximum wage rates in all branches of industry, and introduced a war tax affecting some forty per cent of all industrial workers. In addition, the decree suspended all holiday rights and proposed an increase in tax on luxury items. The aim was to reduce the earnings of German industrial workers by approximately ten per cent, which was intended to be matched by an equivalent reduction in prices in all sectors of the economy apart from agriculture. At the same time, the regime exploited the opportunity to extend the programme of civil labour conscription which had been introduced in 1938. Before the war, 800,000 workers had already been conscripted, of whom 400,000 were involved in the construction of the so-called West Wall. Now, between 1 and 12 September 1939, another 500,000 workers were conscripted and deployed where the labour shortage was most acute.[8] Finally, the Ministry of Labour suspended the legal limits on hours of work.

Within a matter of weeks, however, the Governmment found itself obliged to reverse its tough measures. Between mid-November 1939 and January 1940, they had virtually all either been revoked or drastically modified. The Government had been forced to backtrack on its hard-line programme because of a campaign of passive resistance to its measures by the workforce.[9] The workers' resentment found expression in increased rates of absenteeism and a decline in productivity. Their protest was taken up by Nazi Party and Labour Front officials who were concerned about a deterioration in morale; and it even met with a sympathetic response from some employers worried about deteriorating productivity. Hitler himself had intervened to insist that newly conscripted workers must be employed in firms near their homes since it was impossible to compel workers to live separated from their families. The number of conscripted workers reached a peak in January 1940 of 1.4 million, declining thereafter to 0.68 million in October 1942.

The withdrawal of its hard-line programme out of concern for workers' morale left the Government's labour strategy in some disarray. There were two main problems: 1) an overall labour shortage made increasingly acute by continuing conscription into the Army. Between May 1939 and May 1940, 4.3 million Germans were conscripted into the *Wehrmacht,* of whom over 900,000 came from industry, representing about ten per cent of the industrial work force. 2) The need to transfer labour to those sectors of the economy which were vital to the war effort from those that were not so vital.

To take the second point first: As part of its softer line, the Government had replaced the attempt to reduce wages by a wage freeze. However, by freezing wage rates, the regime had forfeited a mechanism for the reallocation of labour which was to prove highly effective in Britain and, above all, the United States, namely the operation of the market with high wages in the armaments sector attracting labour from other parts of the economy.[10] Furthermore, the problem was compounded by the running down of civil conscription as an alternative tool of labour allocation. In place of these two more effective methods, the regime was obliged to adopt inadequate substitutes – notably the so-called 'combing through' of businesses by roving commissions looking for surplus or inefficiently employed labour and the closing down of businesses which were deemed inessential to the war effort.[11] The problem with these methods was that employers understandably tended to resist the loss of their labour and the closure of their businesses and, what is more, often received support from the local Nazi Party officials who were either concerned at the consequent damage to the local economy or ideologically committeed to the maintenance of small business or both. As a result, such attempts at rationalization of the labour supply proved relatively ineffective. This in turn inevitably made the overall problem of the labour shortage even more acute.

During 1939-41, this situation did not become critical, mainly because the military campaigns were brief and maximum armament production was not in fact required. Indeed, during 1939 and 1940, British armament production was running at a higher level than that in Germany. This was not so much a conscious policy of Blitzkrieg for, during 1939-40, Hitler pressed for a huge armaments' programme. Only the Russian campaign of 1941 was planned as a Blitzkrieg. It was more the result of a continuation of the administrative weaknesses - above all, the lack of coordination and coherent planning - which had bedevilled the pre-war rearmament programme. These weaknesses could only be tolerated because of Germany's military success.

With the reverse in front of Moscow in December 1941, however, the crisis had arrived. It was now apparent that Germany was engaged in a two-front war against major powers which would be likely to last some time. The new situation required a complete overhaul of the administration of the rearmament programme. Above all, as the eastern front gobbled up more and more manpower the labour shortage became critical. In September 1941, there were already more than 2.6 million vacancies - half in agriculture, 50,000 in the mines, and more than 300,000 in the metal industries. And things were going to get worse. Between late May 1942 and September 1944, a further 3.6 million Germans were to be drafted into the Wehrmacht. Between February 1942 and January 1945, 687,000 protected (UK) workers were conscripted from the armaments industry alone.[12]

In January 1942, Hitler responded to this crisis by appointing the Gauleiter of Thuringia, Fritz Sauckel, to the new post of Reich Commissioner for Labour Mobilization. Sauckel was immediately confronted with the problem of where the additional workers were to come from. One solution was a more vigorous enforcement of the combing through and closure programmes, which this time included government and party agencies. However, although this proved slightly more successful than before, it only produced a few hundred thousand redeployed workers, when what was needed was millions of new workers. The question was: where were they to come from ? The regime endeavoured to fill the labour gap by tapping two main sources of new labour: the first, and by far the most important, was foreigners – POWs and foreign workers recruited either voluntarily or by force; the second was German women.

Even before the outbreak of war, the regime had tried to fill the labour gap by recruiting foreign workers – Poles, in particular – to work on the land.[13] Now, Sauckel replaced the predominantly voluntary recruitment practised hitherto by ruthless press-ganging. By 1944, there was a total of 7.6 million foreign workers in the Greater German Reich, 5.7 million of them civilians, 1.9 million POWs. One third of the civilians were women, of whom 87 per cent came from the East. Of the male civilians 62 per cent came from the East. According to some figures, by 1944 one in four of all those employed was a foreign worker. In agriculture the figure was one in two. Indeed, in eastern Germany there were large rural areas where there were twice as many foreign workers as male German workers. In the mining, construction and metal-working industries the figure was one in three. By August 1944, 38 per cent of the miners in the Ruhr were foreign. By that date there were 400,000 foreign workers in Berlin alone –10 per cent of its population. All over Germany there were foreign labour camps.

In fact, the decision to recruit foreign labour on a massive scale was not an easy option for the regime to take. There was very considerable opposition from the Party and the SS to the idea of importing large numbers of foreign workers into Germany, particularly Poles and Russians who were considered racially inferior. In the end an implicit bargain was reached: the Party and the SS accepted the arguments of the technocrats in the Armaments and Labour Ministries on the need for foreign labour. In return, the Party and SS were able to insist on a policy of ruthless discrimination and vicious discipline, particularly with the Russians and Poles. There was in fact a hierarchy among the foreign workers, with West Europeans at the top, who were treated not very differently from German workers in terms of pay and conditions, though they were clearly subordinate to the Germans, to the Poles and Russians at the bottom who were treated appallingly.

How then did the German workers respond to this influx of foreign labour? It is in fact difficult to generalise about the relations between the German and foreign workers.[14] There were cases of brutality by German foremen and supervisors, particularly in the mines, but there were also cases of generosity by German workers, providing food for example. The majority response of German workers appears to have been indifference. Much depended on circumstances – on the particular employer or on whether or not the foreign worker had particular skills. Thus, where foreign workers had skills and performed them well they were sometimes integrated to some extent into the shop floor community.

People's actual experience of workers from the Soviet Union tended to undermine the propaganda sterotypes of the Nazis. Thus, the Nazi Security Service (SD) reported in August 1942:

> The people of the Soviet Union have been portrayed as animals, as bestial. The commissar and the Politruk are regarded as the epitome of subhumanity. The reports about atrocities in the first months of the eastern campaign confirmed the opinion that the members of the enemy army were beasts. People were concerned about what could be done with these animals in the future. Many compatriots thought they should be ruthlessly exterminated. In view of the reports about atrocities committed by escaped Russian POWs, there was some concern that these types could come to the Reich in large numbers and even be employed as labour. But now many compatriots contrast this view with the qualities of intellect and character of the thousands of eastern workers. Workers, in particular, note that these Russians are often quite intelligent, fit in easily, are quick at understanding even quite complicated mechanical processes. Many learn German quickly and are often by no means badly educated. These experiences have undermined their previous image of the people from the East.[15]

There was, however, an insidious aspect to this presence of foreign workers, namely the way in which German workers became involved willy nilly in the racist policy of the Government by the very fact that they adapted to their position as supervisors of a helot population of foreign workers. For some Germans it meant, in effect, promotion. As far as the Nazis were concerned, this had the political benefit of adjusting the Germans to their future role as the superior beings in a post-war 'New Order' in Europe, for which the hierarchy within the foreign labour force provided a useful model.

Despite the appalling wastage of human resources involved, particularly through the virtual starvation of workers from the Soviet Union (quite apart from the inhumanity of their treatment), the Nazi programme of employing foreign labour was undoubtedly an economic success from the German point of view. They formed a crucial part of the German home front and without them Germany would have been unable to contine fighting beyond 1941. Moreover, the extensive employment of foreign labour enabled many Germans to avoid having to perform the hardest and most unpleasant jobs. Thus there was no need for Bevin boys in the mines in Germany; the job was done by Poles or Russians. Finally, the use of foreign labour enabled the regime to refrain from using draconian measures of conscription on women, at any rate until the last stage of the war.

The increased employment of women was the obvious other alternative to foreign labour as a means of closing the labour gap. Attention has often been drawn to the relative failure to recruit German women for the war effort, particularly by comparison with Britain and the United States.[16] However, this interpretation has recently been challenged by Richard Overy who has argued that the concentration on the employment of women in industry (or lack of it) has meant that the extent of the employment of women in other sectors of the economy – on the land or in family businesses – has been overlooked.[17] He claims that in fact more women were employed in Germany than in Britain during the war and that the role of female employment in these sectors made a crucial contribution to the war economy and placed major restraints on the extent to which they could be mobilized for industry.

This is an important corrective. Nevertheless, it is questionable whether it entirely refutes the argument that Germany was less successful at mobilising women into industry, particularly the armaments' sector, than Britain or the United States. For, this argument is not simply an *ex post facto* construction by historians trying to prove the existence of a Blitzkrieg strategy for the years 1939-1942. Rather, it forms a constant refrain among the German officials involved in trying to bridge the labour gap in industry and in the SD reports of popular opinion, particularly among those women who were employed in industry. On 16 February 1944, Field Marshall Erhard Milch,one of the key figures in the War Economy, concluded that there had been 'a total failure in the mobilisation of German women for employment in the armaments' sector.'[18] It was only in December 1944, for example, that systematic attempts were made to train women for armaments work and it was only then that women began to be used for aircraft production.[19] By comparison, in the United States women made up 39 per cent of the labour force in aircraft factories, in the United Kingdom it was 40 per cent.[20] How then did this situation come about ?

At the outbreak of war women were already subject to civil conscription on the same terms as men under the legislation of June 1938 and February 1939.[21] However, the authorities were even more cautious of conscripting women than men for fear of its impact on morale, and up to June 1940 only about 250,000 women had been conscripted, all of whom were already in work, i.e. they were simply being transferred to other work. In fact, the most striking development in German female employment after the outbreak of war was its sharp fall. Whereas in Britain the number of women in regular employment rose by 10 per cent between June 1939 and March 1940, in Germany the number of women in ensured employment fell by 540,000, 300,000 of whom left work between October and December 1939.

The main reason for this fall was the introduction of generous family support allowances for the families of men who had been called up into the armed forces. The authorities were very mindful of the negative effects on morale in the First World War of the inadequate support given to such families. So now they fixed that the wives of combatants would receive up to 85 per cent of their husbands' previous wages plus other benefits such as rent allowances and free health insurance. The average allowance received was in fact 73-75 per cent of former earnings. This compared with 38 per cent in the United Kingdom and 36 per cent in the United States. Women who earned more than one third of the amount of their family allowance had it deducted from the allowance.

The allowance scheme had initially included a stipulation that all recipients should demonstrate that they were taking steps to contribute to their own living expenses, i.e. it was envisaged more as a top-up arrangement. But within weeks of the outbreak of war the authorities had back-tracked and removed this stipulation. The result was that most soldiers' wives who could afford to give up employment did so. They considered the extra money which they could earn above their allowance, i.e. one third, marginal in view of the fact that there was virtually nothing to buy with the money saved. Moreover, by working they subjected their clothes and shoes to excess wear and tear at a time when there was a serious shortage of these commodities. They also increased their calorie consumption at a time of food rationing. This phenomenon of women leaving employment in droves was exacerbated by a boom in war marriages followed by a baby boom. This was encouraged by the Nazi Party agencies on grounds of population policy. Indeed Rudolf Hess publicly encouraged unmarried girls to 'present the Führer with a baby'.[22] But the authorities responsible for labour deployment believed that some of these young women were simply marrying in order to be eligible for family allowances.

Women who had previously worked but had left the work force on the outbreak of war were eventually forced back to work by an unpublished decree issued by

Göring on 20 June 1941.[23] However, in general, the years 1940-1944 were marked by the largely unsuccessful attempts of the officials of the Ministry of Labour, the Nazi Labour Front, Sauckel, and even the Propaganda Ministry, to introduce a tougher line on the mobilisation of women. At last, in January 1943, under the impact of the defeats of Stalingrad and El Alemain, the regime introduced a decree which obliged all women aged between seventeen and forty-five and all men between sixteen and sixty-five to report to their local labour office if they were not already in the armed forces or in full-time employment.[24] Exceptions were made for pregnant women or those who had a child under school age or two children under the age of fourteen. By the end of June 1943, 3,048,000 women had registered with the Labour Office. However, of these only 500,000 women were still in employment in December 1943. Six hundred thousand had secured their release through official channels; many simply abandoned employment without notifying the authorities. Others fixed up cushy office jobs for themselves through their connections. The Labour Offices were more or less powerless to prevent this because their guidelines insisted on kid gloves treatment for women.

We have already noted one of the two main reasons for this relative failure to mobilize German women into the armaments sector – the availability of foreign workers. Foreign workers were generally stronger and had more skills than German women, particularly those not yet employed who tended to be middle-class women unused to factory employment. Certainly they were generally preferred by German employers for whom they had the benefit of being generally cheaper and not subject to the same restrictions on hours of work and types of employment as were German female workers and not requiring special facilities. Having said that, British middle-class women *were* conscripted into factory work. For example, the author's two unmarried aunts, hitherto ladies of leisure, worked for the Handley Page bomber factory in north London from 1943 to 1945, the one as a riveter and the other as her mate !

This was a scenario to which Hitler had strong objections and it was these objections which formed the other main reason. He was influenced by a combination of concerns: firstly, morale–both of husbands and fathers at the front who would object to the conscription of their wives and mothers and of the civilian population at home on whom female conscription would impose an additional burden.[25] Secondly he had racist, sexist, and class objections.[26] A woman who had not been brought up to work in a factory would do more politically for the morale of the population if she looked after her family at home than if she worked in a factory where she would only cause problems. The subjection of middle-class women to a crude factory environment would inflict moral damage. Conscription into industry would cause biological damage and adversely affect women's prime function as mothers.

Until September 1944, Hitler even opposed the conscription of housemaids. For most of the war it was possible for a household to have several domestic servants. Thus, while in Britain the number of domestic servants dropped from 1.2 million to 400,000, in Germany it only went down from 1.56 million to 1.36 million. Overy's point that domestic servants were often not servants as such, but part of a family business has some force.[27] However, he does not take account of the fact that those responsible for labour mobilisation clearly believed that a tougher line should be taken, but were blocked by Hitler who argued not on grounds of economic rationality but from prejudice. He insisted that Germany was not a Communist state and told Sauckel to 'import 100,000 healthy and strong female Ukrainians' instead.[28] In the spring of 1944, Sauckel told Speer that he had repeatedly asked Hitler for powers 'a la Stalin' for the mobilization of female labour but that Hitler had refused with the argument that the 'slim and long-legged German women' could not be compared with the 'dumpy, primitive and healthy Russian women'.[29]

The failure until the last stages of the war to adopt a policy of systematic conscription for women and the restriction of coercive measures to those women who had previously worked, while many of those who had never worked before were able to escape work or find congenial or token employment had serious repercussions on the morale of the female labour force. This is clear from the reports of the SD. For example, the SD reported in August 1941 the comments of female factory workers from Dortmund, who had been recalled to work by the secret Göring decree aimed at those who had left work at the beginning of the war as a result of the introduction of family allowances:

> We can understand that it's necessary for us to go back to work. It will cause us some unpleasant difficulties but there's a war on and we want to do our bit. But why is Frau Director S not conscripted along with her servants. Her little four-year-old son could spend the day in the NSV Kindergarten just like our children. Furthermore, she would learn the simple techniques in the factory just as quickly as we do. Why is there not equal treatment for all compatriots ? The wealthy ladies who did not need to work before are now once again being protected. If that does not change then we shall simply go on sick leave from time to time. Nothing will happen to us.[30]

The point about going on sick leave was an important one. Work discipline among the female workforce was notoriously bad with widespread and persistent absenteeism. This was often not so much a protest against the regime but rather a response to the intolerable burdens placed on working women, many of whom were also obliged to fulfill duties as housewives and mothers in a war situation where such duties were even more onerous than usual. The authorities were aware of this situation and loath to take tough measures against such breaches of discipline. On 13 November 1940, the Ministry of Labour emphasized 'the fear of producing an unfavourable popular response through the harsh treatment of women who are unwilling to work'.[31] The women soon became aware of this as is clear from the woman's comment in the SD report. In fact, the SD showed considerable sympathy for the women's situation. Another report dated 17 August 1942, for example, noted:

> The mood has become tenser as a result of the difficult food situation and the length of the war. It's understandable that women whose men have not been on leave for twelve to nineteen months are not in the best of spirits. One should also not ignore the fact that, after the end of their shift, women still have their household duties to attend to, which are now more onerous than in normal times. In addition, there are worries about the husband at the front so that enough explosive material has been stored up which is liable to detonate if their request for a day off etc. is not respected. Then all warnings and references to the needs of the hour meet with an icy silence.[32]

The problem was that the authorities had no real answer to the complaints of the women about the injustice of their treatment. According to the same SD report:

> The greatest difficulties are faced by the colleagues from the Party and the Labour Front, particularly those who give speeches, who are continually being asked in the factories why one class of women is overburdened while the other is not called upon to make any sacrifices. There is no satisfactory answer to this question since those involved can only refer to the fact that the Führer continues to expect the voluntary commitment of all women. Even the best speakers and propagandists who have continually been calling for efficiency and self-sacrifice have now gradually lost the confidence of the retinue [the Nazi word for the workforce] because they have either had to remain silent in response to this question, which damages the prestige of the Party, or their explanations have lacked uniformity from which the population believes it can deduce the uncertainty of the leadership regarding this question.[33]

What effects did the war have on the millions of women who nevertheless did work ? First, the shortage of males forced the regime to modify its ideological principles somewhat as far as the employment of professional women was concerned.[34] During the first years after 1933, professional women had been discriminated against; now they were welcomed back, though they were still excluded from certain spheres, notably the legal profession. Also far more female students were admitted. The regime felt that highly qualified women would be needed as a stop-gap until the number of qualified males, depleted by the war, had been made up again by a new generation of post-war male students.

Secondly, the war saw a shift towards employment in the service industries and administration.[35] The key factor in this shift from blue to white collar employment was the superior pay and status associated with white collar jobs. Women in office jobs were favoured because male office workers were drafted and, unlike in blue-collar jobs,few foreign substitutes could be employed. The result was that a twenty-two year old single typist in a coal mining firm earned 25 per cent more than a face worker with a family.

Generally, of course, women continued to be paid less than men. Equal pay was introduced in the public sector in September 1939 for women who worked in the same job as men achieving the same performance, a job which was particularly responsible or physically demanding. [36] However, private employers were generally hostile and in the private sector – with the exception of certain piece-rate jobs in particular industries – most women were paid 20-25 per cent less than men.

Although sensitive to the need not to upset wage stability or antagonize male workers, some agencies in the regime were sympathetic to a move towards more equal pay for women, particularly during the last phase of the war when the need to attract women into work made it particularly desirable. In April 1944, Sauckel pleaded with Hitler for equal pay for equal work but he vetoed it. It clearly went against his male chauvinist principles and he no doubt feared male reaction from the shop floor and also from employers. He replied:

The only possibility of removing existing hardships and injustices is for us to win the war so that we reach a position in which all German women and girls can be removed from all jobs which we must regard as unwomenly, which undermine the birthrate, and threaten the family and the nation.[37]

Finally, much was done to protect women workers - more indeed than in the United States or the United Kingdom, where there were far fewer restrictions on what work women could do.[38] Hours of work for women were initially restricted to 48 per week, later raised to 51 in 1942 and then to 56 in 1944 – each time four or five hours less than for men. Night shifts were restricted, whereas in the United States 50 per cent of women were on night shift in 1943. In May 1942, a Mothers' Protection Law was passed which, apart from granting six weeks maternity leave before and after birth, insisted on the provision of creches and nursing rooms in all firms which employed substantial numbers of women. In the United States federally-funded care centres cared for only 120,000 children at their peak in 1944. By contrast, in Germany there were 32,000 creches by 1944, which cared for 1,200,000 children.[39] However, this commitment to women's health and well-being reflected the regime's ideological concern with motherhood as much or more than the need to attract and keep women in the labour force.

As we have seen, the relatively soft line taken by the regime towards female labour mobilization – at any rate up to 1943 – was motivated in large part by concern for morale. At the same time, the ability to take this soft line was in turn dependent on the extensive use of foreign labour. Labour, however, was not the only resource which Nazi Germany was able to plunder from its empire, though it was probably the most crucial. Supplies of raw materials were also important as were – most significant from the point of view of the home front – food supplies.[40] Between 1939 and 1944, Germany imported large amounts of foodstuffs from her empire. In addition, her occupation armies largely lived off the land where they were stationed, a fact which helped to compensate for the burden of feeding the foreign workers employed in Germany. Ironically, she acquired far more from Western Europe than from the putative *Lebensraum* in the East. This was achieved at the expense of the consumption of the occupied territories. These imports enabled the regime to sustain significantly higher levels of food supplies than had been the case in the First World War. [41]

Food shortages had played a crucial role in the deterioration of morale in World War I, when the horrors of the 'turnip winter' of 1916 and the deaths of hundreds of thousands of people through the effects of malnutrition had imposed intolerable burdens on the German people. Moreover, as, if not more, important than the shortages had been the sense of injustice at the inequity of the distribution system. Although rationing had been introduced, it had not functioned effectively and the black market had flourished. In 1939 the German authorities were determined not to make the same mistake again and had, therefore, made plans for a more efficient and equitable rationing system, which was introduced on 28 August 1939. [42]

Whereas Britain limited its rationing mainly to protein foods, milk, and fats and so was able to adopt a uniform system of rationing, since the need for these varies little between individuals, German rationing covered a wider range of foods, including carbohydrates, and so was obliged to adopt a differential system, allocating larger amounts to certain categories which required a higher calorie intake.[43] The scheme initially involved three main categories based on performance: the normal consumer (64.5% of the population), who received 2,570 calories per day, the heavy worker (6%) 3,789 calories, and the very heavy worker (2.3%) 4,652 calories. In addition, there was the *Wehrmacht* (5.9%), children under six (9.6%) 1,871 calories, and children aged 6-14 (11.5%) 2450 calories. From 20 November 1939, a new category was introduced between the normal worker and the heavy workers for those who worked excessively long hours and night workers. The average daily calorie intake per individual per day from 25 September 1939 was 2,672. This compares with 3,206 in 1938 and with an average requirement for the maintenance of full physical health of 2,700. Food rationing was paralleled by rationing of other commodities. Thus, the German population was expected to tighten its belt very considerably and, unlike the measures of the War Economy Decree of 4 September 1939, there was no let-up in the pressure after the victory over Poland, despite the widespread disgruntlement reported by the SD.

In fact, for much of the time workers did not actually receive the norms because of problems of supply and distribution of particular commodities. In the spring of 1942, there was a general crisis in the food supply which caused rations to be cut.[44] However, by the autumn they had been partially restored and it was only in the last months of the war that the food supply position became critical. The war did see an increase in sickness rates, but the deterioration in health was by no means catastrophic and Allied doctors who examined the health of the Germans in the aftermath of the war pronounced it suprisingly good.[45] This was very different from the First World War when the appalling flu epidemic of the winter of 1918-19 wreaked havoc among a debilitated population.

It is clear from the SD reports that morale was significantly affected by food supplies. Thus, after the announcement of the cut in rations in March 1942, the SD reported as follows:

> Several reports state that the announcement of the 'deep cuts' in food supplies has had a really 'devastating' effect on a large section of the population to a degree which is virtually unparalleled by any other incident during the war. Although people are generally aware of the fact that, in order to achieve final victory, the German people will have to adjust to this new situation, relatively few people have been prepared to show the requisite understanding for the new cut in food rations. In particular, the workers in the big cities and industrial areas, who often considered the previous supplies pretty limited, are apparently adopting an attitude which shows no understanding whatsoever for the necessity of this new measure. The mood among these sections of the population has reached the lowest point ever in the course of the war. Numerous compatriots have expressed their disappointment in ironical remarks about the allegedly secure German supply situation and in frank hints about a deterioration in their future work performance. The new restrictions are felt particularly acutely by housewives who find it impossible to feed their families adequately ... In the context of the announcement of a cut in food rations the population is once more becoming increasingly preoccupied with the question of the fairness of the allocation of food and other goods in short supply. People – particularly workers – mention with great bitterness the fact that a large section of the so-called better-off circles can get hold of things in short supply in addition to their food rations through their social connections and their bigger purses. There is widespread concern that after the implementation of the new food allocations, bartering on the Black Market will become even more widespread than hitherto.[46]

In the autumn of 1942, the cuts made in March were partially revoked and a special Christmas bonus was announced as well as concessions to those on leave from the front. Also, Göring made a major speech boasting about the huge resources of food which Germany had conquered in its summer campaign. This produced a significant improvement in morale according to the SD report of 8 October 1942.[47]

Shortages of other commodities could also have quite an impact on morale, but significantly the effect seems to have been worst in the early days when the shortages were not so acute but when people were less inured to them. In the winter of 1939-1940, for example, considerable discontent was reported over shortages, in particular of shoes and coal.[48] The coal crisis was so serious that some firms had to shut down for days at a time and domestic heating was a major problem during what was a severe winter. However, these shortages became much worse later on. In the final months of the war the supply of food and other essential commodities such as gas and even water began to collapse in some areas and yet these shortages did not produce another November 1918.[49]

In a situation in which the supply of most commodities was regulated by rationing wages were clearly less significant as a factor in sustaining morale than in normal times. However, they remained important, particularly since not everything was rationed and the black market became increasingly significant as the war continued. Although the government failed in its plans to reduce wages at the outbreak of war, it did impose a wage freeze with the goal of avoiding inflation.[50] And, despite the fact that it was not wholly successful in sustaining the freeze, it did manage to achieve a remarkable degree of price and wage stability. The cost of living index rose by only 12 per cent between 1939 and 1944 although the money in circulation went up five times from 10.95 to 56.7 billion RM, whereas the Mark had lost half its value between 1914 and 1918. Wage increases were achieved mainly through an increase in hours worked rather than in hourly rates. Up to 1941, there was a slight increase in real earnings for industrial workers; after that date they appear to have declined slightly until, in 1943, they equalled those of 1938, though gross earnings were still higher than in 1939. However, data for real earnings, particularly in the later phases of the war are largely guess- work because of the difficulty of assessing what workers could actually buy with their wages. However, what is clear is that, whereas in the First World War high inflation and a sharp decline in real wages for many social groups contributed much to the deterioration in morale between 1916 and 1918, in the Second World War these did not occur.

Morale was also sustained – for a time at any rate – by the expectations aroused and the opportunities created by the war. In 1940, for example, the German Labour Front published proposals for a new pensions and health insurance scheme – a kind of German Beveridge Plan, though one requiring its recipients to conform to the norms of the 'national community'.[51] Similarly, Robert Ley, the head of the Labour Front, was appointed to head a major housing project for the post-war era, which envisaged the creation of model housing estates.[52] These programmes were portrayed as a manifestation of the express wish of the Führer that 'victory should ensure a better life for every German'.[53]

While these programmes represented hopes for the future, the war also brought benefits, for some at least, in the present. Above all, it increased the possibilities of upward social mobility which had already emerged in the pre-war years – for example, through the rapid expansion of the officer corps in the armed forces and the numerous posts in the expanding bureaucracies required to run the New Order in Europe. Retraining programmes enabled workers to improve their qualifications and thereby increase their pay and acquire better jobs, while many of the remaining German workers who had not been conscripted into the armed forces became supervisors of foreign workers.[54]

The mood of the German people on the outbreak of war was summed up by two post-war historians, one of whom (Helmut Krausnick) had personally experienced it, as 'reluctant loyalty'.[55] The great foreign policy successes of the preceding years – the Rhineland, Munich, Prague etc. had been extremely popular. But the most popular thing about them had been that they had been achieved without war. Only a few fanatical Nazis and naive Hitler Youth members actually wanted a major war. This had represented a significant failure of Nazi indoctrination. However, although the German people entered the war reluctantly, their loyalty to the regime was not in question. For, by 1939, the Nazi regime had acquired a very large reservoir of support which it could draw on when the going got tough. The overcoming of the economic crisis of the early 1930s and the restoration of Germany's international prestige, and the fact that these achievements were associated with an individual who had come to embody not only the regime but, as far as many Germans were concerned, the nation itself – these facts provided a great reserve of strength.[56] By 1939, most people trusted the Führer to know and to do what was best for Germany even if it might not always seem so. It would take a considerable time and a series of major defeats before this confidence was seriously eroded.

In Germany, as in Britain, morale responded to the course of the war, though, as is clear from the British case, not necessarily through the obvious correlation of success with high morale and vice versa. In Germany, however, the high point of civilian morale was reached in the second half of June 1940. Referring to the activities of opposition forces in Germany, the SD reported on 24 June that:

Under the impression of the great political events and under the spell of military success, the whole German nation is displaying an inner unity and close bond between the front and the homeland which is unprecedented. The soil is no longer fertile for opposition groups. Everyone looks up to the Führer in trust and gratitude and to his armed forces pressing forward from victory to victory. Opposition activities meet everywhere with sharp rejection.[57]

However, just as, if not more, important than military victory in creating this mood was the belief that the war would soon come to an end. And, by 7 October, the SD was reporting a change of mood:

It is clear from the Gau reports of the past week that large sections of the population are adopting a completely unappreciative and thoroughly unccoperative attitude which expresses itself in particular in comments about the press and the radio. Impatience with the fact that the 'big blow' against England has not yet occurred predominates. People are already switching their attention to other topics. Even interest in military developments has declined most regrettably. Grudgingly and reluctantly, the population is getting used to the thought of a second winter of war and daily worries, particularly about fuel, have come to the surface.[58]

Although the initial successes of the Russian campaign in June-July 1941 produced a brief mood of confidence, it was soon replaced by growing concern, particularly when, in December 1941, Goebbels announced a public collection of warm winter clothing for the troops on the eastern front. Above all, the military crisis of winter 1941-1942 produced a crisis of credibility for German propaganda.

In some respects it could be said that British propaganda was fortunate in having a war which began with Britain on her beam ends and in which the Government had little choice but to spell out the problems the country faced in blunt terms ('blood, toil, tears, and sweat'). In the case of Germany the position was reversed. She started at the top and then had to cope with a series of ups and downs leading into a steady decline. Moreover, the Nazi regime and above all Hitler's role as Führer had been built on success. It was understandable, therefore, that the leadership tended towards over-optimism in its public comments and was loath to admit to difficulties.. The problem was, however, that the growing gap between the reality, as people perceived it or suspected it, and the picture portayed by Nazi propaganda undermined people's belief in the official media. For example, on 3 October 1941, Hitler announced in a major speech that 'this opponent' referring to the Soviet Union 'is already broken and will never recover'.[59] Six days later, this was confirmed by Otto Dietrich, the Reich Press Chief, who announced to the assembled press that the Soviet Union was 'militarily finished'.[60] In fact, of course, within two months the German armies were reeling back in headlong retreat and, with appeals for warm clothing and generals being dismissed, it was impossible to disguise the crisis that had developed. It was not surprising, therefore, that, on 22 January 1942, the SD reported as follows:

> It is clear from a number of reports that the impact of the public media of guidance is at the moment greatly impaired. Of the various explanations usually given the following are the most frequent:
> People had the feeling that when things were going badly the public media of guidance always preserved an 'official face'. As a result, in such situations large sections of the population no longer regard the press as the best source of information but construct 'their own picture' from rumours, stories told by soldiers, and people with 'political connections', letters from the front and such like, often accepting the craziest rumours with an astonishing lack of discrimination.
> Also as regards the reasons for and implications of the wool collection, the event which has affected the population in the civilian sector more than any other since the beginning of the war, the public media of guidance had preserved their 'official face' in the sense of not giving any answers to the questions about the alleged organizational deficiencies of winter planning and the late timing of the collection, questions that were being asked by everybody.[61]

Once the war started running into difficulties, Goebbels had wanted to adopt a more realistic tone in Nazi propaganda, but in its reports the Army leadership, fearing damage to morale, preferred to disguise reality with euphemism and in this they were supported by Hitler. On 6 January 1943, with the Stalingrad disaster already apparent, Goebbels reflected on the inadequacy of German propaganda hitherto. 'Since the beginning of the war', he told German newspaper editors, 'our propaganda has followed the following erroneous course: first year of the war: We have won. Second year of the war: We shall win. Third year of the war: We must win. Fourth year of the war: We cannot be defeated. Such a development is catastrophic and must on no account be continued.'[62]

Goebbels responded to the Stalingrad crisis with his notorious 'total war' speech of 18 February 1943, in which in a series of ten questions, to which the carefully selected audience shouted 'yes', he called for a commitment from the whole population to wage total war, a kind of Nazi version of Churchill's 'blood, toil, tears, and sweat' speech.[63] The speech was greeted by relief that at last the Government had 'come clean' about the real situation. However, in view of what had happened up till then, people were rightly sceptical about the extent to which the burdens of war would be shared and fearful of the allied response to such a call for 'total war'.[64] Ruhr mine-workers shouted at the British bombers going over:

Dear Tommy, Dear Tommy fly on to Berlin
They're the ones who said yes to him.[65]

As the situation at the front continued to deteriorate, so the SD reported a growing sense of disillusionment with the regime. Thus, on 8 July, 1943, they reported:

> The telling of vulgar jokes detrimental to the state, even about the Führer himself, has increased considerably since Stalingrad. In conversations in cafes, factories and other meeting places people tell each other the 'latest' political jokes and in many cases make no distinction between those with a harmless content and those which are clearly in opposition to the state. Even people who hardly know each other exchange jokes. They clearly assume that any joke can now be told without fear of a sharp rebuff, let alone of being reported to the police. Large sections of the population and even a section of the Party membership have clearly lost the feeling that listening to and passing on political jokes of a certain type is something which a decent German simply does not do...[66]

And yet, despite the increasing disillusionment with the regime, and despite the growing burdens of the war, the German people did not revolt and morale did not totally collapse. Why was this ?

Apart from the points already made about the relative improvement in material circumstances by comparison with the First World War, an important factor was clearly the machinery of terror which was both highly efficient and extremely ruthless and which experienced a tremendous expansion during the war.[67] The war was fought by Hitler from the start as an ideological war, not only abroad against the 'sub-human' Poles and Russians, but also at home in the form of a purging of the 'national body'. All those groups regarded as being 'outside the national community' because they failed to conform to its norms – Jews, Gypsies, the mentally ill and handicapped, habitual criminals and 'asocials', and political offenders were removed from it through incarceration in prison or concentration camp or permanently through extermination.

As far as the question of morale was concerned, the system of terror operated in three main spheres: 1) against breaches of work discipline; 2) against organized opposition; 3) against those deemed guilty of undermining national morale without necessarily being involved in organized opposition.

As far as the category of work discipline was concerned, early on in the war the Gestapo established so-called 'Work Re-education Camps' where persistent absentees and 'slackers' (*Bummelanten*) were sent for periods of 6-8 weeks with the intention of administering a short sharp shock.[68] One gauge of German workers' morale is the fact that the number of German workers arrested each month for disciplinary offences rose by 52% between 1941 and the first half of 1944. In the latter period 20,000 German workers were being arrested each month for labour discipline offences. SD reports referred to the resentment of workers at the unequal distribution of the burdens of the war. However, the re-education camps were increasingly used for foreign workers, whereas Germans tended to be fined or in serious cases sent to prison. In fact, the regime was cautious about cracking down too hard over breaches of work discipline and also could not afford the loss of labour involved in sending people off to prison. In any case, the discipline of male German workers was generally good. An important reason for this was their fear of losing their status as reserved workers and being sent to the front. The majority of disciplinary offences were committed by women and young people under eighteen against whom the authorities felt unable to act toughly for fear of affecting morale. The relationship between the working class and the regime during the war has been summed up as 'the *containment* of working-class discontent rather than any enthusiasm for the regime and its policies'.[69]

As far as the second category – organized opposition – is concerned, the main sources of opposition were the Communists, at any rate after the attack on Russia, and the Resistance movement which culminated in the July 1944 plot against Hitler. They lie beyond the scope of this paper, although from the point of view of morale it must be said that neither had a significant basis of popular support.

Finally, at the outbreak of war, the Nazis introduced a number of measures based on the concept of 'defeatism' (*Wehrkraftzersetzung*). For example, at the beginning of the war, a ban on listening to foreign broadcasts was introduced with those found guilty being sentenced to imprisonment and, in serious cases, where they passed on information which was then construed as 'defeatist', to death. In fact, as the war went on, people making defeatist comments – perhaps overheard by their maid, for example, - were increasingly likely to be sentenced to death. In addition, a number of other offences, such as theft, which were construed as taking advantage of the war situation, e.g. the blackout, received the death penalty. The numbers of executions rose rapidly during the war from 143 in 1939 to 1,146 in 1941 and 5,764 in 1944.[70]

There were thus powerful reasons for people not to draw attention to themselves. As one worker put it: 'Rather than let them string me up I'll be glad to believe in victory.'[71] Added to this was the fact that the regime's virtual monopoly of organization combined with its control of the media ensured that the German people were atomised and deprived of access to alternative sources of information apart from their immediate contacts among family, work colleagues, and friends.[72] They were thus seriously hampered in developing an effective critique, let alone mobilizing a challenge to the regime of the kind that developed between 1916 and 1918.

This process of atomization was aided by the progressive dilution of the work force through waves of conscription of German workers from plants and their replacement by foreign workers, women, or very young workers. Women and young workers were notoriously indisciplined, but it was the indiscipline of individuals and posed no organized threat to the regime.

Nevertheless, it would be a mistake to attribute the lack of a November 1918 solely to the effects of terror, or to portray the Germans as a cowed population. It is significant, for example, that the response of the German public to the July 1944 plot against Hitler was not one of approval and disappointment at its failure, but rather of disapproval and relief.[73] There was a widespread feeling that these officers and top officials had rocked the national boat at a time when it was going through very choppy waters. By that time (July 1944), most people had come to feel that whether they liked it or not – and, as we have seen, many had by then become disillusioned with the regime and even with the Führer – they were bound together to the bitter end.

This sense of national solidarity was generated not so much by a residual patriotism, though this may have existed, but more by fear of the future, in particular of the Red Army, a fear reinforced by a sense of guilt for the conduct of the war in the East and the treatment of the Jews.[74] There was, in fact, a more general sense of complicity with the regime, which, together with a deep physical and emotional exhaustion after five years of war, helped to produce a paralysing belief that there was no alternative, an impression reinforced but not created by the Allied doctrine of 'unconditional surrender'. This situation was vigorously exploited by Nazi propaganda in its attempt to persuade the German people that they were indeed bound to the regime in a *Schicksalsgemeinschaft*, a 'community of fate'. There was thus a widespread feeling that there was no real alternative to staying on board and going over the waterfall together. Moreover, underpinning this relatively high degree of national solidarity was the local solidarity at the work place and in local communities. However, this raises the question of how and to what extent this local solidarity could be sustained under the impact of the Allied bombing campaign.

The bombing campaign had a tremendous physical impact in terms of death and destruction and it grew enormously from year to year. The total bomb load in 1943 was four times that of 1942 and in 1944 five times that of 1943. In February 1942 there were an average of 220 deaths per month from bombing, in the summer of 1942 this went up to 750, in 1943 up to 7,000, and in 1944 there were 5,500 - a drop which may be attributed to a shift in emphasis towards the second front in the West.[75] In four raids on Hamburg carried out within one week between 24 and 31 July 1943 45,000 were killed (40,000 in the firestorm on the night of 27-28th alone).

This compares with the total of 51,509 civilians killed in the United Kingdom by German bombing during the whole of the Second World War.[76] In the main part of the city of Hamburg 56 per cent of the family dwelling units were destroyed during this week and 900,000 people lost their homes. Over one million people fled the city during and in the aftermath of the raid. I mention this week of Hamburg raids rather than the even more destructive Dresden one because it happened much earlier (Dresden was destroyed in February 1945) and is less well-known. What happened to Hamburg in a week was happening to other German cities more gradually but hardly less effectively. In 1944, the city of Cologne, for example, had an air raid warning once a day and an air raid twice a week throughout that year.

The aim of these raids was to demoralize the German people. However, like the much less extensive raids on Britain, they failed. Workers continued to return to work after the raids. Even foreign workers cooperated voluntarily in the fire-fighting and clearing-up afterwards. Only a few took the opportunity to flee. Why was this?[77]

One fact was undoubtedly fear – above all, fear of losing their status as reserved workers and being sent to the eastern front. This need not even be an individual punishment. For, if the plant was unable to keep producing after a raid all the workers would inevitably be liable to conscription. However, there were also material benefits to be gained from continuing work. In order to secure their supplementary rations as heavy or very heavy workers they had to sign on in their plant. Also they could only get replacements for ration cards lost in air raids and compensation for war damage to their homes if they returned to their plants for a signature from their employers. In fact, some firms provided useful help in dealing with the authorities by bulk buying various scarce commodities such as bedding. Employers were anxious to keep their workers, in order not to be closed down.

Last, but by no means least, there were the psychological benefits from carrying on as before. The ordered routine of work provided a point of stability in a world of increasing chaos and a distraction from having to think about the future. A miner commented: 'I look forward to the evening with horror. As long as I am at work I don't remember, but when I get home I'm afraid.'[78]

Thus, while the extreme situation created by mass bombing certainly helped to undermine confidence in the regime as it had been intended to by the Allied strategists of area bombing, at the same time it created an atmosphere in which people became dominated by the priority of the need to survive from day to day. A new form of greeting emerged: 'BU' short for 'Bleib übrig' 'stay alive', literally 'be a survivor'.

This priority of survival through a catastrophe, and increasingly one whose end could be foreseen in the not too distant future, reinforced the tendency for people to keep their heads down for fear of the Gestapo and through sheer exhaustion. As the wielder of power, the Nazi regime benefitted from this. Those people who attempted to opt out of the 'community of fate' by desertion or premature surrender were summarily dealt with by the remaining hard-line supporters of the regime. In January 1945, Himmler imposed the death penalty for any leader of a civil office who abandoned his post without orders. The final weeks saw thousands of hangings and shootings.[79] For the Nazis were determined to prevent another November 1918 and to ensure that their fellow-Germans went over the waterfall with them.

NOTES

1. Cf. T.W. Mason, 'The Legacy of 1918 for National Socialism' in A. Nicholls and E. Matthias (ed.), *German Democracy and the Triumph of Hitler* (London, 1971) and *Sozialpolitik im Dritten Reich.Arbeiterklasse und Volksgemeinschaft*. (Opladen, 1977), pp. 15-41.
2. Cf. Mark Harrison, 'Resource Mobilization for World War II: the U.S.A., U.K., U.S.S.R, and Germany, 1938-1945', *Economic History Review* 2nd. 41 (1988), pp.171-92.
3. For the latest phase of the debate see B.R. Kroener, 'Squaring the Circle. Blitzkrieg Strategy and Manpower Shortage 1939-1942' in W. Deist (ed.), *The German Military in the Age of Total War* (Leamington, 1985), pp. 282-303; R.D. Müller, 'Die Mobilisierung der deutschen Wirtschaft für Hitlers Krieg-führung' in B.Kroener *et. al*, *Das Deutsche Reich und der Zweiter Weltkrieg* Vol. 5/1. *Organisation und Mobilisierung des deutschen Machtbereichs. Kriegsverwaltung, Wirtschaft und personellen Resourcen 1939-1941* (Stuttgart, 1988), pp. 349-689; B.R. Kroener, 'Die personellen Resourcen des Dritten Reiches im Spannungsfeld zwischen Wehrmacht, Bürokratie und Kriegswirts-chaft 1939-1942' in ibid., pp. 693-1002; R.Overy, ' "Blitzkriegswirtschaft"? Finanzpolitik, Lebensstandard und Arbeitseinsatz in Deutschland 1939-1942' *Vierteljahrshefte für Zeitgeschichte* 36 (1988), pp. 379-435; R.Overy, 'Mobilization for Total War in Germany 1939-1941' *English Historical Review* 103 (1988), pp. 613-39; B.R.Kroener, 'Der Kampf um den "Sparstoff Mensch". Forschungskontroversen über die Mobilisierung der deutschen Kriegswirtschaft 1939-1942' in W. Michalka (ed.), *Der Zweite Weltkrieg* (Munich, 1989), pp. 402-17
4. Cf. *Documents on German Foreign Policy* Series D, Vol. VI. p. 225.

5. Cf. W. Deist, *The Wehrmacht and German Rearmament*(London, 1981), pp. 91ff.
6. Cf. H-E. Volkmann, 'Die NS-Wirtschaft in Vorbereitung des Krieges' in W. Deist *et.al.*, *Das Deutsche Reich und Der Zweite Weltkrieg* Vol.1. *Ursachen und Voraussetzungen der Deutschen Kriegspolitik* (Stuttgart, 1979), pp. 364ff.
7. Cf. T. Mason, 'Labour in the Third Reich 1933-1939', in *Past and Present* 33 (1966), p. 20; M-L. Recker, *Nationalsozialistische Sozialpolitik im Zweiten Weltkrieg* (Munich, 1985), pp. 26ff; L. Herbst, *Der Totale Krieg und die Ordnung der Wirtschaft. Die Kriegswirtschaft im Spannungsfeld von Politik, Ideologie und Propaganda 1939-1945* (Stuttgart 1982), pp. 103-26.
8. Cf. S.Salter, 'The Mobilisation of German Labour, 1939-1945. A Contribution to the History of the Working Class in the Third Reich' (D.Phil. thesis, Oxford University, 1983), pp. 15-16.
9. See the references in fn.7.
10. Cf. A.S. Milward, 'Arbeitspolitik und Produktivität in der deutschen Kriegswirtschaft unter vergleichendem Aspekt' in F. Forstmeier and H-E. Volkmann, (ed.), *Kriegswirtschaft und Rüstung 1939-1945* (Düsseldorf, 1977), pp. 88-9.
11. Cf. Salter, (above, note 8), pp. 12ff; Kroener, 'Die personellen Resourcen..', (above, note 3), pp. 757ff.; W.F. Werner, *"Bleib übrig". Deutsche Arbeiter in der nationalsozialistischen Kriegswirtschaft* (Düsseldorf, 1983), pp. 81ff.
12. Cf. Salter, (above, note 8), p. 6.
13. On foreign labour see E.L. Homze, *Foreign Labour in Nazi Germany* (Princeton, 1967), and, above all, U. Herbert, *Fremdarbeiter. Politik und Praxis des "Ausländer-Einsatzes" in der Kriegswirtschaft des Dritten Reiches* (Berlin-Bonn, 1986).
14. Cf. Herbert, (above,note 13), pp. 205ff.
15. Cf. H. Boberach (ed.), *Meldungen aus dem Reich. Die geheimen Lageberichte des Sicherheitsdienstes der SS 1938-1945* Vol. 11 (Herrsching, 1984) pp. 4084-5.
16. E.g. by Albert Speer in his memoirs, *Inside the Third Reich* (London, 1970), pp. 220-1.
17. Overy, "Blitzkriegwirtschaft ?" (above,note 3), pp. 425ff.
18. Cf. W.Bleyer, *Staat und Monopole im totalen Krieg* (East Berlin, 1970), p. 125.
19. Cf. D. Winkler, *Frauenarbeit im "Dritten Reich"* (Hamburg, 1977), p. 150.
20. Ibid., p. 181.
21. For the following see, ibid., pp. 85ff and 176ff, and L. Eiber, 'Frauen in der Kriegsindustrie. Arbeitsbedingungen, Lebensumstände und Protestverhalten' in M. Broszat *et. al.*, *Bayern in der NS-Zeit. Vol III. Herrschaft und Gesellschaft im Konflikt* (Munich, 1981), pp. 574ff.

22. Cf. G. Lilienthal, *Der "Lebensborn e.V." Ein Instrument nationalsozialistischer Rassenpolitik* (Stuttgart-New York, 1985), pp. 132ff.
23. Cf. Winkler, (above, note 19), p. 109.
24. Ibid., pp. 134ff.
25. Cf. Salter, (above, note 8), pp. 37-8, 52ff.; T.W. Mason, 'Women in Germany 1925-40: Family, Welfare and Work', *History Workshop Journal* 2 (Spring 1977), pp. 18ff; Winkler, (above, note 19), pp. 105, 110ff.
26. For the following see Winkler, (above, note 19), pp. 114ff.
27. Overy, "Blitzkriegwirtschaft?" (above, note 3), p. 428.
28. Winkler, (above, note 19), p. 143.
29. Ibid.
30. Cf. Boberach (ed.), (above, note 15), vol.7, p. 2639.
31. Cf. Winkler, (above, note 19), p. 99.
32. Boberach (ed.), (above, note 15), vol.11, p. 4100.
33. Ibid., p. 4102.
34. Winkler, (above, note 19), pp.124-5; J. McIntyre, 'Women and the Professions in Germany 1930-1940' in A.J. Nicholls & E. Matthias (eds.), *German Democracy and the Triumph of Hitler* (London, 1971), pp. 212ff.
35. Winkler, (above, note 19), pp. 126ff.
36. For the following see ibid., pp. 164ff.
37. Ibid., pp. 172-3.
38. For the following see ibid., pp. 154ff.
39. Cf. L.J.Rupp, *Mobilizing Woman for War. German and American Propaganda 1939-1945* (Princeton, 1978), p. 171.
40. Cf. H-E. Volkmann, 'Landwirtschaft und Ernährung in Hitlers Europa 1939-1945' *Militärgeschichtliche Mitteilungen*, 35 (1986), pp. 9-74 and A. Milward, *War, Economy and Society 1939-1945* (London, 1976), pp. 259-71.
41. Cf. L. Burchardt, 'The Impact of the War Economy on the Civilian Population of Germany during the First and Second World Wars' in Deist (ed.), (above, note 3), pp. 40-70.
42. On the lessons learnt from the First World War see M. Kutz, 'Die agrarwirtschaftliche Vorbereitung des Zweiten Weltkrieges in Deutschland vor dem Hintergrund des Weltkrieg 1-Erfahrung' *Zeitschrift für Agrargeschichte und Agrarsoziologie* 32. H.1, pp. 59-82.
43. Cf. Werner, (above, note 11), pp. 44ff. On the comparison with Britain see K.G. Fenelon, *Britain's Food Supplies* (London, 1952), pp. 77-8.
44. Cf. Werner, (above, note 11), pp. 194ff.
45. Ibid., pp. 160ff, 300ff.

46. Cf. H. Boberach (ed.), (above, note 15), vol. 9. pp. 3504-5.
47. Ibid. vol. 11, pp. 4291-2.
48. See, for example, the SD reports of 8 and 27 December 1939 and 8 January 1940 in ibid. , vol. 3, pp. 552-3, 608, 622-3.
49. Cf. Werner, (above, note 11), pp. 329ff.
50. On the development of wages policy see ibid., pp. 34ff, 105ff, 220ff; Salter (above, note 8), pp. 116-156; Recker, (above, note 7), pp. 26-57, 82-97, 193-249. On prices and wages see also D. Petzina, 'Soziale Lage der deutschen Arbeiter und Probleme des Arbeitseinsatzes während des Zweiten Weltkrieges' in W. Dlugoborski (ed.), *Zweiter Weltkrieg und sozialer Wandel. Achsenmächte und besetzte Gebiete* (Göttingen, 1981), pp. 73-79.
51. Cf. Recker, (above, note 7), pp. 98-127.
52. Cf. ibid., pp. 128-54.
53. Quoted in N. Frei, 'Der totale Krieg und die Deutschen' in idem (ed.), *Der nationalsozialistische Krieg* (Frankfurt/New York, 1990), p. 291.
54. Ibid, p. 292 and M. Roseman, 'World War II and Social Change in Germany' in A. Marwick (ed.), *Total War and Social Change* (London, 1988), pp. 58-78. On the expansion and social transformation of the officer corps see B.R. Kroener, 'Auf dem Weg zu einer nationalsozialistischen Volksarmee' in M.Broszat, *et.al.* (eds.), *Von Stalingrad zur Währungsreform. Zur Sozialgeschichte des Umbruchs in Deutschland* (Munich, 1988), pp. 651-82. On workers see L. Niethammer, 'Heimat und Front. Versuch, zehn Kriegserrinnerungen aus der Arbeiterklasse des Ruhrgebietes zu verstehen' in idem, (ed.), *"Die Jahre weiss man nicht, wo man sie heute hinsetzen soll"*. *Faschismuserfahrungen imRuhrgebiet* (Berlin-Bonn, 1983), pp. 97-132;
55. By Helmut Krausnick and Hermann Graml in H. Krausnick and H. Graml, 'Der deutsche Widerstand und die Allierten' *Vollmacht des Gewissens* 2 (Frankfurt, 1965), p. 482. See also W. Deist, 'Überlegungen zur "widerwilligen Loyalität" der Deutschen bei Kriegsbeginn' in Michalka, (above, note 3), pp. 224-39.
56. Cf. I. Kershaw, *The Hitler Myth. Image and Reality in the Third Reich* (Oxford, 1987), pp. 143ff.
57. Cf. Boberach (ed.), (above, note 15), vol. 4, p. 1305.
58. Ibid., vol. 5, pp. 1645-6.
59. M. Domarus (ed.), *Hitler, Reden und Proklamationen 1932-1945* (Wiesbaden, 1973), vol. 2, p. 63.
60. Cf. W.A.Boelcke, *Wollt Ihr den totalen Krieg. Die geheimen Goebbels Konferenzen 1939-1943* (Stuttgart, 1969), p. 245.

61. Cf. Boberach (ed.), (above, note 15), vol. 9, p. 3195.
62. Ibid., pp. 417-18.
63. Cf. H. Heiber (ed.), *Goebbels-Reden* (Düsseldorf, 1972), vol. 2, pp. 172ff; G. Moltmann, 'Goebbels' Rede zum Totalen Krieg am 18 Januar 1943', *Vierteljahrshefte für Zeitgeschichte* 12 (1964), pp. 12-43.
64. For a discussion of the response to Goebbels' speech see G. Moltmann (above, note 15), and M. Steinert, *Hitlers Krieg und die Deutschen. Stimmung und Haltung der deutschen Bevölkerung im Zweiten Weltkrieg* (Düsseldorf-Vienna, 1970), pp. 334ff.
65. Steinert, (above, note 64), p. 362.
66. H. Boberach (ed.), (above, note 15), vol. 14. pp. 5445-6.
67. On Nazi terror see H. Buchheim *et.al.*, *Anatomy of the SS-State* (London, 1968) and the relevant sections in *Deutschland im Zweiten Weltkrieg* 6 vols (East Berlin, 1975-1985).
68. On the relationship between the working class and the regime and specifically work discipline see Salter (above, note 15), pp. 172-242, 285-94 and 'Structures of Consensus and Coercion: Workers' Morale and the Maintenance of Work Discipline 1939-1945' in D. Welch (ed.), *Nazi Propaganda* (London, 1983), pp. 88-116; W.F. Werner (above, note 11), pp. 26ff, 72ff, 171f, 318ff. On female work discipline see ibid., pp. 92ff. On young people see D. Peukert, *Inside Nazi Germany. Conformity, Opposition and Racism in Everyday Life* (London, 1987), pp. 145-74.
69. Cf. S. Salter, 'Germany' in S. Salter and J. Stevenson (ed.), *The Working Class and Politics in Europe and America 1929-1945* (London, 1990), pp. 99-124.
70. See the figures in W.Ruge and W.Schumann (ed.), *Dokumente zur deutschen Geschichte 1943-1945* (Frankfurt, 1968), p. 143.
71. Cf. Werner, (above, note 11), p. 341.
72. Cf. Salter, (above, note 69), p. 118.
73. Cf. Frei, (above, note 53), pp. 296-7.
74. See, for example, the report of the Stuttgart office of the SD dated 6 November 1944 in J. Noakes and G. Pridham (ed.), *Documents on Nazism 1919-1945* (London, 1974), p. 669.
75. Cf. Werner, (above, note 11), p.257.
76. Cf. M. Middlebrook, *The Battle of Hamburg. The Firestorm Raid* (London, 1980), p. 328.
77. For the following see, in particular, Werner, (above, note 11), pp. 259ff, 350ff.
78. Ibid., p. 266.
79. Cf. ibid., p. 354; Frei, (above, note 53), p. 298, and J. Stevenson, 'Resistance' to 'No Surrender': Popular Disobedience in Württemberg in 1945' in F.R. Nicosia and L.D. Stokes (ed.), *Germans Against Nazism. Essays in Honour of Peter Hoffman* (Berg, 1990), pp. 351-67.

4

THE SOVIET UNION

Mark Harrison

The Character of the Eastern Front

Germany's campaign against the USSR, which began on 22 June 1941, became the greatest land war in history. By the winter of 1942 its front line stretched more than 1,000 miles from the Arctic Ocean to the Caucasus. The opposing sides mobilised tens of millions of soldiers, and hundreds of thousands of aircraft, tanks and guns, during four years of bitter fighting.

During 1941, Germany military power reached its zenith. The *Wehrmacht* had occupied the territories of a dozen European countries; only Britain still resisted. Now Hitler sought to realise the long-standing Nazi ambition of expansion into the Baltic, the Ukraine and European Russia itself. By September, German forces had taken the Ukrainian capital of Kiev and stood before the gates of Leningrad and Moscow.

Soviet resistance, at first unexpectedly weak, now strengthened. For the time being the Germans advanced no further, although Leningrad was blockaded and Moscow was directly endangered. Soviet counter-offensives outside Leningrad and Moscow, stiffening through the winter, denied Germany the chance of a lightning victory. The Germans were caught off balance, unprepared for a protracted struggle.

Having temporarily lost the initiative, Hitler tried to win it back during 1942 with a new offensive to the south. His forces advanced to Stalingrad and the edge of the Caucasian oilfields. On the Soviet side there were fresh setbacks. Only at the end of 1942 was a real Soviet recovery marked with the encirclement and destruction of German forces at Stalingrad. This decisive stroke brought the war to its turning point. For Germany the long retreat now began. Hitler mounted only one more big offensive in the east, at Kursk in July 1943; this battle ended in another decisive

Soviet victory, which sealed the fate of German occupation in eastern Europe. The slow, costly but inexorable advance of Soviet forces continued against unremitting German resistance until the final battle of Berlin in 1945.

This huge war had several main features which determined its impact upon civilian life in the USSR.[1] Germany's war in the east was first of all a war for *Lebensraum* – living space for German colonial settlers. It was also a war to win guaranteed supplies of food and raw materials for German workers and German industries. These were to be won at the expense of the indigenous Slavic races who were destined by German plans, some for eastward deportation or starvation, the rest for menial labour as Germany's helots.[2] The peoples of the USSR therefore faced a bitter war for national survival.

Another feature of the war became the tremendous productive effort on each side. This was to a large extent a measure of the failure of the Blitzkrieg. German plans had intended a lightning war ending in a quick victory before the USSR could mobilise its larger economy, avoiding the necessity for significant German sacrifice. The Soviet denial of German victory turned the war into a protracted struggle. Eventual victory would now belong to the side that could wield the greatest volume of resources.

The two sides waged the struggle with unique intensity. On the eastern front as a whole there died three fifths of the war's total dead, which reached well over 50 millions.[3] Soviet national losses are now officially estimated as 26-27 millions, or one in seven of the pre-war Soviet population. Of these, civilians probably made up the majority.[4] Soviet civilians died in an extraordinary variety of ways. Some died under fire on the front line as it crossed their homes. Others died, whether blockaded in Leningrad, or at a distance from the front line, perhaps under bombardment by aircraft and distant shellfire, and also perhaps more commonly in the Soviet interior from overwork, hunger and disease. Still others died for the same reasons under enemy occupation; there, they were also killed as Jews, commissars, partisans and hostages, and additionally in Germany itself as slaves.

Civilian Life

For nearly all civilians, life in wartime was very hard. Just how hard depended on whether they spent the war in occupied territory or under Soviet control, and what was their employment and social status (e.g. peasant, industrial worker, government official). There was also tremendous movement between regions and economic and social positions – just in 1941-2 there were 25 million homeless refugees to be fed and housed. On the whole I shall not write about the worst extremes – about life under German occupation, in Leningrad, or in labour camps or internal exile – which have been ably surveyed in authoritative works.[5] Rather, I shall concentrate on more typical, everyday trends.

The Urban Economy

War production. Soviet rearmament had already pushed munitions output to a relatively high peacetime level before war broke out. In the late 1930s Soviet defence factories were producing a full range of modern weapons of a quality and quantity to compete with Germany, and their rate of output was rising rapidly. The war years saw further huge increases. By the wartime peak in 1944, weekly Soviet output would stand at 750 aircraft and 400 armoured fighting vehicles, 2,500 guns and mortars, 45,000 rifles, and 4,000,000 shells, mines and bombs.[6]

The wartime expansion of war production proceeded in two phases. In the first phase (from mid-1941 to the end of 1942) munitions output raced ahead in an uncontrolled way which, although essential to the country's immediate survival, carried huge costs and did considerable damage. The absence of controls meant that different lines of war production got out of balance with each other – thus the output of guns outpaced shell production, and a persistent shell famine ensued. The supply of aircraft and armour fell behind, partly because of the high proportion of factories being decommissioned and put on wheels for transfer from the battle zones to the interior regions. At the same time, the concentration on war production ignored trends elsewhere in the economy which pointed in the other direction. If defence output climbed, everything else was collapsing. Traditional priorities failed to protect the output of coal, steel, electric power and industrial machinery, which plummeted. German successes in capturing territory were only partly to blame. On the Soviet side the pursuit of war production at any price took further resources away from the civilian infrastructure and hastened its decline.

As long as the civilian economy pointed downward, the Soviet capacity to maintain supply of the war effort remained in doubt. There was a constant danger that munitions factories might be forced to halt production because of shortages of steel and power, or rations for munitions workers. In the winter of 1941/42 war production faltered. The chasm between the huge and multiplying needs of the Army, and the restricted supplies of war goods available, now reached its widest.

In 1942, war production would accelerate again, but its basis in the civilian economy would remain unstable through the following winter. With 1943 nearly everything began to turn up. Imbalances between different lines of war supply were put right, and the civilian economy began to recover, strengthening the basis for war production as a whole. Defence output rose towards its peak in 1944. Some lines of output were even cut back – for example, the Army now had as many guns and mortars as it needed.

Civilian production. Maintenance of some residual level of civilian economic activity was essential for the war economy. War production was not, and could not be, self-sufficient. Defence factories could not operate without metals, fuels, machinery and electric power. Nor could they operate without a workforce, and their workers likewise could not live without food, clothing and shelter. The Army itself could not operate without inputs supplied directly from the civilian economy. In addition to munitions, it needed the means of military construction and operations in huge quantity – food rations, petrol and aircraft fuel, transport services, and building materials.

In fact, the civilian economy suffered a catastrophic reverse. With 1942 the output of civilian industry fell to less than half the pre-war benchmark – and went on falling, because for most of 1942 things were still getting worse, not better. There was a downward spiral. To the south, territory was still being lost; most of the key factories evacuated from the south and west were still out of commission; there were persistent problems with the coordination of different branches of the economy, the matching of factory outputs with inputs, the reconciliation of military and civilian freight requirements, the specialisation of regional economies.

During 1942 the pattern of priorities changed. It was no longer enough to pursue war production at any price. The stabilisation of civilian industry and transport became just as vital to the war effort as making aircraft, guns, tanks and bullets. Stabilising the civilian economy required new resources. And for the time being there were practically none to be found, because existing resources were already dangerously overstretched, because territory was still being lost, and because Allied aid had not reached a significant scale. This made the task more or less impossible, and in economic terms 1942 would be remembered as a year of desperation and panic measures.

Soviet economic leaders were already used to operating under conditions of shortage, and of the unreliability of central supply. In peacetime, factory managers had already learnt the virtues of self-reliance, turning to local resources for survival. Better for the factory to have its own toolroom, machine shop or foundry than have to rely on other factories and regions for components or materials that might never arrive. The supply of imported goods was typically least reliable. As wartime shortages took these circumstances to new extremes, self-reliance became a dominant characteristic of economic life. As central supplies ran out, every factory and locality was forced into still greater self-sufficiency. Cut off from foreign trade, the economy as a whole became a self-sufficient enclave. For some branches, however, self-reliance was meaningless. The consumer industries could not avert a collapse of output by turning to 'local resources'. There were no local resources left over for making cotton frocks or cups and saucers when everything had already been preempted by the needs of war production and heavy industry.[7]

With 1943 the condition of the civilian economy began to improve (this was true of all its branches except food products). The basis of the Soviet war effort had been stabilised. The situation was less threatening, but not yet free of danger. The situation in agriculture and food processing remained dreadful right through 1944, and hunger continued to undermine the efforts of the workforce.

Employment. The productive effort which supplied the Soviet front depended on the number of workers available after meeting the needs of the army, and their hours and intensity of work. When war broke out, the balance between demand for workers and their supply was completely upset. On the supply side the number of potential soldiers and workers was slashed by many millions because of the millions of soldiers and the tens of millions of civilians killed or abandoned in early battles. At the same time, on the demand side several millions of additional soldiers and war workers were required almost overnight.[8]

The Soviet economy had entered the war with its industrial workforce already fully employed. There was extensive regimentation backed up by the emergency labour laws of 1938 and 1940; these had already increased normal hours of work and reduced freedom of movement from one job to another. With the war came more controls; normal leisure time and holidays were cut immediately, while hours of work in industry rose from an average of 41 hours before June 1940, and 48 hours thereafter to 54-55 hours in 1942.[9] Existing harsh penalties for minor lateness and absence from work were applied widely, and new penalties were added when defence industry were placed under military discipline in December 1941.[10] In the winter and spring, other measures provided for the fullest mobilisation of the working population through universal liability to perform either military or civilian service.

These measures, undertaken from above, were met with a ready enough response from below. There was an immediate flow of volunteers for war work, including many hundreds of thousands of housewives, college and school students, and pensioners. The response from below extended to massive participation in or-ganised programmes such as the emergency tasks of industrial evacuation and conversion, and the industrial movements of 'socialist emulation' – individuals and groups pledged to double and triple fulfilment of work norms, overcoming the multiple obstacles to high productivity entrenched in the pre-war industrial system.[11] Lower level responses were also represented in recruitment into war work from the village, Russia's traditional labour reserve.

Such measures were at least relatively obvious and straightforward. Far more difficult was the maintenance of numerical coordination between the three main subgroups of the working population: the soldiers, the war workers who supplied them with munitions, fuel and other goods, and the civilian workers who kept everyone alive with food and other basic necessities. At first there was chaos in the labour market, with different rival military and civilian agencies competing to recruit workers for different purposes. New, more centralised institutional controls were required to overcome this; they were worked out in the course of war mobilisation, and it took nearly 18 months to get them right.[12]

Productivity. The only positive trend was in output per worker in the munitions industries, which increased sharply and continued to improve throughout the war.[13] The main factors accounting for this were a switch from small batch production to flow production, and the mobilisation of reserve capacities; the latter included reserve capacities deliberately created as a matter of pre-war defence policy, 'concealed' reserves of idle time resulting from the operation of the industrial planning system, and the unused leisure hours of the workforce. This productivity gain certainly eased difficulties in 1942-3 by cutting the direct employment requirements of war production; its importance was magnified by the disastrous record of other economic sectors, where productivity sagged.

Low output per worker in agriculture, and the setback to productivity in every branch except specialised munitions work, inevitably limited the Soviet mobilisation of resources. If productivity losses had been avoided, or if the productivity gap between industry and agriculture had been limited to western European or north American proportions, millions of workers would have been freed for war work in industry or frontline duty.

During 1942 it became more and more difficult to get the right proportions between numbers employed in combat, war work and the civilian economy. The problem was that, of those not taken by the army, too many had become munitions workers, leaving too few to carry on with producing food, steel, fuel and power. The reserves of labour in inessential employment had run out; remaining kinds of civilian employment in construction, transport, agriculture and government service were all essential to the war effort, and all carried highest priority. The relative priorities of war work became more and more finely graded and, at times, even outranked the priority of military needs.

Stricter controls on the mobilisation process, and the stabilisation of the civilian economy, came more or less together at the end of 1942. Economic management became more centralised, and the anarchistic rivalry between different wartime claims on resources was brought under control. At the same time other conditions also lightened the situation in the domestic economy, especially the victory at Stalingrad which eased the military pressure and put to an end the erosion of Soviet territory, and the swelling volume of Lend-lease shipments of weapons, industrial goods and foodstuffs.

The Urban Community

Food. In wartime most civilian households and consumers were never far from the knife edge which separated sufficiency from starvation.[14]

By November, 1941, food rationing was general for almost half the country's population. The rationed foods were bread, cereals, meat, fish, fats and sugar; the only staple foodstuff not to be rationed was potatoes. Most important was bread, which supplied 80-90 per cent of rationed calories and proteins. Bread was issued daily, other foods three times a month. Bread was the only foodstuff for which the rationing authorities did not permit substitutes to be issued – as, for example, powdered eggs could be substituted for meat (however, there was frequent resort to inferior ingredients in baking). Any failure of the bread supply was treated as a police matter.

Not everyone got the same, and there was considerable differentiation by age and working status (in ascending order – adult dependents, children, office workers, industrial workers, war workers, coal face workers). However, none of these except war workers in the most dangerous occupations got enough to live on from rations alone.

There was not enough to go round. Most people went hungry, and suffered the physiological consequences – loss of weight and wasting of body tissues, accompanied by a compensating reduction of metabolic pace. Deaths from starvation included not only a million Leningraders but a wider circle of unnumbered victims in the interior of the country. However, with preservation of basic sanitary and medical services, there was no great excess mortality from disease.

Rations alone were not sufficient to sustain life, and most had to look to unofficial sources as well (except for Leningraders, who lacked any surrounding farmlands). These now made the difference between life and death. Thus, workers and householders too had to practice self-reliance, in the shape of sideline farms and allotments. Another important unofficial source was peasant food surpluses sold in the unregulated urban food markets.

Morale. National feeling, long recognised as a decisive factor in modern warfare, was also of great importance to the Soviet war effort. At the same time, patriotic considerations did not automatically point everyone in the same direction. We know, after all, that in the communities which fell under enemy occupation a significant number identified with the invader and became collaborators. Among them were some evidently driven by a mistaken patriotism, who believed that the nation would fare better under German than Soviet rule.[16] Their motives for doing so were doubtless complicated, and the dividing line between self-interest and sincere national feeling is not easily drawn. The basis for sincere belief was soon undermined by experience of German occupation policies of plunder and enslavement, but Vlasov's Russian Liberation Movement could still meet with some popular support in the occupied USSR in 1943.[17]

When we look at those who remained loyal to the Soviet state and committed themselves to its preservation, whether in the interior or behind enemy lines, we do not really know with any precision what provided the effective motivation for them to do so. Why did Slavic and non-Slavic communities from the Ukraine to the Far East join in resistance to Hitler's war? To what extent were they driven to do so by political authority, and would they have chosen the same freely? What cause were they defending - that of their leader Stalin, the Soviet state, the nation or ethnic group? To what extent was their participation in Soviet wartime institutions differentiated by ethnic affiliation?

In answer to these questions historians still have little to offer but intelligent speculation. This is partly a problem of sources, for the whole subject of patriotism and collaboration has remained a large 'blank space' in Soviet historiography. But there is also the historical fact that Hitler's stance towards the eastern territories was so unappealing as to provide only a very weak test of the Soviet population's true loyalties and national feeling.

Whatever its determinants and character, Soviet national feeling was probably a big factor in the civilian war effort.[18] If for no other reason, this was simply because compulsion could not do everything, and the scope for substituting monetary incentives was also very limited. Wartime experience in construction would show that military style organisation without attention to worker morale would not give good results. Issuing orders in agriculture and mining, too, had little effectiveness when other conditions for success were absent, and what was done was often done in spite of the coercive instincts of authority. Likewise, wage premiums and cash bonuses probably had much reduced effect on worker behaviour in wartime. This is because, in official shops, there was little or nothing to buy above the ration until 1944; as for the free market, goods were available sometimes at hugely inflated prices (which must have motivated some to work harder for cash, while deterring others from seeking to buy), or were available at other times only for barter.[19] However, the authorities found that giving out extra rations to war workers was a powerful incentive to participate and perform reliably.

One result of the food shortage (and this was found everywhere in World War II, not just in the USSR) was 'food crimes'. These covered all sorts of misdemeanours and felonies from petty theft to largescale corruption. Government food stocks sometimes found their way to the black market. Ration coupons were forged, stolen (from the authorities and from individuals), bought and sold.[20] Associated with food crimes were both social and private costs. Social costs were shared out in the shape of reduced ration entitlements. Sometimes, however, the full burden fell upon the individual, especially in the case of private theft. In Leningrad the authorities refused to replace stolen ration cards before the end of each month, in order to discourage falsely reported losses. In the winter of 1941/42, to have a ration card stolen in the first weeks of the month meant death, unless the victim received support of family or friends. All food crimes were punished severely, often by shooting.[21]

Food supplies were among the determinants of morale, but there were many intervening factors, and the relationship was always complex. Certainly loss of civic morale did not follow inevitably from food shortage and hunger.

For example, in the territories of eastern Poland and the Baltic region absorbed in 1939-40, many welcomed the German occupation without having suffered any great shortage of food or other goods. On the other hand the Leningrad population suffered quite extraordinary hardship, with hunger-related deaths numbered in tens of thousands per month at the worst times; individuals suffered every variety of physical and moral atrophy. Yet there was no breach of collective morale – no panic, no looting, as would be experienced in Moscow itself, and no surrender. The Moscow events of October 1941, themselves provide an instructive example. Consumer shortages did not prompt the looting and other breaches of public order in the city. The 'panic' was sparked off by the evacuation of central government offices, which stimulated the people's fear that their leaders had deserted them.

The Village

The collective farm. Under the pressures of war the collective farm (*kolkhoz*) system was in some respects intensified. There was more compulsory labour, and pressure on farms in the interior to extend sowings. Historians have argued over the success of these measures, sometimes seeing them as counterproductive.[22]

In some ways, however, the agrarian regime was relaxed. When the pressure for results was greatest, for example during the harvest, there was often greater readiness to reward the farmworkers first and take the state's share afterwards. There was also a tendency for a kind of privatisation to encroach on the collective farm itself; more decisions were taken on a family basis, families took over responsibility for *kolkhoz* livestock and equipment, and family allotments extended their margins onto *kolkhoz* land. These trends would have to be stamped out at some cost after the war.

Production. In agriculture 1941 was already terrible, and in 1942 things got far, far worse. In that year total agricultural output fell to two fifths of the pre-war level. In the meantime, the population under Soviet control had only fallen by one third.

In wartime, farm labour was exceptionally difficult. The main causes were the loss of the best agricultural land in the southern regions, the loss of horses and tractors, and the disappearance of young men from the agricultural workforce.

Those who remained carried on a bitter struggle. Men and women both worked harder than in peacetime, with more time worked on the collective, and with fewer breaches of discipline. But harder work failed to sustain output per worker. Output per worker in agriculture in 1942 was well down on the prewar level, which was already miserably low.

Food. The extent of wartime consumer sacrifice on the part of collective farmers is another 'blank space' in Soviet historiography, with little hard research to fill the gaps in our knowledge. Certainly, food output per farmworker had fallen, while the share of total grain and meat output taken by government had risen.[23] The farm population was left with a reduced share in a smaller total than before the war.

Collective farmers did not have the privilege of a guaranteed ration which was nominally available to urban dwellers. They relied for the most part on the one significant unrationed foodstuff. Potatoes played the same role in the village diet as bread in the towns. Potatoes were supplemented by milk for proteins, fats and vitamins and, in the final resort, by grass.[24]

The wartime treatment of collective farmers was very harsh. Even before the war, the attitudes of authority to the consumer needs of the village had operated according to harsh and arbitrary norms. Compulsory state purchases of food 'surpluses' were based on official assessments of potential farm capacity, not real farm output. Farm payments of grain to state-owned machine tractor stations in return for machinery services were based on percentages of the crop before harvesting, not after it had been gathered and stored in barns. In wartime the arbitrary confiscation of food from farm stocks was intensified, and procurement was carried on in the style of a military campaign against the peasants right through 1944.

Not all sacrifices were imposed on peasantry from above. Collective farmers accepted wartime privations, in part, in order to help feed husbands and children who had gone to work in munitions factories and to fight in uniform. There was some inequality in the burden, however. Food produce was fantastically scarce but those who had any to spare could take it to the markets where urban dwellers went to find their own means of survival. There the seller could get up to 12 or 13 times the prewar return on food produce.[25] On this basis, a few became significantly wealthy in cash terms. But they did not become materially better off, since there was nothing to be bought in the village for cash.

State and Society

Civil and Military Leadership

Soviet wartime government remained in civilian hands. There was only Marshal Voroshilov to represent the military in Stalin's war cabinet, and his personal influence generally declined. The army as an institution was too busy fighting the Germans to take on any new roles in the making of Soviet domestic or foreign policy.

However, the character of civilian control over the military did change. In the pre-war years Stalin had established absolute personal authority over the armed forces, and decided or supervised everything from grand strategy to details of military appointments and munitions policy. The removal of professional autonomy from military leaders and institutions had been greatly facilitated by the armed forces purge of 1937-8, which was accompanied and followed by huge numerical expansion of Red Army personnel. The purge had eliminated a substantial fraction of the experienced officer corps, and terrorised their survivors and replacements.

Replacing the purge victims, and at the same time recruiting to meet the needs of the huge expansion of 1938-40, resulted in a dramatic lowering of army officers' professional standards and experience.

These things had a powerfully negative influence on wartime military performance. Not least was the lack of restraint on Stalin's propensity to make mistakes in 1941-2. Having wrongly anticipated German moves, he failed to make appropriate dispositions of his forces; even when German intentions had become obvious, he still showed incapacity to organise defence in depth. As time went by, professional soldiers began to win back a louder voice in operational matters. Stalin was required to dictate less and listen more (but still arbitrate, if necessary, between conflicting professional assessments). All the same, he retained absolute control over grand strategy and diplomacy. And even in operational matters the ideology of Stalinism still left characteristic traces right through to the last moment of the war, for example in the failure to anticipate casualties while planning operations, and in the setting of arbitrary objectives regardless of the huge cost in lives and technical means which would be paid to attain them.[26]

Uncontrolled Economic Mobilisation

Civilian authority was changed by the war in more ways than one. Governmental morale was badly damaged by the outbreak of war, since the general view was that enough had been done in diplomacy, rearmament and deployment of armed forces on the Soviet-German border to deter German aggression for the time being. For a few days Stalin went through the motions, apparently believing that the scope of the conflict could still be limited. But it was Molotov, not Stalin, who had to break the news of the attack to the Soviet population on the radio. After a week Stalin retreated in depression to his country residence near Moscow. Senior Politburo members visited him to propose that he should form and head a war cabinet. Evidently he thought they had come to arrest him. Mikoian recalled afterwards: 'He looked at us beseechingly and asked "Why have you come?" One felt that he was alarmed, but was trying to keep calm.' Molotov put the proposal. 'Stalin looked at him with some surprise, but after a pause said "Good." '[27] After that he was back in the saddle, but things turned from bad to worse and his determination was not yet restored. In October, 1941, facing the possibility that Moscow would be taken, Stalin tried to surrender to Hitler, offering the Baltic, Belorussia, Moldavia and part of the Ukraine in return for peace.[28] Hitler, scenting victory, refused.

Government did not disintegrate, but its administrative effectiveness was seriously weakened. Formal mechanisms for resource allocation became irrelevant.

While the *Wehrmacht* ate up Soviet territory, including the country's most important military-industrial centres, economic planners went on writing factory plans and coordinating supplies. But the factories and supplies only existed on paper. Meanwhile, Army requirements for new supplies of munitions and soldiers, just to replace early losses, hugely exceeded plans. The gap between needs and resources could not be papered over by any plan, and grew dangerously.

What really carried out the essential tasks of war mobilisation and managed the war economy through the first period of the war was a system of informal leadership. The key roles fell to individual leaders – Stalin's deputies, members of the Politburo and war cabinet. Kaganovich, Kosygin, Shvernik and others headed a crash programme to evacuate war industries from the war zones to the interior, which was carried out without any planning beforehand, as an inspired piece of improvisation. Other powerful individuals – Beriia, Malenkov, Malyshev, Mikoian, Molotov, Voznesenskii – armed with unlimited personal responsibility, took on key tasks of industrial mobilisation and conversion. All this was carried on regardless of economic plans and attempts at high-level coordination, which anyway bore no relation to the needs of the situation.

These powerful individual leaders did not do everything themselves. Their activities would have been quite ineffective if they had not been met by a response from below. Initiative from below was represented both in the evacuation of assets, especially farm stocks, and in the conversion of factories to war production. Initiative from below did not mean that there was no organisation or forethought; the conversion of civilian capacities to wartime needs did not come out of the blue, and was supported by pre-war planning carried out in factories, municipalities and industrial branch administrations. The point was that people did not adopt an attitude of 'wait and see', but went straight over to wartime tasks without needing instructions from the Kremlin.

However essential under the circumstances, uncontrolled mobilisation on this pattern was extremely costly. In 1941, the defence industries were saved, and the supply of munitions expanded rapidly, but everything else was left to look after itself and lapsed into a state of chaos. This was no basis for a sustained war effort. As for 1942, the intolerable strains in the civilian economy were not just the product of successful German offensives, but were actually made worse by the forced, unbalanced character of mobilisation in the previous year. The relocation of the western and southern factories for making guns, tanks, shells and aircraft in the Urals and western Siberia had shifted the centre of gravity of war production hundreds of miles to the east. This effort alone had cost huge resources of civilian transport and construction. But now additional costs presented themselves. These remote regions were utterly unready for such accelerated development. They lacked most things necessary for recommissioning the evacuated war factories – additional workers, housing and food supplies, transport links, electric power, sources of metal products and components, and any kind of commercial and financial infrastructure. To make good these shortages cost the economy dearly.

Much of the cost was met straight away, by huge Soviet civilian sacrifice, in terms of immediate creation of a supportive infrastructure. Some costs were met by the United States through Lend-lease shipments, which acquired a massive scale in 1943-4. Other costs – for example, long-term ecological damage to the Urals and western Siberia, arising from the region's crash industrialisation – were hidden for many years.

The informal, uncoordinated system of emergency leadership by individual members of the war cabinet and Politburo, which had managed the transition to a war economy at the highest level, lasted until the end of 1942. In November, workforce controls were centralised in a single government agency (the Committee for Registration and Allocation of the Workforce); soon after, personal war production responsibilities of individual war cabinet and Politburo members were devolved upon a new, powerful cabinet subcommittee, the GKO (war cabinet) Operations Bureau. After this, the formal procedures for compiling and implementing economic plans were gradually brought back to normal operation, diminishing the scope for powerful individuals to run the economy by decree. Wartime plans began to incorporate objectives of reconstruction and rehabilitation, which sometimes also included consideration of post-war requirements.[29] Overriding panic measures and crash programmes became less frequent, although they did not disappear, especially in food and agriculture policy where the situation remained critical right through 1944.

Measures to Strengthen Civilian Morale

A critical wartime task was that of unifying Soviet society around the patriotic cause. In order to achieve this, the Stalinist regime moved away from pre-war emphasis on internal struggle against the enemy within and the need to purge hostile elements. The campaigns against the pre-war oppositions of Left and Right were wound down. A few military and economic leaders imprisoned as a result of the pre-war purges were rehabilitated and taken back into official posts.

Stalin himself, in speeches and decrees, offered major concessions to Russian national feelings. In the autumn of 1941 he began a deliberate rehabilitation of the image of the Army in Russian history before the Soviet era, altering its role from one of imperialist oppression to one of national liberation. In the summer of 1942 the renewed status of the Army officer corps was further confirmed by abolition of the commissars responsible for political supervision of professional officers, and by restoration of many pre-revolutionary privileges of rank. In 1943 the Russian Orthodox church was another beneficiary of renewed national traditions, when a new concordat was promulgated between the Soviet state and the Russian Orthodox church. The agreement provided for restoration of the holy synod, and greater freedom of religious expression. Meanwhile, as Russian national sentiment strengthened, anti-German feeling was also strongly promoted. All these trends were objectively reinforced by the fact that, with occupation of the western republics and the Ukraine, Russia was now more than ever the dominant partner in the Soviet family of nations.

But the break with peacetime was far from complete. A characteristic element of continuity lay in Moscow's persistent distrust of civilian morale and civilian values. The wartime behaviour and decisions of Soviet leaders suggest that they were continually prey to fears about the imminent breakdown of public order; whether or not the fears were exaggerated, the consequences were often cruel. Thus, in the face of enemy advances Stalin delayed the evacuation of noncombatants first from Leningrad, then from Stalingrad. He preferred to incur additional civilian casualties, rather than give a signal of retreat. Another, more infamous example was the punitive treatment of minor nationalities (for example, the Volga Germans, and Crimean Tatars); where a minority sided with the German invaders, the whole ethnic community was punished by deportation under atrocious conditions.

In general, the peacetime apparatus of repression was kept active and in good working order. Numbers held in forced labour camps and colonies shrank, mainly because of shockingly high wartime mortality, but the proportion of 'counter-revolutionaries' (i.e. those held under Article 58 of the RSFSR criminal code) rose slightly.[30]

Stalinism and the Price of Victory

Once Stalin was seen everywhere as the great Soviet war leader, the Generalissimus who symbolised the military destruction of Nazi expansionism and the confirmation of the USSR's post-war great power status. More than anything, the Soviet victory in 1945 was seen as validating Stalin's rule. As a modernising statesman who changed both his own country and the world, Stalin invited comparison with Bismarck, Napoleon or Peter the Great.

Over the years, a variety of revelations and reinterpretations has eroded this image. Now Stalin's contribution to history appears more sordid, even criminal. Modern historical writing tends to emphasise the price which the USSR paid for Stalin and Stalinism in World War II as well as before and after.

Reformist Soviet historians of the war period have condemned Stalin on a variety of counts, which could be summed up as follows.[31] His pre-war policies of industrialisation and collectivisation were too wasteful of human life and labour, and needlessly overstrained the economy. The ceaseless purging of the 1930s left Soviet society demoralised and divided against itself. Stalin's foreign policies were too opportunistic; first he underrated the Nazi threat, then failed to win potential allies to a policy of collective security against Germany; his turn to appeasement of Hitler in 1939 was ultimately counterproductive. The concentration of diplomacy and military policy in Stalin's hands undermined Soviet security; his mistakes opened the way for the *Wehrmacht* to the gates of Moscow and Leningrad in 1941, and to Stalingrad in 1942. The Stalinist belief that the human individual was no more than a passive cog (*vintik*, literally 'screw') in the machine of state also had practical consequences: a cheapening of human life, indifference to casualties in planning and executing military operations, and post-war concealment of the huge cost of victory in Soviet fatalities, both military and civilian. Irresolute in defeat, Stalin proved vindictive in victory; after the war he condemned the few returning Soviet prisoners of war, declared 'traitors to the motherland' because they had allowed themselves to fall alive into German hands, to years of further suffering in internal exile and labour camps; he renewed his authority by imposing fresh sacrifices on society and launching new purges.

Such a comprehensive verdict is part scholarly evaluation of the Soviet past, part political statement about the Soviet future. In reality, it may not be easy to disentangle the historical role of Stalin and Stalinism from what might have transpired without them. The indictment is not so much a finished judgement as a set of working hypotheses which we must continue to research and refine, and be ready to modify or reject. In fact, the historiography of the USSR in World War II will continue to evolve, and what is written above is best seen as a report of work in progress.

NOTES

1. Some of the ideas and evaluations contained in this paper are developed at greater length by John Barber and Mark Harrison, *The Soviet Home Front, 1941-1945: a Social and Economic History of the USSR in World War II* (London, 1991).

2. Alexander Dallin, *German Rule in Russia, 1941-1945* (London, 1957), pp. 310-13.

3. The leading Soviet demographer B. Urlanis, in his *Wars and Population* (Moscow, 1971), p. 294, gave a detailed analysis of worldwide premature deaths totalling 50 millions, on the basis of a Soviet figure of 20 millions.

4. A total of 26.6 million excess deaths is the result of an official demographic revaluation by E. Andreev, L. Darskii and T. Khar'kova, 'Otsenka liudskikh poter' v period Velikoi Otechestvennoi voiny', *Vestnick statistiki*, 10 (1990), pp. 25-7. Soviet wartime military fatalities have now been reported officially by the Chief of the Soviet General Staff, M.A. Moiseev, 'Tsena pobedy', *Voennoistoricheskii zhurnal*, 3 (1990), pp. 14-16, as 8,668,400 (a figure which may well, however, prove to be an underestimate). If these two figures are reliable,then a residual figure in the region of 18 million civilian deaths is left by subtraction.

5. Dallin (above, note 2); T.J. Schulte, *The German Army and Nazi Policies in Occupied Russia* (Oxford, 1989); Harrison E. Salisbury, *The 900 Days: The Siege of Leningrad* (London, 1971); Alexander Solzhenitsyn, *The Gulag Archipelago, 1918-1956*, 3 vols (London, 1974-8).

6. On wartime production see Mark Harrison, *Soviet Planning in Peace and War, 1938-1945* (Cambridge, 1985), pp. 109-64; also id, 'The Volume of Soviet Munitions Output, 1937-1945: A Re-evaluation', *Journal of Economic History*, 50 (1990), pp. 569-89.

7. Harrison, *Soviet Planning* (above, note 6), pp. 204-9.

8. On wartime labour a standard work is A.V. Mitrofanova, *Rabochii klass SSSR v gody Velikoi Otechestvennoi voiny* (Moscow, 1971).

9. According to N.A. Voznesensky, *War Economy of the USSR in the Period of the Patriotic War* (Moscow, 1948), p. 91, in 1942 the industrial worker's hours exceeded those worked in 1940 by 22 per cent.

10. Viktor Zemskov, 'Na rabote. Sorokovye, "trudovye"', *Soiuz* (18 May 1990), p. 9.

11. L.S. Rogachevskaia, *Sotsialisticheskoe sorevnovanie v SSSR. Istoricheskie ocherki. 1917-1970 gg.* (Moscow, 1977), pp. 175-212.

12. Harrison, *Soviet Planning* (above, note 6), pp. 185-91.

13. For Soviet and comparative evidence see Harrison, 'Soviet Munitions Output' (above, note 6), p. 576.

14. U.G. Cherniavskii, *Voina i prodovol'stvie. Snabzhenie gorodskogo naseleniia v Velikuiu Otechestvennuiu voinu (1941-1945 gg.)* (Moscow, 1964); A.V. Liubimov, *Torgovlia i snabzhenie v gody Velikoi Otechestvennoi voiny*

(Moscow, 1968); William Moskoff, *The Bread of Affliction: The Food Supply in the USSR during World War II* (Cambridge, 1990).

15. Moskoff (above, note 14), pp. 226-9
16. John Barber, 'The Role of Patriotism in the Great Patriotic War', paper to Moscow conference on 'Russia and the USSR in the XX Century' (April 1990).
17. Catherine Andreyev, *Vlasov and the Russian Liberation Movement: Soviet Reality and Émigré Theories* (Cambridge, 1987), pp. 47-50.
18. For more discussion see Harrison and Barber (above, note 1), chapter 9.
19. See also Moskoff (above, note 14), chapter 8.
20. K.S. Karol, *Solik: Life in the Soviet Union, 1939-1946* (London, 1986), pp. 94-5; Moskoff (above, note 14), chapter 9.
21. Salisbury (above, note 5), p. 533; Moskoff (above, note 14), p. 176.
22. Iu.V. Arutiunian, *Sovetskoe krest' ianstvo v gody Velikoi Otechestvennoi voiny* (Moscow, 1970), pp. 18-20, 86-96.
23. Mark Harrison, 'Stalinist Industrialisation and the Test of War', *History Workshop Journal*, 29 (March 1990), p. 84.
24. Arutiunian (above, note 22), p. 361.
25. Voznesensky (above, note 9), p. 102.
26. *Istoriki sporiat. Trinadtsat' besed* (Moscow, 1988), p. 314; V.I. Kozlov, 'O liudskikh poteriakh Sovetskogo Soiuza v Velikoi Otechestvennoi voiny 1941-1945 godov', *Istoriia SSSR*, 2 (1989), p. 132.
27. A.I. Mikoian, 'V pervye mesiatsy Velikoi Otechestvennoi voiny', *Novaia i noveishaia istoriia*, 6 (1985), p. 98. Mikoian's story is repeated, in slightly different terms, in Dmitrii Volkogonov, *Triumf i tragediia. Politicheskii portret I.V. Stalina*, vol. II, part 1 (Moscow, 1989), p. 169.
28. Nikolai Pavlenko, 'Tragediia i triumf Krasnoi Armii', *Moskovskie novosti*, 19 (7 May, 1989), pp. 8-9. Pavlenko cited Marshal Zhukov as firsthand witness to this attempt, initiated by Stalin on 7 October, 1941. Volkogonov (above, note 27) vol. II, part 1, pp. 172-3, places the episode as early as July 1941, but in this he is apparently mistaken.
29. Harrison, *Soviet Planning* (above, note 6), pp. 175-85.
30. Aleksandr Dugin, 'GULAG glazami istorika', *Soiuz* (9 February 1990), p. 16.
31. On recent views of Stalin in wartime, see R.W. Davies, *Soviet History in the Gorbachev Revolution* (Basingstoke and London, 1989), pp. 100-14.

5

THE UNITED STATES

Neil A. Wynn

The USA may appear to fit oddly among the fifty-year 'celebrations' of the coming of World War II of which this volume forms part. Not only did the United States enter the war later, in 1941, but the American experience, and the civilian experience especially, also seemed so different from that of other participants – distant from the conflict, America was not directly subject to attack nor to the horrors of war experienced by the populations of Europe and Asia. At the war's end most other countries emerged poorer and weaker, while America emerged richer and stronger. This very fact was recognized then, and now, and at the time caused the resentment summed up in the British description of GIs as 'over-fed, over-paid, over-sexed and over here'. Some American historians, while obviously not accepting the explicit criticism, confirm something of this view. John P. Diggins in his recent survey of the forties and fifties, revealingly titled *The Proud Decades*, describes the war as 'the most popular war in American history', and Studs Terkel entitled his oral history of the war, *"The Good War"*. One of his contributors, a Red Cross worker, recalled 'The war was fun for America' – 'a hell of a good time'.[1]

While certain aspects of this view may be accurate, it tends to over-simplify and suggest the war had little dramatic effect on America. I want to suggest that it had a significant impact not just on America's economic and international standing but on society as a whole, and that while the nature of this impact may be subject to some debate, it nonetheless shares some of the same characteristics of civilian populations in war elsewhere, even though its long-term consequences were different. However, I also think that in the search for 'turning-points' in history too much can be made of the impact of the war, and that it needs to viewed within the broader perspective of both the 1930s and late-1940s.

The significance of the war years for America was for a long time overlooked either because it was assumed to have little significance, or because it was lost sight of between the Depression and Cold War/Affluent Society. In the late 1960s and 1970s, however, there was a change and suddenly a series of studies claimed the war years as especially significant. In addition to scholarly general studies such as Richard Polenberg's *War and Society: the US 1941-45*, John Morton Blum's *V Was for Victory*, there were more 'popular' works such as Richard Lingeman's, *Don't You Know There's a War On?* and Geoffrey Perrett's, *Days of Sadness, Years of Triumph*. Several monographs examined the impact of war on black Americans, women, labour, management relations, propaganda, and Hollywood – the last two often appearing to be the same.[2] All of these have in common the tendency to see the war as marking a divide in modern American history, a point often made implicitly in studies of postwar America such as William Chafe's *The Unfinished Journey: America since World War II*, which begins with a chapter on 'The War Years'. Indeed Chafe writes that 'wartime mobilization set in motion developments that would help transform American society – for the next four years, *and for generations to come*' [italics mine]. A recent article with a narrower perspective makes a similar point when it begins, 'For many southerners World War II was a great divide' which 'reshaped their society'. [3]

These views echo those of Polenberg who had earlier written that 'World War II radically altered the character of American society and challenged its most durable values.' It was the war, Polenberg argued, that turned America into a middle-class nation.[4] Such claims relate not just to the war years but also, of course, serve to reassess the 1930s. Geoffrey Perrett suggested the war was the closest to a real social revolution America experienced and that it brought 'more desirable social change than did six years of the New Deal'.[5] In the latest study of the New Deal Tony Badger seems to concur: 'World War II' he writes 'was the juggernaut that ran over American society'.[6]

The transformation (and contrast with the thirties) was most obvious in the sphere of economics and economic organization. The war resulted in a booming economy and a move towards state-directed capitalism which began as early as 1940 as America became the 'Arsenal of Democracy'. The American GNP increased three-fold after 1941 and more industrial plant was built in three years of war than in the previous fifteen years of peace. Fifteen million people entered the armed forces and ten million extra were added to the labour force. Shortages of labour and of materials brought both new opportunities and greater central control to determine priorities and allocate scarce resources whether human or physical.

Throughout the war people spoke of the three allied dictators, Stalin, Churchill, and Roosevelt, and certainly governmental bureaucracy and executive control increased in America with the War Powers Acts of 1941 and 1942 and the creation of more than 30 war agencies. However, politics continued as usual throughout the war and Congress continued to function to some extent as a check on excessive presidential power. The maintenance of the Constitution unamended during the war was perhaps one indication of the conflict's lesser impact on the country. Equally, and perhaps surprisingly given the American experiences of World War I and those of Allied powers in World War II, the growth of governmental authority was not immediate, but a gradual development. Only in 1942 did the second War Powers Act confer the authority to allocate priorities and resources to the President, and only then was a supreme body, the War Production Board, established to carry this out.

While some commentators pointed to the dismantling of New Deal agencies as one of the most significant effects of the war, those agencies were replaced by the more than thirty new war agencies dealing with all aspects of society. Nonetheless, if 'Dr New Deal' was, as Roosevelt suggested, replaced by 'Dr Win-the-War', the centrality of the federal government's role in American life was confirmed and consolidated by the war as government spending rose from less than 10 per cent of GNP to over 30 per cent and as the federal deficit rose from a high of $4.43 billion in the 1930s to one of $57 billion at the height of the war.[7] In the postwar years the political issue was to be about the *size* of government rather than its basic role. Roosevelt's Economic Bill of Rights of 1944, and the subsequent Employment Act of 1946, committed government to a degree of intervention to ensure maximum employment, and the social welfare aspects of the New Deal were now generally accepted by both political parties.

Much of the New Deal was, of course, no longer necessary during the war due to full employment. Unemployment reached the lowest level ever since World War I in 1943, but it is worth noting that there were still over three million unemployed in 1942 and that it took almost three years of war to eradicate the last vestiges of the Depression. Agricultural production increased 50 per cent and farm income rose 200 per cent during the war: as one woman recalled with possibly some exaggeration, farmers to whom she had paid out $4 per week on relief in the 1930s were worth a quarter of a million dollars at the war's end.[8] The average weekly wage rose from $24 in 1939 to $45 in 1945, and real wages rose by an average of 50 per cent or more as the workforce worked longer hours for higher wages.[9] Contrary to popular imagination, however, there were shortages in America and rationing was introduced from 1942 onward. Beginning with petrol (to save rubber initially), rationing was extended to cover some 20 essentials by 1944, including sugar, meat, coffee, and even whisky. Even though rationing was limited and sometimes intermittent, one quarter of Americans polled in a survey thought occasional resort to the black market was justified.[10]

Despite rationing there were few really severe shortages and most Americans were probably better off than before. As John Kenneth Galbraith noted, 'Never in the history of human conflict has there been so much talk of sacrifice and so little sacrifice.'[11] Indeed Americans not only appeared to prosper but the gap between haves and have nots seemed to close. While the incomes for the top fifth of the population rose by 23 per cent, that of the bottom fifth rose by almost 70 per cent.[12] One worker from Kentucky recalled moving from having no electricity, no plumbing, and no telephone to having 'money to buy any kind of food I wanted. We had a second-hand car ...' She also remembered being able to go out for meals for the first time, pointing up the contrast with the 'hungry thirties'.[13] Pent-up demand and wartime savings ensured that this continued; by 1948 one investigator reported that members of a local of the formerly militant United Auto workers now owned their own homes and had become consumers rather than 'have-nots'.[14]

Wartime memories also included a sense of psychological unity and talk of 'togetherness'. Future president Richard Nixon could accept the boredom of work in the Office of Price Administration before he went into military service because 'we felt we were part of a bigger cause'. Other Americans spoke of 'a great coming together of people, working as a team', and recalled that 'a shared sense of commonality grew with war'.[15] In his much acclaimed study of *Country Made By War: From the Revolution to Vietnam*, Geoffrey Perrett wrote of the effects of the war which reached into 'the fissures of a divided, insecure nation and bound it together as nothing else could'.[16]

Such positive views of the war's effects, and the impressions and memories which contribute to them, blur the realities of wartime tensions and conflicts. Wartime affluence obscured the persistence of poverty and also the concentration of wealth (rather than just incomes) which increased rather than diminished through the war. Labour unions gained in numerical strength and saw their members achieve higher earnings; they were also subject to wage controls and freezes which resulted in an outbreak of strikes involving three million workers in 1943, despite an official no strike pledge. The strikes in turn led to the passage of the restrictive War Labor Disputes Act, the model for the postwar Taft Hartley Act which has applied to American unions ever since. Equally the involvement of labour in government during the war, and increasing bureaucratization, coupled with obvious economic gains encouraged a non-confrontational, even conservative, attitude among some labour leaders which continued in the Cold War era.

The experience of labour points up the conflict between heightened in-group identity and out-group conflicts; 'If you weren't in this group you were really an outsider', recalled one woman. The same person pointed out that fear and anxiety were as much a part of American war experience as elsewhere.[17] Even though not subject to direct attack other than Pearl Harbor and the limited shelling of California (and the launching of a few bombs on balloons which landed in the forest of Washington state), many Americans feared worse. Ten million people were active in the Office of Civilian Defense preparing for bombing raids or invasions which never took place; as one inhabitant of Portland, Oregon, recalled 'Nobody knew what was going to happen, and there was always this fear of attack.' One Californian remembered living 'constantly with the fear we might be invaded or bombed' and spending hours in an improvised bomb shelter in a hall closet listening to the gramaphone.[18] The real victims of this fear were the 112,000 Japanese Americans on the West coast (out of a total Japanese-American population of 127,000) who were rounded up and re-located in concentration camps in 1942, losing an estimated $400 million worth of property and possessions in the process. Divisions among the Japanese between critical and non-critical factions resulted in a riot in which two people were killed. Insult was added to injury when the draft was applied to American citizens in the camps and those who refused to serve were jailed. Some 12,000 Japanese Americans did, however, serve in the Army, and the two Japanese-American battalions which served in Italy were among the most decorated in the military. Once the military threat had passed in 1944, a process of gradual release began which ended in 1945. After the war some 5,700 Japanese-Americans re-nounced their citizenship, and 7,000 were repatriated to Japan. The treatment of the Japanese Americans was supposedly based on the fear of possible sabotage; the absence of such sabotage was presented as evidence of their cunning and the application of relocation even to American citizens was justified on the basis of 'once a Jap, always a Jap', revealing the deep-seated racism which lay behind the move.[19]

Other racial conflicts surfaced during the war: Mexican American youths were the victims of attack in the Zoot suit riot in Los Angeles in 1943. Here racism was compounded by other resentments as servicemen were particularly evident in attacks on the outrageously dressed civilians. Something of the ambiguity of the war's impact was also evident in the black experience. African Americans were initially excluded from the 'Arsenal of Democracy' – first to be fired in the Depression, they were now last to be hired - in 1940 only 240 blacks were employed in the entire aircraft industry.[20] In the armed forces blacks were segregated, kept in limited roles, and excluded from the the Marines and Air Corps. The combination of black protest and wartime necessity in terms of propaganda and labour demands led to concessions in the form of an Executive Order in 1941 forbidding discrimination in war industry and the subsequent expansion of the black military role. By the end of the war a million blacks had served in the forces and segregation had been significantly challenged. Experiments in integration took place in the Army in 1944 during the crisis of the Battle of the Bulge, and the Navy found that once black manpower increased in number segregation was no longer practicable. Racial prejudice in the 'armies of democracy' proved an embarassment overseas and, following the re-introduction of the draft in 1947, President Truman called for an end to segregation in all the American armed forces.[21]

At home the migration of African Americans exceeded the 'Great Migration' of World War I as 1.8 million blacks moved to the North and West where their numbers in skilled and semi-skilled industrial occupations doubled as new job opportunities opened up in war industries. This was not an immediate development, but again one which occurred only as labour shortages began to develop after 1942, presidential orders notwithstanding. At the start of 1942 only 3 per cent of all people involved in war production were black; a year later this had doubled, and by the end of 1944 8.3 per cent (still below their proportion in the population) of war workers were black. By the end of the war aircraft companies among others had 'completely altered their policies in the face of all-out war, the need to utilize all available manpower, government pressure, and obvious morality and decency'.[22]

Such gains have to be balanced against resistance to change. In 1943 there were over 240 race riots or racial incidents in some 47 cities, the worst occuring in Detroit where 25 blacks and nine whites died after five days of rioting. In 1944 the employment of eight black trolley drivers in Philadelphia led to a strike by white workers which only ended after 8,000 troops had moved into the city. In Harlem in 1943 black anger exploded in a riot indicative of the new black mood.[23] The challenge to prejudice was manifest in the threat of a march on Washington by blacks in 1941, the constant protest about discrimination throughout the war, and in the renewed threat of a civil disobedience campaign after the war.

These actions built upon a base of growing organization and protest in the 1930s and upon the new place of blacks within Roosevelt's Democratic Party. White support for the attack on racism was articulated by a variety of white writers, celebrities, and politicians, and wartime actions were taken further by Harry S. Truman when he established a Commission on Civil Rights in 1946, condemned race violence in a public address to the NAACP in 1947, and began the process to end discrimination and segregation in the armed forces and civil service in 1948.[24] While substantial achievements may have been few, Truman indicated the racial agenda for the future and within six years the Supreme Court issued its historic ruling against segregation in schools. Many of the early black civil rights campaigners in the late 1950s such as Medgar Evers were to point to the significance of the war years in shaping their attitudes.[25]

If black Americans seemed to advance during the war the picture for American women is less clear, and one must attempt to separate images from reality. In advertising and government propaganda the ubiquitous American wartime heroine was of course, Rosie the Riveter (NBC's Commando Mary was less successful!). As one woman recalled, 'The war years offered new possibilities. You came out to California, put on your pants and took your lunch pail to a man's job.'[26] There clearly was some dramatic change – a survey of the shipbuilding industry in 1941 found a total of 36 female workers; in 1943 there were 160,000. All told more than eight million women joined the labour force, an estimated three million more than would have done so normally. The proportion of women in the labour force rose from 25 per cent to 36 per cent during the war. More significant, 75 per cent of new women workers were married and 60 per cent were 35 or older.[27] Several states now removed the laws (often introduced in the 1930s) prohibiting the employment of married women as teachers, and there continued to be a general change in the distribution of the female workforce towards older, married women in the post-war years.

Most long-term gains in women's employment were in areas already associated with female work and there tended to be a concentration in white collar clerical work rather than the much publicised shipyard or other heavy work. All changes met, however, with continued resistance and opposition. A fear of so-called 'New Amazons' was widely evident and discrimination persisted. Women were effectively denied top positions, and despite equal wage policies were paid on average 40 per cent less than men. Even more, wartime employment gains often appeared temporary – two million women were laid off at the war's end, and the proportion of women in the labour force fell back down to 29 per cent. However, the percentage of women in the labour force was still higher after the war than it had been before, and by the early fifties was growing again and was soon above 30 per cent.[28]

Paradoxically government propaganda which had stressed patriotic duty in getting women out to work, now did the same to get them back into the home. Work, particularly for married women and mothers, was stressed as exceptional and in the war and postwar years 'the suburban ideal of companionate, child-centered marriages with little scope for careerism' became a dominant stereotype.[29] The *Ladies*

Home Journal could state that the nation's number one task at the end of the war was to 'make it better, easier, cheaper, and safer to have at least three babies a piece'.[30] It is worth bearing in mind too that if Rosie the Riveter was one stereotype encouraged by the war, just as powerful among men was the widely used 'pin-up', an image which dominated wartime movies in the form of Jane Russell and others. Nonetheless for at least one woman 'defense work was the beginning of my emancipation as a woman. For the first time in my life I found out that I could do something with my hands besides bake.' That she doubtless spoke for many was indicated in polls in which women expressed a strong desire to stay in work at the war's end.[31]

If some women found independence, albeit temporary, they also experienced the hardship and suffering borne of loneliness, anxiety, and emotional strain in addition to the problems of coping with demands of work and home. Dellie Hahne recalled 'the misery of war': 'Pregnant women who could barely balance in a rocking train going to see their husbands for the last time ... women coming back from seeing their husbands, travelling with small children'.[32] Marjorie Cartwright recalled her marriage to a sailor in the 7th fleet: 'I lived alone for four years during the war and they were the most painful, lonely years I think I will ever spend.'[33]

While separation was disruptive perhaps even more so was the wartime migration of population. Over twelve million people moved out of state and another thirteen million moved within states during the war. Over a million entered California, the location of half the nation's shipbuilding and aircraft industry. Many of the centres, large or small, were overwhelmed. While major cities like San Francisco and Detroit grew by more than half a million each, the naval town of Portsmouth, Va., grew from 4,500 to 48,000; the population of Seneca Falls 70 miles south west of Chicago rose from 1200 to 6500 as workers came to build landing craft on the river shore.[34] In all cases the problems were much the same only different in scale and emphasis. There were conflicts between old inhabitants and newcomers, blacks and whites, and these rivalries were often compounded by social problems resulting from overcrowding of homes, schools, and recreational facilities. When Ford established a massive new plant at Willow Run outside Detroit, a trailer park sprang up housing 32,000 people in conditions which could only be described as squalid. Another 15,000 in-migrants to Detroit lived in dormitories, lodgings, or hotels. Little wonder that Detroit was a centre of both labour and racial conflict during the war.[35]

Children and the family were often seen as the greatest victims of wartime disruption. Children did appear to occupy an ambiguous position in wartime society – denied an active role in war, they had little awareness or understanding of the forces affecting their lives and yet were perhaps more susceptible to emotional pressures, fears and anxieties. *The Washington Post* observed in 1944 that 'From Buffalo to Wichita it is the children who are suffering most from mass migration, easy money, unaccustomed hours of work, and *the fact that mama has become a welder on the graveyard shift*' [italics mine].[36] As if to reinforce particular stereotypes of women and to confirm the temporary (and undesirable) effects of war, child-related problems were often associated with the wartime activities of women. Considerable attention was given to 'eight-hour orphans' and latch-key orphans and a great deal of discussion focused on juvenile delinquency which appeared to rise during the war – sometimes by 20 per cent or more.[37]

Particular concern centred on female crime and the sexual misdemeanours of 'patriotutes, V-girls, cuddle bunnies' and 'Allotment Annies'. Such behaviour was attributed to the attraction of uniforms, the excitement of life near army camps, dance halls, and beer parlours, and a desire to participate in the war in some way. It was also explained by the breakdown of normal social controls due to the absence of fathers in the forces, mothers working in industry, an increase in teenage employment, or just the move from familiar surroundings.[38]

As well as the heightened social and moral concerns evident here, there is too some indication of the emotional and psychological effects of the war. John Costello in his study of *Love Sex and War* in Britain and the United States writes of 'war aphrodisia' and notes a rise in illegitimacy in America from 7 per 1000 births in 1939 to 10 per 1000 in 1945. There was also a rise in legitimate birthrates during and after the war reflecting the increase in marriage rates – the highest ever in 1941 at 12.6 per 100,000 of the population. Marriages were clearly spurred on by the onset of war either as a way to try to beat the draft, or as couples contemplating marriage decided that there was no point in waiting longer. Marriage also ensured financial provision for female partners as the incidence of 'Allotment Annies' made all too clear. Whatever the cause, the increase in marriage was to some extent off-set by the rise in divorce which reached its highest level in 1946 and was not to be equalled again until the 1970s.[39] Those that married in haste perhaps repented at leisure: as one of Terkel's contributors recalled, 'I don't think I'd have married so foolishly, if it weren't for the war ...'[40] For others war provided the money, or the break, which made divorce a possibility.

These statistics reveal something of the confusion and excitement which the war engendered. Amidst it all there remained a strong fear of the future. Most Americans were affected by a 'depression psychosis', a belief that the Depression would return after the war. The Department of Labor predicted possible unemployment of 12-15 million and even more conservative estimates put the figures at 5-10 million.[41] In the event those fears were not to be realised. Continued high government spending in waging the Cold War and through payments to veterans under the Selective Serviceman's Re-Adjustment Act or GI Bill, described by one veteran as 'the American Dream', which enabled eight million former servicemen to go to college or school and millions more to buy homes or businesses, combined with consumer demand and wartime savings to produce the Affluent Society very quickly.[42]

After years of turmoil and change stretching back to 1929 Americans were more than willing to settle for this. With the war as an example, reformers now sought to eradicate social inequality not by redistribution of wealth but by encouraging economic growth; ordinary Americans sought security and stability in a similar fashion. As Betty Friedan put it of women, 'we were all vulnerable, homesick, lonely, frightened. A pent-up hunger for marriage, home, and children was felt simultaneously by several different generations, a hunger which in the prosperity of postwar America everyone could suddenly satisfy.' The combination of anxiety about the future and fear of the past produced what historian Sara Evans called the 'ferocious pursuit of private domesticity'[43]; the conservatism it underpinned was to dominate the whole of suburban society of the 1950s and justify the repression of anything which threatened it at home and abroad.

Thus, although certain wartime experiences were the same, the war which brought radical political changes in other countries such as Britain and France, combined with the post-war international situation to produce a conservative climate in the United States. While this could be explained by differences in cultural outlook or by reference to the period of American reform in the 1930s, it also points to the effect of fighting total war in distant lands. If World War II *was* the 'Good War' for America it was perhaps because the United States felt some of the stresses and strains of conflict and shared some of the consequences without suffering the most obvious costs of massive physical and human destruction experienced by other nations.

Notes

1. Studs Terkel, *"The Good War": An Oral History* (London, 1985), p. 10; John P. Diggins, *The Proud Decades: America in War and Peace, 1941-1960* (New York, 1988), p. 14.
2. Richard Polenberg, *War and Society: The United States, 1941-1945* (Philadelphia, 1972); John Morton Blum, *V Was For Victory: Politics and American Culture During World War II* (New York & London, 1976); Richard Lingeman, *Don't You Know There's a War On? The American Home Front*

1941-1945 (New York, 1970); Geoffrey Perrett, *Days of Sadness, Years of Triumph: The American People, 1939-1945* (New York, 1973); Neil A. Wynn, *The Afro-American and the Second World War* (New York & London, 1976); Karen Anderson, *Wartime Women: Sex Roles, Family Relations and the Status of Women During World War II* (Westport, Conn., 1976); D'Ann Campbell, *Women at War with America: Private Lives in a Patriotic Era* (Cambridge, Mass., & London, 1984); Nelson N. Lichtenstein, *Labor's War At Home: the CIO in World War II* (Cambridge, Mass., 1982); Howell John Harris, *The Right to Manage: Industrial Relations, Politics & American Business in the 1940s* (Madison, 1982); Allan M. Winkler, *The Politics of Propaganda: the Office of War Information* (New Haven, Conn. & London, 1978); Clayton R. Koppes & Gregory D. Black, *Hollywood Goes to War: How Politics, Profits and Propaganda Shaped World War II Movies* (New York & London, 1987). The latest addition to works on aspects of World War II in America is Allan Berube, *Coming Out Under Fire: The History of Gay Men and Women in World War II* (New York, 1990).

3. William Chafe, *The Unfinished Journey: America Since World War II* (New York, 1983), p. 3.

4. Polenberg (above, note 2), p. 4, and idem, *One Nation Divisible: Class, Race, & Ethnicity in the United States since 1938* (Harmondsworth, 1980), pp. 61-6.

5. Perrett (above, note 2), p. 11.

6. Anthony J. Badger, *The New Deal: The Depression Years, 1933-1940* (London, 1989), p. 310.

7. Ibid, p. 115.

8. Terkel (above, note 1), p. 10; Diggins (above, note 2), p. 17.

9. Perrett (above, note 2), pp. 353-5.

10. Mark J. Harris *et al.*, *The Homefront: America During World War II* (New York, 1984), p. 64.

11. Galbraith in Terkel (above, note 1), p. 323.

12. Polenberg (above, note 4), p. 64.

13. Harris *et al.* (above, note 10), p. 37.

14. Samuel Lubell, *The Future of American Politics* (1965), quoted in Robert H. Zieger, *American Workers, American Unions, 1920-1985* (Baltimore & London, 1986), p. 135. Also see Harris *et al.* (above, note 10), p. 241.

15. Stephen E. Ambrose, *Nixon: The Education of a Politician, 1913-1962* (New York, 1987), p. 102; Harris *et al.* (above, note 10), pp. 74, 80.

16. *A Country Made By War* (New York, 1989), p. 438.

17. Harris *et al.* (above, note 10), p. 74.

18. Ibid, pp. 69, 72-3.
19. The treatment of the Japanese-Americans is fully dealt with in Peter Irons, *Justice At War: The Story of the Japanese American Internment Cases* (New York, 1982) and Roger Daniels, *Concentration Camp, USA: Japanese Americans in World War II* (New York, 1971).
20. Wynn (above, note 2), p. 41.
21. See Richard M. Dalfiume, *Desegregation of the US Armed Forces: Fighting on Two Fronts, 1939-1953* (New York, 1968).
22. William J. Schuck, 'History of the Mobilization of Labor for War Production' (1946), manuscript in National Archives, Washington, D.C., Record Group 211, p. 64.
23. Dominic J. Capeci, *The Harlem Riot of 1943* (Philadelphia, 1977); Harvard Sitkoff, 'Racial Militancy and Interracial Violence in the Second World War', *Journal of American History*, 58 (1971), pp. 661-81; Robert Shogan & Tom Craig, *The Detroit Race Riot: A Study in Violence* (New York, 1964); Allan M. Winkler, 'The Philadelphia Transit Strike of 1944', *Journal of American History*, 59 (1972), pp. 73-89.
24. See William C. Berman, *The Politics of Civil Rights in the Truman Administration* (Columbus, Ohio, 1970), and Donald R. McCoy & Richard T. Ruetten, *Quest and Response: Minority Rights and the Truman Administration* (Kansas, 1977).
25. See Wynn, (above, note 2), p. 125, and Henry Hampton & Steve Fayer (ed.) *Voices of Freedom: An Oral History of the Civil Rights Movement* (New York, 1990), pp. xxiv-xxvii.
26. Harris *et al.* (above, note 10), p. 121.
27. See Wiliam H. Chafe, *The American Woman: Her Changing Social, Economic, and Political Roles, 1920-1970* (New York, 1972), pp. 135-80; Campbell (above, note 2), pp. 72-83; Carl M. Degler, *At Odds: Women and the Family in America* (New York & Oxford, 1980), pp. 418-19.
28. Chester W. Gregory, *Women in Defense Work During World War II* (New York, 1974), p. 183; Chafe (above, note 27), pp. 181-2.
29. Campbell (above, note 2), p. 4.
30. See Leila J. Rupp, *Mobilizing Women for War:German and American Propaganda, 1939-1945* (Princeton, 1978), pp. 160-6.
31. Harris *et al.* (above, note 10), pp. 128-9; Rochelle Gatlin, *American Women Since 1945* (London, 1987), p. 4.
32. Terkel (above, note 1), pp. 118-19
33. Harris *et al.* (above, note 10), p. 190.

34. Terkel (above, note 1), pp. 309-10; Seneca is the subject of Robert J. Havighurst & Gertha Morgan, *The Social History of a War Boom Community*, (New York & London, 1951).

35. See Alan Clive, *State of War: Michigan in World War II* (Ann Arbor, 1979).

36. *Washington Post* quoted in John Costello, *Love, Sex and War: Changing Values 1939-45* (London, 1985), p. 265.

37. Polenberg (above, note 2), pp. 149-50.

38. Lingeman (above, note 2), pp. 90-2, 100-1.

39. Costello (above, note 36), pp. 13, 30, 277.

40. Terkel (above, note 1), p. 122.

41. Davis R. B. Ross, *Preparing for Ulysses: Politics and Veterans During World War II* (New York, 1969), pp. 34-5.

42. Ibid., p. 124.

43. Betty Friedan, *The Feminine Mystique* (New York, 1974), p. 174; Sara Evans, *Born to Liberty: A History of Women in America* (New York & London, 1989), p. 237.

6

JAPAN

Ian Nish

Civilians in Japan suffered from a long war and had the sense of the imminence of war which lasted much longer. What the Japanese describe as the Great(er) East Asian War began in December 1941 and the full horrors of total war reached the Japanese cities with the bombing campaigns of the last year of war. But what the Japanese call the North China Incident and later the China Incident were in essence the beginnings of a war against China which lasted from July 1937. There were few families which did not have sons called up for service at the front and were not affected by this war in other ways. But even before the China War, there were calls for national mobilization at every level because of Japan's isolation in the world which affected the life-styles of civilians. Emergency mobilization plans covering the whole of the Japanese economy were discussed from the Manchurian Crisis of 1931 onwards.[1]

Many Japanese civilians had a sense of impending crisis as the state made increasing demands on them over the decade from September 1931. It is sufficient to record that for the major military-naval operation which began in 1937 there was an immense need for emergency funds in addition to the budgets for which the army and navy had been competing in previous years. From this time a massive control of the economy began which affected all civilians. In March 1938 the Diet passed, despite stiff opposition, the national mobilization law which gave the government tremendous powers to intervene in the economy, including powers to conscript labour. Japan, which had already experienced a tightening of political controls for two years, came under a war economy from that date. The government placed short-term funds under its control and regulated corporate accounts. Industry had to concentrate on war needs. The old concentration on the production and export of cotton goods came to an end, depriving Japan of foreign exchange. For example, the Toyota Company, which had originally been a cotton machinery enterprise, converted its production increasingly to motor vehicles which were required for the China campaign. This was a typical sort of switch, partly commercial to meet changing patterns of trade and partly national to meet the demands of a regulatory government.[2] A Cabinet Planning Board was established in October 1937. Among other actions it imposed a limit on imports in order to save foreign currency and set priorities for the importation of essential goods for army use.

Something of the atmosphere of the times is captured in the letters of Richard Storry, a young professor of English at Otaru Commercial College in Japan's northern island of Hokkaido. Four months after the start of the China Incident he sent his parents a letter which illustrates the attitudes of civilians as he saw them.[3] In order to avoid Japanese censorship it was handed to a P. and O. skipper calling at Hokkaido ports.

> The army started the fuss in N. China and the navy began it all in the Shanghai area, so I am heartily against this business. But I dare not say so in my normal letters as police surveillance in this country reaches incredible dimensions; the land is stiff with police spies who keep the closest watch on all foreigners.
>
> At the beginning, in July, one heard criticisms of the aggressive policy against China. Some students here wrote an article in the college paper attacking the government for its "fascism". This caused a stir, and since then students, whom I know well, have said how much they disliked the power of the military, but it is not safe to rely on these signs of dissatisfaction. The country at large, with the successful war on, supports the government ... Intelligent Japanese, who in their hearts condemn the war, cannot protest. The Conservatives like it because it rouses the "National Spirit" and develops Emperor worship. The army likes it because they like fighting. Big business imagines it will get rich by the war and young men have no idea, as a whole, of criticising their elders whom from youth up they are taught to regard as their betters. The women of course don't count. ...
>
> I have been and am treated well. Even with this trouble on, the Japanese students are mostly friendly, and my acquaintances are if anything more kind and generous to me than before. The police are petty tyrants, much disliked by foreigner and Japanese alike.
>
> As I look at my students, either in a lecture room or as they drill and do manoevres in the snow, my heart aches at the pity of this war, and the wars that will come upon them. But they think it no tragedy, their greatest glory is to die in the service of the Emperor, collectively they become a very terrible fighting machine, and as they die they shout "Banzai, long live the Emperor".

Storry's experience as a foreigner in an academic atmosphere and in an agricultural part of the country may not have been typical. The first twelve months of the China Incident were a period of success for Japanese arms. In July 1938 Storry had to report: 'Personally I hardly feel any effect of the war'. But the campaigns ran into trouble thereafter – what one writer calls 'the China Quagmire'.[4] This was a situation into which the Japanese armies were more and more drawn without coming any closer to achieving a peaceful settlement. The civilians at home were not fully aware of Japan's deteriorating fortunes, unless they had a family member involved at the front.

Civilians soon became aware that they would be affected by the total war that was developing. Government controls involved rationing, the introduction of a coupon system, central fixing of wages and prices and police campaigns against black-marketeering. The production and sale of luxury items was prohibited. Within the family there was no sugar and no sweet things were available for children. For the rest of the war period they had to be content with sweet potatoes.

Moreover, the civilians were called upon for belt-tightening and sacrifices in their daily lives. For example, we are told that the first day of every month was designated as 'Service Day for the Development of Asia' when the people had to rise early in order to visit the Shinto shrines. During that day restaurants and bars were compulsorily closed; and civilians were required to eat the simplest and poorest meals.[5] They had to be taught to 'control their appetites' for the war effort. The spartan life-style of many Japanese families became more and more restricted as the war progressed.

Japan passed her next turning-point in the year 1940. Not, as we might expect, in 1939. When the war in Europe broke out in September 1939, Japan was numb: numb because the Japanese army had sustained a frightful defeat at Nomonhan; numb because of the Nazi-Soviet Pact; numb because of the threat by the United States to end her Trade Agreement with Japan and thus threaten economic sanctions. As a result of this numbness, Japan declared her strict neutrality in the European war. Japan, like some European countries, passed through a period of 'phoney war'.

1940 began symbolically with the celebration of the 2600th anniversary of the origins of the Japanese empire, the coming to the throne of the legendary emperor Jimmu. The war in China was static; the war in Europe was moving in favour of Germany. Political dissent and anti-nationalist sentiments were driven underground. Politicians who criticized the China campaign were expelled from the Diet. The government resorted increasingly to propaganda on Japan's New Order in East Asia and the Great(er) East Asia Co-prosperity Sphere.[6] While opinions may differ on this, it would appear that these doctrines had greater impact in boosting morale at home than they did overseas. Political parties were in effect merged into a larger unit when the Taisei Yokusankai was founded in October. Agencies like the Foreign Ministry which were on the whole internationalist in complexion were purged and had their wings clipped and the range of their activities reduced. Neighbourhood watch groups (tonari-gumi) began to ensure at the local level the loyal pursuit of national objectives or, as some Japanese have called it, 'ultra-nationalism' (etsu-kokka-shugi). As a result of all this, the population was cowed. The people had been infused with 'the national spirit' from their earliest schooldays. But even this was tightened up with the introduction of national education in April 1941.

The Japanese education system had served an important purpose in the creation of the nation-state. It now had an essential role in moulding the thinking of children towards the war and, by that means, influencing the attitudes of families. In the spring of 1941 a major tightening took place when the traditional Shogakko (elementary school) was abolished and a new Kokumin Gakko (National School) substituted. The objects of the new education were set out in the Kokumin Gakko-rei. Its prime purpose was to organize primary education in order to achieve the 'way of the empire' and 'the basic training of the nation'.

The practical consequences of this may be seen in some of the changes in curriculum which writers have described. School textbooks (tokuhon) were already standardized and approved by the Ministry of Education. They carried strong ideological overtones in their stories and the morals to be drawn from them. For example, songs to the tune of Auld Lang Syne which were deeply rooted in the pre-war educational system were now prohibited for use in the classroom as they were considered to be over-sentimental or too western in ideas. Songs that carried echoes of foreign tunes were to be discouraged. Instead the approved songbooks included the national anthem, Kimigayo, and songs commemorating Empire Day, Kigensetsu, the Russo-Japanese war, the Rescript on Education and other national events.[7] It may not be too much to say that this all served the purpose of creating a nationalistic education in order to fit the children for the disciplined life as soldiers and dedicate them to the war effort.

Needless to say, these reforms in the educational field applied also to physical education. Apart from military drills, which had been incorporated in the curriculum for boys' education, special encouragement was given to training in the martial arts. For some time past the Education Ministry, which dominated the public sector of education, had been commending the martial arts as something uniquely Japanese and as a form of training which would increase the sense of national identity among the young. Kendo (fencing) was made compulsory for boys. Just before the war with China broke out, a nation-wide programme of judo training was formally introduced; and judo, archery and naginata were offered at girls' secondary schools as optional subjects. By 1941 these arrangements passed from the high school to the elementary school level as boys at the top of elementary schools were specially instructed in judo and kendo. Two years later the physical education syllabuses of schools were completely modernized for schools at each level from elementary school to college and instruction in the martial arts was made compulsory.

This emphasis was in accord with the educational ceremonials which increased in the war years. The Education Rescript (*Kyoiku chokugo*) which had been promulgated by the Emperor Meiji in 1890 was officially and ceremonially read out in all schools. It brought home to the children, in spite of the difficulty of its language and concepts, that the fundamental character of the Japanese nature was loyalty and filial piety and the need for self-sacrifice of the individual for the state. While this was something that had been built into the school system over many years, it naturally acquired a special relevance for Japanese during the war years. It encouraged the notions of national self-sufficiency and self-confidence, especially on the home front.

When the emperor issued his rescript on 8 December 1941 declaring war against the United States and Britain, a new phase of Japan's war effort began. Initially there was great popular exuberance, the exuberance of military success and of economic achievement. Thus, rubber and oil which had previously been scarce suddenly became plentiful because of the conquests of Malaya, Indonesia and Burma. But this was short-lived. Merchant shipping became scarce and Japan lost the command of the seas by the end of 1942. She even had to appeal to Germany to ask whether she could think of some way of absorbing some of the raw materials from her newly-acquired territories.[8] Setbacks in the war effort were concealed. Partly losses such as the defeat in June at the Battle of Midway were not adequately reported to headquarters. Partly military defeats were presented to the people as 'strategic withdrawals'. How far the people understood how the war was going is still hard to tell.

But the civilians were in no doubt about the hardships which the war was causing to their everyday life. Scarcities of food have been vividly portrayed by Lady Toshiko Marks, herself a schoolchild in wartime Japan:

In 1942 the main foods (rice, miso, soya beans, salt, sugar etc) and clothes (cotton, wool, leather etc) came under government control and people could acquire these foods only through rationing. Clothes became unobtainable.

In early 1943 people started suffering from a desperate shortage of food. Even rationed food was at a minimum and starving people had to go either to the black markets or to nearby farmers in order to get extra food: sweet potatoes, radish, carrots, eggs, flour and anything else to supplement the rations.

Children were often taken - or sent by their mothers - to carry food, since small children seemed to escape the checks of the 'economic police'.[9]

Gradually food grew more and more scarce. Rice, the staple of the Japanese diet, had traditionally been imported to about one-quarter of Japan's needs. With the coming of war the number of people involved in agriculture dropped, while the demand of the armed and emergency services for supplies increased. The allied blockade of the seas exacerbated the problem and communication with Manchukuo, a major supplier of soya beans, and China grew more and more difficult. When the bombing of Japan began in earnest, the fairly rudimentary network of arterial railway lines was frequently dislocated. All in all, there was a deterioration on all fronts.

Food shortages led to malnutrition and disease. By the end of the war the Japanese civilians were down to a starvation diet – and one with nutritional limitations. Fish was increasingly in short supply. Vegetable and fruit cultivation which was labour-intensive had to be neglected. Dependent on night-soil and comparatively primitive, vegetable production was reduced by 81 per cent. Disease of many sorts from diarrhoea to scabies and tuberculosis spread alarmingly. The medical profession was reduced and hospitals were no longer able to cope. Medicines and dressings were seriously lacking. If there had been the prospect of release from these predicaments, morale might have been kept up, but the leaders knew – and the people may have had an inkling – that the situation could only go from bad to worse. The gamble that the military and naval leaders had initially taken on a successful short war had been shown to be illusory. The victims were the Japanese people. It is estimated that civilians in Japan suffered more than in any major belligerent country.[10]

A new chapter in the experience of Japanese civilians began with the coming of air-raids to Japan's home islands. The first Doolittle raid on Tokyo in April 1942 was experimental from the American side and an unexpected and unwelcome development for the Japanese government. It was also a new experience for Japanese civilians who had thought that they would be immune from the aerial bombing of the European war. Air-raid precautions were introduced immediately and children were required to carry gas masks wherever they went. Towards the end of 1943, well-to-do people started to move privately to their ancestral roots (furusato) in the countryside. This was intended to avoid the expected air-raids in the cities and to come closer to the sources of foodstuffs. After the capture of Saipan, the Americans were able to attack Tokyo, some 1350 miles away, with their B29 Superfortresses. The first of these attacks took place in June 1944 and they became more regular from October onwards. On 9-10 March 1945 the first full-scale incendiary attack on Tokyo took place. Great as was the devastation, it has to be said that many families had by this time left the capital and schools were already suspended. It was the fathers who were left to cope with the emergency. Air-raid shelters came too late to be of great service and were of simple construction. When the incendiary bombings spread to 66 other prefectural cities, food supplies dried up, communications became uncertain and absenteeism spread to ordnance factories. Professor Coox has reckoned that

> the B-29s destroyed 40 per cent of Osaka and Nagoya; 50 per cemt of Tokyo, Kobe and Yokohama; and 90 per cent of Aomori. At least 241,000 persons died, and 313,000 were injured in the raids against the homeland. Conventional bombing killed almost as many people as did the two atomic bombs in August.[11]

Japan had a formidable airforce; but its fighters were unable to intercept the waves of incoming bombing. It suffered from shortages of aviation fuel and from an inadequate early warning system. The military authorities were inclined to conserve their air resources in order to prepare for the *kessen*, the expected 'decisive battle' including the allied invasion of Japan's home islands.

Considering the volume of air attacks and the danger of the impending invasion, it is surprising how slow the Japanese bureaucracy was in addressing the problem of civil defence. It seems to have been overconfidence about Japan's invulnerability that led to the long delays. It was not until November 1943 that government plans for evacuating important sections of the population were announced. There were hopes that one million evacuees from Tokyo who were not required for industry could be moved to the countryside by September 1944. Just short of two million people had been moved by the spring of the following year out of a notional population of 8-9 millions. By this time the transport network was hardly able to service a major evacuation programme. This meant that much reliance had to be put on the provision of air-raid shelters for civilians in the city areas. Here too the plans were very late in appearing. Theoretically every citizen of Tokyo had a shelter to go to; but the protection which they afforded was questionable and their appropriateness for protection against incendiary bombing was doubtful. It is perhaps true that the inadequate provision of civil defence – for whatever cause – made little difference in face of the intensity of carpet-bombing of Japanese cities carried out in the spring and summer of 1945. As Dr Gordon Daniels writes,

> It is impossible to refrain from some mention of the policy of the Japanese towards their own civilians. The time and effort they directed towards air-raid prevention was surely wholly inadequate and the failure to evacuate Tokyo with more urgency, and to devote more resources – when they were still available – to shelters, seems to show culpability of a high order.

He ends with what might be an epitaph for the Japanese experience during the war years: the 'rulers chose their own prestige before the welfare of their own citizens.'[12]

The *kessen* which was so much feared came ever nearer with the American capture of Iwojima in March 1945 and the savage battle of Okinwawa which followed. The prime minister, General Koiso, resigned on 5 April just before the surrender of the Germans, Japan's only remaining ally. Admiral Suzuki replaced him with a conviction to prepare for the worst but also to cultivate the paths of peace. For the helpless civilian, it was apparent that the *kessen* would have to be fought with a shortage of manpower and of weapons. However the authorities shuffled the manpower, the resources of Japan's home islands were inadequate. The Voluntary Military Service law which passed the Diet called up for service all males between 15 and 60 and all females between 17 and 40. The propaganda of resistance was formidable. The Japanese were told that, while the Americans were decadent, the Japanese had a spiritual strength which would carry them through. The resistance of Okinawa showed that the Japanese army had what might be called a 'Tiger in its Tank'. Would a similar power of resistance exist among the civilians? The allies may have thought so. Certainly they prepared elaborate measures for counter-propaganda. The aircraft that flew to Japan jettisoned large quantities of leaflets, telling the Japanese what was going on in the war and calling on them for surrender. In short, Japan's eight years of war brought untold suffering to her civilians.

But the sufferings of civilians seems to have had comparatively little impact on the government's decision for peace. As we survey the agonized discussions which took place in the decision-making bodies in July and August, we must conclude that the voice of the civilians went largely unheard. The cabinet and the army were reluctant to accept the allied terms calling for unconditional surrender. These had been reiterated in the Potsdam declaration of 26 July:

> We call upon the government of Japan to proclaim now the unconditional surrender of all Japanese armed forces... The alternative for Japan is prompt and utter destruction.

The prime minister decided to react to this by *mokusatsu* (silence). Ten days elapsed. Then the atomic bomb was dropped on Hiroshima on 6 August; the Soviet armies entered Manchuria and Korea two days later; and on 9 August the second atomic bomb was dropped on Nagasaki in the western island of Kyushu. The Potsdam declaration was accepted at a joint meeting of the cabinet and the military high command in the presence of the emperor during the night of 9-10 August. But it was accepted only with significant reservations. For the people at large who were left in the dark, much depended on the broadcast by the emperor which took place on the morning of 15 August. Since an imperial message by radio had never been heard before, the people, we are told, expected a speech of exhortation, calling for final effort and sacrifice. Instead they heard a message which they barely understood because it was spoken in court language. It announced that Japan had decided to effect a settlement and accept the provisions of the Allied Declaration. Bewildered, the people bowed, sang the national anthem and proceeded methodically with their daily business. Martial law did not have to be declared.[13]

The sacrifices of Japan's civilians were borne stoically. Initially they had been relieved by news of military success – in China, at Pearl Harbour and Singapore. Thereafter morale was kept up by blatant suppression of the truth. The notion that Japan was fighting 'the Great East Asian War' was a powerful inducement to accept hardships. The final months of the war were a time of great agony and suffering. It was during this period that most of the civilian casualties were caused. These have been estimated at 300,000 dead and 25,000 missing in Japan's main islands.

An essential source of information on all aspects of the wartime experience of Japanese civilians is the United States Strategic Survey for the Pacific. During the summer of 1944 the Joint Chiefs of Staff had authorized studies into the allied bomber offensive against Germany. While the prime purpose was a military one, related to the effectiveness of the armed services, it extended to civilian morale, to physical damage caused and to the economic effects, broadly construed. One of its subsidiary objectives was to give guidance on the war against Japan, then entering a critical phase. By the summer of 1945 the decision had been taken to carry out a strategic bombing survey for the Pacific battle-zone on a much broader basis than the European survey. The teams began arriving in Tokyo on 4 September, two days after General MacArthur had taken the Japanese surrender. They were able to issue questionnaires and interview essential personnel almost immediately. These were to cover not just the metropolitan areas of Tokyo, Osaka and Nagoya but also Iroshima and Nagasaki. Japanese government had survived at both a central and provincial level, even if it was in a state of shock, and seems to have made the pragmatic decision to collaborate with the survey. So the survey was remarkable for its comprehensiveness and for the first-hand impressions which it was able to collect so soon after the event. Since relatively few Japanese documents survived the bombing campaigns, the information obtained from other sources was vital to an understanding of how the civilians were affected by the war (among other things). The survey teams were able to return to the United States by the end of 1945. Their reports began to appear from July 1946.[14] While some of their conclusions were speculative and controversial, it is hard to overestimate the value of these – and also the British report on the atomic bombing[15] – as historical sources. A non-Japanese must write with reserve of the wartime attitudes of Japanese civilians which he cannot know at first hand. Sources are scarce and can be slanted out of respect for hindsight.

In the aftermath of war the lot of the civilians was even worse. In a sense we know rather less about this for, while the agonies of the wartime period were vigorously studied in the Strategic Bombing Surveys, post-war experiences – and expectations – are rarely charted. Certainly the destruction of the means of transport had a great impact on the normally mobile life-style of the Japanese – on the railways the main lines and subsidiaries had been broken; buses with charcoal burners on the rear for fuel operated sparingly; the *densha* (street-cars) in the cities gave a solid, if slender, service; and German-style bicycles were the only reliable means of travel. In the city-centres only stone or brick building survived. There was for a while a natural reluctance to re-establish bomb-destroyed areas like Hiroshima. Since shops were fewer and access to the countryside was difficult, food supplies were extremely difficult. The black market which had developed during the war expanded after the peace-making. The *katsugiya*, the itinerant merchant plying his trade between country districts and the cities, was a common figure on Japanese railway stations carrying black market rice, while the small coastal craft were often found to be carrying the other staple of the Japanese diet, fish.

Despite their ordeal, the Japanese civilians survived. Sir Peter Parker, who served in Japan in 1945 and 1946, describes his visits to a Japanese family who revealed that they had a contingency plan for mutual suicide if the occupation proved to be as savage as was predicted.[16] Such was the Japanese image of the enemy that wartime propaganda had created. Despite the intense relief that the family had survived the war, they were still willing to take each other's lives in the face of an invader. One may reflect that Japan, in the period down to the surrender, was not under any form of military occupation and that the cruelties and hardships imposed on her people were the result of the actions of their own leaders and not of a conquering invader. Down to the end of the war the Japanese civilians accepted their lot uncomplainingly. While there was a peace movement in the summer of 1945 which consisted of influential civilians,[17] there were no serious uprisings against the government collectively or individual assassination plots against the leaders (though there had been many instances of assassinations successful and unsuccessful in Japanese politics of the 1930s.)

NOTES

1. M.A. Barnhart, *Japan Prepares for Total War: The Search for Economic Security, 1919-41* (Cornell, 1987), pp. 34, 37-8.
2. G.D. Allinson, *Japanese Urbanism: Industry and Politics in Kariya, 1872-1972* (California, 1975), pp. 88ff.
3. Dorothie Storry, *'Second Country': The Story of Richard Storry and Japan, 1913-82* (Ashford, 1986), pp. 41-3.
4. Ibid., p. 47. See also J. W. Morley (ed.), *The China Quagmire: Japan's Expansion on the Asian Continent. 1933-41* (Columbia, 1983).
5. Toshiko Marks, 'Life in Wartime Japan' in *International Studies* pamphlet, LSE, IS/89/197 (1989), pp. 1-2.
6. I. H. Nish, 'The Great East Asian Co-Prosperity Sphere' in K. Neilson and R. A. Prete (ed.), *Coalition Warfare: An Uneasy Accord* (1983), pp. 125-42.
7. Ury Eppstein, "School Songs before and After the War: From 'Children Tank Soldiers' to 'Everyone a Good Child'", *Monumenta Nipponica*, 42 (1987), pp. 435-6.
8. A. Coox, *Japan: The Final Agony* (New York, 1970), p.55.
9. Nish (above, note 6), pp. 139-41.
10. Toshiko Marks, 'Children's Life in Wartime Japan', *Proceedings of the Japan Society* [of London], 112 (1989), pp. 66-7.
11. A. Coox in P. Duus (ed.), *Cambridge History of Japan*, vol.6, *The Twentieth Century* (Cambridge 1989), p. 369.
12. G.Daniels, 'The Great Tokyo Air Raid, 9-10 March 1945', in W. G. Beasley (ed.), *Modern Japan* (London, 1975), p. 131.
13. The best account is still to be found in R. J. C. Butow, *Japan's Decision to Surrender* (Stanford, 1954), esp. chs.8 and 9.
14. G.Daniels (ed.), *A Guide to the Reports of the United States Strategic Bombing Survey* (London, 1981).
15. British Government Inspection team (including the Government of India), *The Effects of the Atomic Bombs at Hiroshima and Nagasaki* (London, 1946).
16. P. Parker, *For Starters: The Business of Life* (London, 1989), p.33.
17. Butow (above, note 13), p. 75 and *passim*.

7

ITALY

Toby Abse

Italy's experience in the Second World War was an extraordinary one and one in which the home front was in many ways far more important than the front line. Italy, unlike her allies Germany and Japan, both of whom fought on until the bitter end, with their armed forces and civilian populations maintaining their loyalty to their rulers long after military defeat had become inevitable, collapsed because of events on the home front, not events on the battle fields. Italy, alone amongst the Western European countries, was occupied by both sides after September 1943, by the Germans in the north and the Anglo-Americans in the south.Whilst the two occupations were very different in character, nobody can deny, particularly after the valuable information and acute insights made available by David Ellwood's magisterial work on Italy between 1943 and 1945, that the Allied occupation of the south was an occupation too, that the co-belligerency of the Italian monarchy on the side of the Allies did not amount to a great deal in practice.[1]

It is impossible to discuss what occurred on the Italian home front between June 1940 and July 1943 without making some mention of Italian attitudes towards war, and towards the nation state, during the earlier decades of this century, attitudes whose almost incredible persistence were so recently confirmed by the popular, as opposed to governmental, reaction of Italy to the Gulf War. The Risorgimento may have created Italy but it failed to make Italians. The Libyan War of 1911 did not evoke the same national enthusiasm as colonial wars, such as the Boer War, did in other countries.[2] In fact it provoked widespread disorder and unrest at home. There is a certain irony, given his later militarism, in the fact that it was Mussolini's leading role in these protests that first gave him nation-wide fame. A few years later, it was anti-militarism that sparked off the insurrectionary rioting of the *Settimana Rossa*, the Red Week of June 1914, which swept the Romagna, the Marche and a number of important localities in Northern Italy. After the *Settimana Rossa*, the Italian government was well aware that to enter any war on the side of Austria-Hungary, as its treaty obligations dictated, would have led to the downfall of the House of Savoy. Hence in the months between August 1914 and May 1915 the choice facing the Italian government was between neutrality and intervention on the side of the Triple Entente; entry into the war on the side of the Triple Alliance was never seriously considered. When Italy entered the war in May 1915, the decision was imposed upon a Giolittian majority in parliament and a pacifist majority in the country by the King and a few leading ministers such as Salandra and Sonnino, supported by an extremely vocal but relatively small movement of interventionists in the piazzas.

The First World War may have been regarded as a unifying national experience by Mussolini or pro-war intellectuals like Marinetti or D'Annunzio but it was perceived very differently by the mass of the population, who were far more attached to their village, city, province or region than to the abstract and largely rhetorical concept of the nation. The bulk of the Italian army during the First World War was recruited from the peasantry, since the majority of industrial workers were needed for the war industries where they were subjected to military discipline and intensified exploitation within the factories. The peasants in uniform and the elderly, young and female peasants left behind to farm the land all experienced the war negatively, as a massive disruption of their everyday lives for purposes about which they knew little and cared even less.

In short, Italy had not by 1914, or even by 1918, experienced the transformation that Mosse has suggested was a Europe-wide phenomenon, the nationalisation of the masses.[3] Nor had peasants been turned into Italians in the way Eugen Weber's peasants were turned into Frenchmen.[4] The gap between *paese legale* and *paese reale* remained almost as wide as it was in 1860. The Socialists' hostility to the war, far from isolating them from the masses, brought them unprecedented popularity amongst the peasantry in hitherto Catholic and politically apathetic regions like Umbria. Those war veterans who turned to Fascism did so because they were petty bourgeois or bourgeois war veterans, steeped in nationalist ideology, not because they were war veterans as such.

The Fascist regime set up by Mussolini after the March on Rome in October 1922 sought to eliminate these popular traditions of pacifism and anti-militarism associated with socialism and anarchism and instead to instill into the Italians an exaggerated nationalism and a rampant militarism. The Abyssinian War of 1935-36 seemed to suggest that Mussolini's experiment had succeeded, that the masses had become identified with the nation, that every worker and every peasant was now prepared to glory in the triumph of Italian arms. May 1936 is generally accepted as being the high point of consensus for the Fascist regime, with even former anti-fascists welcoming the Italian victory.[5] However, the Abyssinian War was fought a long way from Italy and was over relatively quickly without the population at home being fully aware of the difficulties the army had been faced with or the way in which poison gas had been used to subjugate badly-armed Africans. Moreover the League of Nations' sanctions, ineffective as they were in practice, had led the Italian people to rally behind their government, to feel in some sense the victim rather than the aggressor.

Later in 1936, the Rome-Berlin Axis was formed, with Mussolini, rather than Hitler, acting as its initiator. This alliance with Germany never aroused much enthusiasm among the Italian people. Even before the *Anschluss,* the Italians regarded Austrians and Germans as one and the same, and as their historic enemy, the enemy of the Risorgimento and of the First World War. While the Catholic Church gave its whole-hearted backing to Italian involvement on Franco's side in the Spanish Civil War, this war never aroused the popular enthusiasm that the Abyssinian War had, and may if anything have strengthened anti-fascist sentiment, leading Mussolini to organise the assassination of the Rosselli brothers who had put forward the slogan 'Today in Spain, tomorrow in Italy'. Mussolini's return from Munich in 1938, bearing news of peace rather than war, brought him a rather more rapturous reception from the crowds than even he would have liked.

In September 1939 Mussolini made various excuses about raw material shortages and failed to enter the war on Hitler's side as the Pact of Steel suggested he ought. The successive wars in Abyssinia and Spain had eroded rather than increased Italy's military capacity. In June 1940 it looked as if Hitler was winning the war and Mussolini felt he had better bring Italy into it as quickly as he could if he was to gain any territory for his country in the 'New Order'. It has been argued, especially by Macgregor Knox in *Mussolini Unleashed,* that Italian public opinion supported Mussolini in this decision.[6] Even if one concedes that this might have been the case, and it certainly can not be ruled out that it was so, for one has only to remember the almost universal rush to support Marshal Petain in France in June 1940 to realise the rapid changes of mood that occurred among the peoples of Europe during that fateful month, this new-found enthusiasm for war, and for war on the side of the hated Germans, did not last.

It is a commonplace that one of the principal differences between the First and the Second World Wars was the much greater degree of civilian involvement in the Second. Of course the First World War too had led to an expansion of the war industries and the militarisation of labour in Italy, as has been mentioned above. In this sphere there was more similarity than difference between the two wars as they affected Italy and in any case the switch from peacetime to wartime production in Italy had to a large extent started in 1936, not 1940, with Abyssinia, not the fall of France. In the years 1935-39 11.8 per cent of Italy's national income had been spent on war preparations, compared with Nazi Germany's 12.9 per cent and the mere 6.9 per cent in France and 5.5 per cent in Britain.[7] Admittedly, Italy pushed this up to 18.4 per cent of national income in 1939-40 but such a level of mobilisation was not really sustainable. The agreement between Agnelli and Mussolini to plan the development of war production reached on 24 October 1940 only achieved its targets in 1942. Italy's war economy proved less successful in the Second World War than in the First. If the 1938 figure for industrial production is represented as 100, 1940 saw Italy achieve 110, before falling back disastrously to 89 in 1942 and 70 in 1943.

The most conspicuous phenomenon associated with the outbreak of war was not a switch from car-production to tank- production at FIAT, which had already started in 1936, but the entrance of women into a labour market from which the Fascists had quite consciously sought to exclude them during the inter-war years.[8] It is no accident that on 5 June 1940 previous Fascist legislation discriminating against women was rescinded and replaced by a decree allowing the substitution of female for male personnel in the public administration. This had results in a wide variety of sectors – women were seen driving trams as well as staffing the post offices. Even in large factories like FIAT in Turin or Pirelli and Falk in Milan, where at least some of the male workforce were protected from the call-up, the lower grades included an increasing number of women, generally the wives and daughters of men who had been sent to the front. Women were the most mobile and marginal segment of the labour force and could be taken on and sacked with equal rapidity. The increased female participation in the labour force was not confined to either white collar or industrial employment. As had already occurred in the First World War, women had to substitute for men in agricultural labour as the army made its habitual demands on the peasantry. The enormous dependence of the landowners in some areas on female labour as early as 1941 can be seen from the successful agitation of the female landless labourers in the provinces of Bologna, Modena and Ravenna, an agitation that achieved victory on the wages front, despite both the habitual repression of the dictatorship and the increased severity of war-time decrees affecting labour. Miriam Mafai has emphasised the subjective as well as objective dimension of the female entry into the Italian labour force during the war, stressing the feelings of independence and personal responsibility it generated, especially amongst those women whose husbands or male relatives were away at the front.

Food, or rather the lack of it, was a crucial aspect of the Italian experience of the Second World War.[9] The appearance of rationing was a sign of the imminence of war. In May 1939 restrictions were imposed on the serving of coffee in bars, although these were not observed at all strictly in the early years of the war, at least as far as regular clients were concerned. September 1939 saw a rather more serious restriction when the sale of meat was forbidden for two days a week, though it must be realised that large sections of the population could rarely afford meat at the best of times. Nonetheless, despite these privations, there was no hunger during the first year of the war, or rather it was confined to the groups among the Italian population who had never eaten enough and were used to living on a miserable diet of bread and soup. Some aspects of rationing in this early portion of the war had a rather paradoxical effect. For the peasants of the Italian hills and mountains, who had no tradition of using sugar as part of their everyday diet, the sugar ration was an unexpected gift. They quickly learnt to put it to one side and sell it to those city dwellers, newly evacuated to the country, who seemed to have an inexhaustible need for it. Although from the autumn of 1940 pasta was rationed, with a maximum of 2kg per head per month, rather less than previous consumption figures, pasta was also available on the black market at relatively low prices which took the sting out of rationing. As the war went on the situation deteriorated, with further restrictions in 1941. February 1941 brought a change in pasta rationing, with regional diversification, involving the use of either rice or polenta as substitutes depending on the traditions of the region. In March 1941 a growing meat shortage led to all customers being obliged to register themselves with a particular butcher rather than being allowed to pick and choose. In the autumn of 1941 bread itself was rationed – 200 grams per head per day. This gave rise to a lot of discontent and the regime reacted in November by increasing the bread ration for various categories it considered to be more deserving (or perhaps to have more potential for rebelliousness) – for instance the quota for miners and dockers was raised to 500 grams. The dire economic situation made such politically expedient decisions difficult to sustain for any length of time and in March 1942 the standard bread ration was reduced to 150 grams a head. As the economic crisis deepened regional anomalies became ever more apparent. One glaring example was that in the early months of 1942 cheese was rationed in Milan but still freely available in Rome.

A black market, a universal phenomenon in wartime Europe, began to be organised in Italy in the winter of 1941-42. During the winter shortages started to bite and prices started to rise very rapidly indeed. On the black market flour and pasta cost ten times their legal price, and even the less sought after, because already expensive, meat reached 8 times its legal price. Women were absolutely central in the organisation of a black market once the peasantry began to engage in a massive clandestine trade in the cities. Countrywomen brought food into the cities to urban women. Since the female black-marketeers of the countryside took a smaller risk in selling ten kilogrammes of flour to one woman, rather than one kilogram each to ten women, urban women were rapidly drawn into the black market as intermediaries and distributors as well as simple customers. By the spring of 1942 a contemporary survey carried out by Professor Luzzatto Fegiz of the University of Trieste estimated that 2½ million Italian families, approximately ten million people, were suffering from real hunger.[10] The rationed black bread that was being distributed to the Italian people in 1942 was no longer the pure bread of prewar days but a strange almalgam that included such admixtures as potatoes and rice flour. War increased the gap between rich and poor, and the gap between city and country. In the countryside food consumption remained at more or less the prewar level. Life for those deprived by poverty or geography of ready access to the black market, particularly for the poorer sections of urban society, became harder and harder. By January 1943 a Biella factory worker's ration card could only enable him to obtain food whose calorific value was an inadequate 1000 calories a day.

Important as food shortages were in their effect on civilian morale, what really brought the war home to Italian civilians in the most deadly way possible was the bombing.[11] The impact of the bombing on the Italians cannot be measured in purely numerical terms, that is in terms of the casualties caused by it. In the entire course of the Second World War 64,000 Italians were killed in bombing raids, only very slightly more than the 60,000 killed by bombs in Britain and far far less than the number of German civilians killed in Allied bombing raids which totalled somewhere between 600,000 and 700,000. Furthermore of those Italian civilians killed in the Allied raids, only 21,000 had been killed by 8 September 1943, about half the British total of such fatalities by that date. The crucial point is that the reaction of the Italian population to the bombing raids was very different from that of the British population to the German bombs or of the German population to the Allied bombs. In Italy bombing raids did not have the effect of unifying the population behind their own government and increasing their hostility towards the war-time enemy, which was the majority reaction in both Britain and Germany (one has to emphasise 'the majority reaction'; for there were outbreaks of mass panic at certain times and certain places in those two, more nationalistic and more bellicose, countries as well). In Italy the bulk of the anger aroused by the bombing was not directed, as the Fascist authorities had hoped, at the targets continually vilified in government propaganda, the British and the Americans, who were after all genuinely responsible for the casualties in the most immediate direct and physical sense, but towards the Fascist regime and its alliance with Nazi Germany.

In part this can be explained in terms of the inadequacy of the regime's preparation for the bombing, which was in such marked contrast to the propaganda it had churned out for some years about the overwhelming superiority of that most Fascist and most modern of Italy's three armed services, the airforce. It may have been the case that if the organisation of bomb shelters had been seen to be both efficient and socially just, that if all Italians had been treated equally, mass disaffection from the regime might have been prevented.In reality the chaotic and inefficient evacuation of the major cities of the North that followed the bombing raids only added to discontent amongst the urban population that was already on the increase for the reasons mentioned earlier, namely food shortages and unequal access to the black market. The evidence from police reports, which drew heavily on a network of informers, and from the reports of the officials employed to censor the war-time mail of both soldiers and civilians shows how rapidly popular discontent with the war grew, even though at first most of this discontent did not take the form of coherent political anti-fascism and in some cases never evolved into this. The ambiguity of popular feeling is plain in the police reports from Milan in 1943 in which references to attitudes of the following type recur – 'Why don't they go to Rome? Instead of bombing us, why don't they drop their load on Palazzo Venezia and the Quirinale?'[12] This could be interpreted as political anti-fascism, as hostility to the highest political authorities which happened to be situated in Rome in the buildings referred to in the quotation or it could be interpreted as pure Milanese anti-Rome localism or it might be seen with equal validity as an uneasy mixture of both these sentiments. It is very interesting that after the first bombing raid on Rome on 19 July 1943 police sources spoke of what they described as the 'monstrous feeling' of satisfaction of the rest of the country.

Given the extent to which the population, especially the lower classes, identified the Fascist regime with its head, with Mussolini, the remarks made about his speeches during these years give a good indication of popular morale. As early as June 1941 police informants report Mussolini being described as 'a man in decline', by February 1942 they were saying 'he's old' and by August 1942 – 'he's finished'.[13] The reaction to Mussolini's broadcast of 2 December 1942, which caused panic by urging the rapid evacuation of bombed cities, was an even more interesting one. Police informers reported that it was widely believed that 'the voice heard on the radio is not the Duce's voice'.[14] In short, the myth of the Duce himself as an all-powerful leader had started to crumble. This was a myth that had some currency amongst sections of the population who were not committed fascists but were willing to ascribe much of the inefficiency and corruption of the regime to Mussolini's subordinates, not to the dictator himself, rather as people in earlier centuries had always blamed their troubles on the King's evil advisers, rather than on the King himself. In this respect there does seem to have been some parallel between Fascist Italy and Nazi Germany, about which Ian Kershaw in *The Hitler Myth* has reached rather similar conclusions.[15]

These subterranean currents of discontent that in 1941 and 1942 expressed themselves in grumbling on the trams or slogans written on walls late at night rose to the surface in the spring of 1943. The outbreak of mass strikes in Turin and Milan in March and April 1943 was one of the most remarkable episodes in Italy's wartime experience, more remarkable in comparative perspective than the Resistance itself.[16] These strikes preceded the King's dismissal of Mussolini on 25 July by some months and can not be linked in time with the disaffection of the traditional elites – the army, navy, aristocracy, the monarchy, to some extent the industrialists – to which the King's action gave concrete expression. The working class acted alone, to some extent under the leadership of the clandestine Communist Party, but without any support from the other social groups. The workers' action may be seen as prompting the subsequent action of the elites who began to feel that if they did not act to remove Mussolini by conspiracy the workers would remove him by mass strikes and demonstrations and such events would lead to dramatic social and not just political change, sweeping aside capitalism along with Fascism. It should also be emphasised that the strikes broke out before the Allied landings in Sicily and not as a result of them – no Italian territory had been invaded in March. It is arguable that the strikes' organisers were more influenced by the course of the war in the East – by the Soviet triumph over the Nazis at Stalingrad – than by that of the war in the West – Italy's defeats in North Africa. While by 1943 the regime was identified in the popular imagination with the increasingly hated Germans, unlike the later mass strikes of 1944, those of 1943 were directed against a native Fascist regime, not against German occupation – showing once again both the very fragile basis of Mussolini's conversion of the Italians to nationalism in 1936 and the enormous strength of the old repressed subversive traditions which had outlasted twenty years of Fascist dictatorship and which now identified themselves with the Soviet Union.

The 45 days between 25 July 1943 and 8 September 1943 were another unique episode in Italy's wartime experience. The mass of the population greeted Mussolini's overthrow by the King with rejoicing, assuming it meant the end of the Fascist regime and the end of the war that the regime had unleashed, and from which the vast majority of Italians, whatever their initial reaction in June 1940, now wanted to withdraw as rapidly as possible. The power of the Fascist Party as an organised force was broken literally overnight. In the recent and rather heated historiographical debate over whether the events of 1943-45 can be regarded as a civil war and not simply as a war of national liberation, those who regard the conflict that took place in northern Italy between 8 September 1943 and 25 April 1945 purely as a war of national liberation, in which the partisans of the Republic of Salò were collaborationists whose relationship with their German masters was essentially as servile as that of their French counterparts after 1942, place a great deal of emphasis on the fact that there was no attempt by the fascists to take up arms in defence of their Duce or their beliefs in the period between 25 July and 8 September.[18] However, one might argue this was in part because the monarchist-military dictatorship of the King and his new Prime Minister Badoglio gave no signs of wanting political liberty or social change – soon after the initial wave of popular rejoicing had faded, the security forces were once again quite ready to fire on working-class crowds, employing not just warning shots but ones clearly designed to kill – in Bari 23 people were killed and 70 injured when the army opened fire on the crowd in Piazza Roma.

The popular desire for peace, which had been expressed at the start of the 45 days by the 4000 Innocenti workers of Milan, who had marched through the city carrying placards demanding an immediate end to the war and by the women of Genoa distributing red carnations to the soldiers, was left unsatisfied. First, to almost universal dismay, the King and Badoglio announced their intention to carry on fighting on the German side and then they engaged in long drawn out secret negotiations with the Allies. Meanwhile, in mid-August, when the Torinese and Milanese workers went on strike to demand an immediate peace and an end to the German Alliance, the authorities reluctantly released some political prisoners but simultaneously responded with more bloodshed and a wave of mass arrests.

The Germans reacted to the changing political and military situation far more quickly than either the indecisive Italian King or the puzzled Italian people and started moving large numbers of troops into Italy. When on 8 September Badoglio announced the armistice which he had signed with the Anglo-American forces before fleeing south with the King, absolutely no serious attempt had been made to organise military or civilian resistance to the Germans who had been steadily strengthening their position throughout the 45 days, implementing contingency plans for the occupation of Italy first drawn up ten days before the fall of Mussolini. Given the disgraceful lack of leadership at the top, it is hardly surprising that the Italian army disintegrated with the mass of conscripts going home as fast as they could. It is also at the very least highly probable that the demonstrable failure of the conservative forces led by the King and Badoglio to maintain a functioning bureaucratic, military and police apparatus for more than a few weeks, was bound to have contributed to a revival of sympathy for Mussolini amongst some of those who had previously served the Fascist regime, as civil servants, policemen or soldiers, and that the King was thus partially responsible for the degree of collaboration the Germans obtained after 8 September, which might otherwise have been more strictly confined to ideologically committed fascists.

The period between 8 September 1943 and 25 April 1945 saw Italy divided into two, a German-occupied north and an Anglo-American-occupied south, even if the boundaries between the two sectors changed to the Allies' advantage as the war progressed, with a painful slowness that showed that Italy was far from being the soft underbelly of Churchill's imagination. Obviously the two occupations were very different in character. The German occupation of the north was an horrifically brutal one, whilst the Allied occupation of the south was relatively mild by the standards of occupation regimes. Nonetheless, the ignominious flight of Badoglio and the King to the south gave them little moral authority and in the early days of the Allied campaign before the capture of Rome in June 1944, the Allies had more control over the day to day life of civilians than the King had. As Ellwood has emphasised, constant arguments between the British and the Americans over their goals in Italy, together with the huge gap between the high-flown directives issued at the top and the capacity to implement them on the ground meant that any occupation policies not directly related to the course of the military campaign were pursued in a fairly haphazard and inefficient manner.[19] Ellwood points out that by and large the Allied officers used to fill the lower levels of the Allied military government had no economic or technical qualifications and that they were all too frequently given this role because their former commanding officers in the field thought they were fit for little else – in other words they were often the rejects and misfits rather than the cream of the officer corps.

The general line of the British government was to maintain 'the continuity of the state' – to use Claudio Pavone's classic formulation - as far as possible, both because of Churchill's lifelong fear of left-wing subversion and because it was felt that if the existing state disintegrated completely, the Allies would have the whole burden of running the country.[20] The Americans were in theory more committed to reforms and had far less regard for the monarchy, because of their own republican tradition, but from 1944 onwards, as the Communist threat came to the fore within the Resistance, a lot of their earlier crusading zeal evaporated. In any case it was the British rather than the Americans who dominated day to day administration, particularly after the Americans withdrew a large part of their army from Italy to transfer it to operations in France in 1944. Whilst official British attitudes were far more vindictive than American ones, with Eden in particular being notoriously anti-Italian, American material assistance for Italian reconstruction did not in practice arrive in any quantity before the end of the war. Allied, particularly American, troops' spending in Italy further boosted inflation and played its role in wrecking the currency. In accordance with southern tradition the old notables continued to run things under the occupation just as they had done before Fascism and during Fascism – the change of regime did not mean a change of ruling class. Where a purge of Fascist officials was conducted in Sicily, most of the latter-day anti-fascists were in reality mafiosi with good links with the Italian-Americans who had arrived in quantity in the American army. It is also worth noting that there was no Fascist resistance to the Allied occupation, even though neo-fascism was to put down roots in the south after 1945, and this lack of support for Mussolini in areas outside the German occupied zone has been adduced as an argument against Pavone's 'civil war' interpretation of events in the north between 1943 and 1945. In short, whilst southern Italy, unlike the north, did not experience anything worse than the poverty, confusion and dislocation that are the usual products of an unsuccessful war, neither did it experience any movement of national rebirth or renewal that was in any way analogous with that in the north.

In the North the Germans restored Mussolini, whom they had rescued from the top of a mountain in the Abruzzo, to nominal power in the Italian Social Republic or Republic of Salò as it was more popularly known. German occupation policy in Italy was characterised by serious internal conditions that reflected the increasing rivalry between the various military and bureaucratic hierarchies that co-existed within the power structure of the Third Reich.[21] The heads of the *Wehrmacht* favoured a very harsh occupation policy hoping to exploit Italy to the maximum and callously including in their calculations the possibility of completely destroying the country, in much the same way as territories in Eastern Europe had been reduced to starvation and chaos. The *Auswärtiges Amt* under Ribbentrop's leadership believed in a more flexible policy that made use of Italian collaborators. This of necessity would have to be a more prudent and softer policy in order that Germany's Fascist collaborators were not stripped of all credibility in the eyes of Italians. Ribbentrop's milder line was not advocated out of greater humanity but because any other one would have deprived his men of authority; if Italy had been dominated by a military administration which could have given orders to the Prefects, military power would have been absolute and Ribbentrop's diplomats would have had no role to play.

The question of which German organisation or personality was to be in charge of Italy was never resolved during the twenty months of the occupation. Ribbentrop's attempt to ensure he obtained the dominant position in Italy was blocked from the very beginning not only by Speer and Sauckel, who sent their representatives to Italy with broadly defined tasks and extraordinary powers, but also by the *Wehrmacht* who set up a 'provisional' military administration (which lasted until May 1945) to assure the functioning of the Italian economy. From September 1943 there was a continuous struggle between the *Auswärtiges Amt* and the *Wehrmacht* for the political control of Italy. The diplomats wanted a policy of collaboration that employed strong but indirect pressure on an Italian government, whose independence was to be purely formal. The military men did not believe in political solutions, but in an occupation regime directed by a military administration in which there would be no role at all for an Italian government.

The principal internal contradiction of the German occupation regime was that Hitler had very typically given full powers to both the representative of the *Auswärtiges Amt* and that of the *Wehrmacht*, leaving the way open for the more ruthless and capable of the two to eliminate his internal adversaries. The victor proved to be Ambassador Rahn, an expert in organising collaborationism from his days in France, Syria and Tunisia. By February 1944 Rahn had got the upper hand over his rival General Toussaint, making sure that the military administration never got the legislative power it had so desperately desired. Rahn's authority was based on Hitler's instructions of 10 September 1943 not to interfere with Italian sovereignty on a formal level.

Some other organisations which had operated in Italy on their own initiative ever since the armistice were only partially subordinated to Rahn. Amongst these was Speer's ministry represented by Leyers. Initially Leyers' aim was to dismantle Italian industrial installations and to transfer both their raw materials and their machinery to the Reich. But after February 1944 this policy was completely overturned.The productive capacity of Northern Italy had to be exploited to the maximum degree possible because the Axis's transport system was breaking down and the bombing of German factories was proving increasingly devastating. As a result Leyers worked with Rahn to maintain the level of production in German-occupied Italy and to try and keep the Italian workers calm. They got involved in a furious argument with Sauckel who had an ever greater need for foreign workers to fill the gaps in production caused by the call-up of numerous German workers in the last phase of the war. Sauckel in agreement with Hitler had planned at the beginning of 1944 to deport more than three million Italian workers to the Reich, starting with one million in the first four months of 1944. Whilst this figure may seem incredibly high, it must be remembered that Sauckel had achieved his objectives in Poland, Russia and even to some extent in France and Holland.

Sauckel failed in Italy because Rahn, Leyers and even the SS General Wolff, Himmler's representative in Italy, had other objectives and therefore did not want to stir up discontent among the Italian workers who had already been working for some time for what were now in reality German war industries, even if the Nazis never expropriated Italian capital and respected the property rights of men such as Agnelli, Pirelli and Donegani. On 4 July 1944 Leyers protested against the compulsory call-up of Italian workers by the German authorities, pointing out that it had caused grave damage to the war economy because workers had disappeared from the factories and the number of partisans had increased to a level that put public order in danger. Even the SS General Harster claimed that there were not enough German police to implement the policy, whilst the Italian Fascist police and army could not be trusted to carry it out and were in certain instances actively sabotaging it. In an important meeting on 4 July Rahn got the agreement of all the principal German representatives in Italy that the compulsory labour call-up be suspended and one week later Hitler himself appoved this decision.

German campaigns to obtain Italian volunteers ready to go to work in Germany yielded poor results. As a direct consequence the deportation of Italian prisoners and captured partisans was stepped up. A third possibility remained open to the Germans, that of indiscriminate deportations of civilians, which were carried out in the form of a man-hunt, organised it ought to be stressed not by the SS but by the *Wehrmacht*. In the province of Bologna in August 1944 of 7400 men arrested by the Germans, 5600 were deported to the Reich.[22] Only 1 per cent were volunteers, 10 per cent were partisans and a startling 89 per cent were ordinary civilians evacuated by the *Wehrmacht* from areas near the front line. In the zone under the control of the 14th Army 23,000 men were registered as fit for work and promptly arrested. More than 4000 of these civilians were dispatched to forced labour in the Reich, while more than 7000 were conscripted to work for the Germans in Italy. The same army captured more than 14,000 men in October 1944 but after 2 months the Germans decided to abandon these vicious measures because they had led to too worrying an increase in the number of partisans. In November 1944 SS General Wolff banned 'other attempts at man hunts,because he, the man in charge of public order in Italy, would have otherwise had to pay the price'.[23] Sauckel's megalomaniac policy had proved a failure – instead of rounding up 1½ million men in 1944, he had only obtained 75,000 men, despite the employment of a variety of methods ranging from prizes for volunteers to indiscriminate round-ups.

While Rahn achieved his objectives in relation to forced labour, he was less successful in restraining his rivals in other fields. Rahn explicitly opposed the transfer of methods used in the war in the East to Italy. The *Wehrmacht* General Kesselring adopted quite a different attitude to partisan warfare. The same Kesselring who in his memoirs talked without any justification of the sincerity and honesty of the German army issued an order on 12 January 1944 that the term 'hostage' not be used in public statements and that 'the killing of hostages should no longer be made known'.[24] With this order the *Wehrmacht* in Italy abandoned any remnant of respect for international law and adopted the arbitrary methods of pure terrorism, already all too familiar in the East. It would be wrong to make too simplistic a distinction between the actions of the *Wehrmacht* and the actions of the SS during the German occupation of Italy. Each force was to some extent internally divided. While the SS General Wolff may have appeared relatively moderate, SS units like the 16th Armoured Division which included the notorious Major Reder received direct orders from Himmler to adopt a ferocious approach to the partisans, orders which would clearly have over-ridden any more measured instructions from their immediate superiors.

The capacity of the Republican Fascist regime to pursue any policy that the Germans disapproved of or even to veto any German policy unwelcome to Mussolini was more or less non-existent. The most obvious illustration of Mussolini's political impotence was the fate of his socialisation policy, an objective embeddeded in the very name of the Italian Social Republic as well as in the theses of the Verona Congress, the only major political gathering organised by the Republican Fascist Party.[25] Mussolini's reversion to dreams of some sort of socialisation or workers' control was a product of his anger against the industrialists whom he regarded as having betrayed him, despite everything that he had done to repress the workers on their behalf. This policy may have been based on a desire for revenge, just as his resurgent anti-clericalism and his resurgent republican fervour owed much to the belief that the Church and the King had betrayed him, but it was as sincere as any other belief that he held during the last twenty months of his life. Yet, despite frequent rhetoric about socialisation, Mussolini was unable to implement it, because the Germans in general and the SS in particular were determined that it be blocked as dysfunctional in terms of the German war economy, which they believed would have fewer problems with Agnelli than with the militant FIAT workers who had already shown their teeth in the spring of 1943. Conversely, the extermination of the Jews, the most obvious example of a policy for which the bulk of Italian Fascists had shown no enthusiasm prior to 1943, and towards which Mussolini had at the very least been ambivalent, was put into rapid operation by the German occupiers on Italian soil. Whilst the Fascist regime had introduced racial laws in 1938, it had not only made no effort to slaughter its own Jews in the years before July 1943 but it had even acted to protect the Jews of Yugoslavia, Greece and Southern France against their German persecutors and the Germans' local accomplices.[26] The wholesale offensive against such Jewish communities as those of Rome and Ferrara, even if it involved some Italian informers, motivated by greed, and a certain number of ideologically committed extreme fascist fanatics, was primarily the product of German will-power and organisation, and was actively or tacitly opposed by the bulk of the Italian population, who sheltered the majority of the country's Jews during the German occupation.

Having outlined German occupation policy and indicated the major limitations on Mussolini's freedom of action, one can not avoid commenting on the debate as to whether the violent events that occurred in Northern Italy between September 1943 and April 1945 are best described as a civil war or as a war of national liberation. It seems reasonable to suggest that both descriptions have some validity. To some extent it was a war of national liberation. The Italian Resistance was far more united in its wish to defeat the Germans than it was on any matter relating to domestic policy. The Italian fascists had not taken up arms against the King during the 45 days and did not organise a Resistance against the Anglo-Americans in the south – in other words, it is hard to envisage the Italian Social Republic outside the context of German occupation and objectively the forces of Salò behaved very similarly to collaborationist groups elsewhere in German-occupied Europe. On the other hand it was not just a war of national liberation. The Republic of Salò had 150,000 men in its police force in April 1944. This was at least as many men as the Resistance had at its disposal. The General Staff of the Kingdom of the South estimated on 16 September 1944 that there were 82,000 partisans in German-occupied Italy and another 30,000 in regions that had already been liberated. In short the number of Italians involved in some form of military action on each side was roughly equal, a factor that gives some validity to the idea of a civil war. The fiercely ideological nature of the war between Italians was more reminiscent of the Spanish Civil War than of any war fought between nation states. Some historians have also suggested that the ruthlessness with which the war was fought on both sides is a typical feature of civil wars. Some quantitative illustration of the level of violence can be seen in the rise in the number of homicides in Turin from 66 in 1939 to 3204 in 1945, in Bologna from 48 in 1939 to 1749 in 1945 and in Venice from 50 in 1939 to 1239 in 1945. The fact that the description 'civil war' had been adopted by neo-fascists since 1945 and was more frequently used by the supporters of Mussolini than by his opponents during the actual events being discussed does not deprive it of historical meaning. Certain groups in the Resistance, particularly the Action Party, made a regular use of the term and if the majority of the partisans did not employ it by the end of the war, this owed a lot to a very determined effort by the Communist leadership to eliminate any reference to either civil war or class war from the vocabulary of their members or sympathisers. Pavone's description of the war as being simultaneously a patriotic war, a civil war and a class war is a more accurate description of what actually occurred at the time. In this context civil war and class war were not synonymous – members of the same class and even the same family were often divided by ideology, whilst there were occasions when partisans motivated by a desire to settle scores with the rich and powerful applied the description 'fascist' to men whose connection with the Republic of Salò, if not the pre-1943 Fascist regime, was often either non-existent or very slight indeed.

The efforts by Mussolini's regime and its German controllers to conscript the Italian peasantry of military age played a major role, perhaps the crucial role, in creating an armed resistance movement in the countryside, since any civilian of military age who either failed to answer the call-up or deserted from the Salò forces was liable to be shot on sight by the Germans or their more fanatical Italian collaborators. Most deserters chose to arm themselves in self-defence, although their willingness to engage in any offensive action against the Germans and certainly any action that took them beyond their immediate neighbourhood was often strictly limited. Without the large layer of young peasants of military age, the more committed nucleus of anti-fascists, principally workers from the Communist Party and intellectuals from the Action Party, would never have been able to build up a mass resistance movement in northern Italy in 1944 and 1945, so it is rather absurd to carry cynicism about men's initial motives for taking up arms too far, particularly when the major ideological influence on the apolitical, that of the Catholic Church, was being exerted in favour of obedience to constituted authority in the autumn of 1943, as will be shown in due course. In any case there were areas in which certain peasant families had as strong a left-wing political tradition as any urban working-class community, areas where the memory of the great agrarian struggles of the *biennio rosso* of 1919-20 and their subsequent repression by the fascist squads had lingered on. This phenomenon was particularly marked in Emilia-Romagna. Participation in the Resistance in regions such as Emilia was not limited to young males; young women were also drawn into Resistance activities, because the Germans were far less likely to regard them with the deep suspicion they reserved for young Italian men of military age. Although these women, often the daughters of old socialist militants or the sisters of men already in the Resistance may have started their Resistance careers as carriers of messages and of supplies, since these supplies often included arms, the leap from auxiliary activities to active participation in the armed struggle did on occasions occur, and in any event lesser degrees of participation exposed them to the same mortal risk as any male Resistance member.[30]

Another aspect of Italian peasant behaviour during 1943-45, and one which is worthy of wider attention than it has often received, was the willingness on the part of very large numbers of peasants to assist and shelter escaping Allied prisoners of war, who had taken advantage of the chaos that followed 8 September 1943 to begin a long journey towards the Allied lines. Any peasant sheltering an Allied prisoner of war was liable to the same penalty at the hands of the Germans or the forces of Salò as any partisan – in other words these peasants too were risking their lives. This phenomenon whose proportions may well have reached the same order of magnitude as more strictly defined Resistance activity emerges very clearly from the memoirs of Stuart Hood and Eric Newby and has been studied with more rigour and some anthropological insight by Roger Absalom.[31]

While the Italian Resistance did not reach Yugoslav proportions, it certainly became a more impressive force than its French counterpart, if only because of the slow rate of the Allied advance up the Italian peninsula, which came to a grinding halt in both the winter of 1943-44 and the winter of 1944-45. Nor was Resistance in Italy confined to the countryside. Whilst there was a limited amount of urban guerrilla activity and terrorist attacks on the Germans, most of the urban resistance in Italy took the form of strikes. The epic strikes of 1943 set a precedent for the mass strikes of 1944, the most impressive strikes organised anywhere in Nazi-occupied Europe. The workers in northern Italy, who had regained sufficient confidence to engage in mass actions in the spring of 1943, after nearly two decades of sullen acquiescence, showed even greater courage in confronting the German occupiers in 1944. The strikers openly demanded an immediate peace and an end to war production for Germany, making no effort to disguise their political goals behind an economic facade. The numbers who participated were extraordinarily high - 300,000 workers in the province of Milan alone.[32] The strike spread beyond the industrial triangle of Turin, Milan and Genoa to the textile factories of the Veneto and the central Italian cities of Bologna and Florence. Militancy was not confined to the higher-paid male workers who had traditionally been in the forefront of Italian strikes; in fact on this occasion women and lower-paid workers played an extremely prominent role in the agitation.

Precisely because the demands of the strikers were political, not economic, many participants felt that when the strikes failed to lead to an immediate insurrection, as some Communist leaders had suggested they would, nothing much had been gained from the struggle and a great deal had been lost, since 2000 workers had been deported to Germany as a collective punishment. It was undoubtedly the case that the deportation of the most active working-class militants to Germany occurred with the connivance or the enthusiastic assistance of industrialists or their factory managers who supplied lists of the most dangerous subversives, lists that the Germans would not have had on their own account and even the police might well have been unable to compile. There were exceptions like Lancia's widow, who strenuously defended her employees against the Germans and managed to save some of them from deportation, but the majority of industrialists were only too happy to be rid of such trouble-makers, illustrating yet again that the events of 1943-45 have to be seen in class as well as national terms.

Despite their ambiguous outcome, the strikes did a great deal to sustain the morale of Resistance groups in the countryside at a very difficult time. German behaviour in the Italian countryside during the last years of the war was typical of Nazism at its most brutal. The SS battalion commanded by Major Walter Reder exterminated whole villages. Reder's notorious 'march of death' began on 12 August 1944 at Sant' Anna di Stazzema where he organised the killing of 560 men, women and children and ended on 1 October 1944 at Marzabotto where 1830 people were massacred by the Germans.[33]

The Church's attitude to the events of 1943-45 requires a special mention.[34] The initial stance of many bishops in the autumn of 1943 emphasised obedience to authority, not only 'legitimate authority' like the Kingdom of the South but also 'constituted authority' such as the Italian Social Republic, so as to avoid the greater evil of what was variously described as 'civil war' or 'fratricidal war'. On 25 December 1943 Pius XII, who failed to make any public statement on the German round-up of Roman Jewry, vigorously condemned the activity of the Roman GAP, resistance commandos who had resorted to terrorist tactics in the struggle against the brutal German occupation of the capital. While the Church hierarchy's attitude became more ambivalent in the course of 1944 with condemnations of the Germans and the Italian Social Republic starting to accompany the condemnation of the partisans' alleged excesses, the Church never wholly committed itself to the cause of the Italian Resistance, even if many individual parish priests did. The Church tended to see the events of 1943-45 as a civil war.

There were regional variations in bishops' responses in the spring of 1944, with some emphasising German atrocities and others laying more stress on the behaviour of the partisans, while yet others, perhaps understandably, refrained from making any public pronouncement on such matters in the belief that to do so would only make a difficult situation even worse. Although there were differences of attitude between the higher and the lower clergy, with many parish priests siding with their communities against the Germans, Catholics joining the Resistance often experienced great moral conflict because of the Catholic Church's predominant emphasis on obedience to constituted authority, rather than the demands of the individual conscience, an emphasis reinforced by the years of alliance between the Church and the Fascist regime that had followed the Concordat of 1929.

The two movements of mass strikes in the factories and large-scale armed Resistance in the countryside were co-ordinated by a central Resistance leadership, the CLNAI, in which the Communists played a leading role but were flanked by a number of other forces – the Action Party, the Socialists and, to a far lesser extent, Christian Democrats and Liberals. This leadership was able to mount a national insurrection in northern Italy against the retreating German forces in April 1945, and thus take charge of the cities in advance of the Allies who arrived a week or two later. This was a largely symbolic action, since by this stage Togliatti had made it very clear to the northern Communists like Longo and Secchia that there would be no seizure of power, that they were fighting a war of national liberation, not preparing to carry out a socialist revolution. Equally significant in symbolic terms was the killing of Mussolini by the Italian partisans before the Allies were in a position to capture him. Both the national insurrection in the cities of the industrial triangle and the shooting of Mussolini, followed by the public hanging of his corpse in the centre of Milan, can be seen as ways of restoring Italian honour and national self-confidence.

The home front in northern Italy may have been marked by panic and defeatism in 1940-43 but from 1943 to 1945 northern Italians displayed a great deal of remarkable heroism. However, the civilians of the south experienced this war, like so many other wars before it, as a natural disaster, as inevitable as an earthquake or a volcanic eruption, not as something in which they were active protagonists. Therefore, once again, the gap between north and south remained unbridged and the Resistance did not have the impact which some northerners had hoped for - the dream of a Second Risorgimento proved every bit as illusory as the dream of socialist revolution that had sustained so many northern Resistance cadres during the bitter winters of 1943-44 and 1944-45.

Notes

1. David Ellwood, *Italy 1943-1945* (Leicester, 1985).
2. Maurizio Degl'Innocenti, *Il socialismo italiano e la guerra di Libia* (Rome, 1976).
3. George L. Mosse, *The Nationalisation of the Masses: Political Symbolism and Mass Movements in Germany from the Napoleonic Wars through the Third Reich* (New York, 1975).
4. Eugen Weber, *Peasants into Frenchmen: The Modernization of Rural France 1870-1914* (London, 1977).
5. Denis Mack Smith, *Italy: A Modern History* (Ann Arbor, 1969), p. 452; Martin Clark, *Modern Italy 1871-1982* (London and New York, 1984), p. 282; Edward R. Tannenbaum, *Fascism in Italy: Culture and Society 1922-1945* (London, 1972), p. 89.
6. Macgregor Knox, *Mussolini Unleashed 1939-1941: Politics and Strategy in Fascist Italy's Last War* (Cambridge, 1982), pp.108-12.
7. Valerio Castronovo, 'L'industria di guerra 1940-1943' Francesca Ferratini Tosi, Gaetano Grassi and Massimo Legnani (ed.), *L'Italia nella seconda guerra mondiale e nella resistenza* (Milan, 1988), pp. 237-56.
8. Miriam Mafai, *Pane nero: Donne e vita quotidiana nella seconda guerra mondiale* (Milan, 2nd edition, 1989), pp. 43-72. There is a growing literature on the attitudes towards, and legislation affecting, women during the Fascist regime, of which the following is a representative example: P. Meldini, *Sposa e madre esemplare: Ideologia e politica della famiglia durante il fascismo* (Rimini/Florence 1975); Maria Antonietta Macciocchi, *La donna "nera", "Consenso" femminile e fascismo* (Milan, 1976) and Lesley Caldwell, 'Reproducers of the Nation: Women and the Family in Fascist Policy', in David Forgacs (ed.), *Rethinking Italian Fascism* (London, 1986), pp. 110-41.
9. Mafai (above, note 8), pp. 73-98.
10. Ibid., p. 94.
11. Nicola Gallerano, 'Gli Italiani in guerra 1940-1943: Appunti per una ricerca', in Tosi, Grassi and Legnani (ed.) (above, note 7), pp. 307-24.
12. Ibid., p. 316 (translation Abse).
13. Ibid., p. 320 (translation Abse).
14. Ibid., (translation Abse).
15. Ian Kershaw, *'The Hitler Myth': Image and Reality in the Third Reich* (Oxford, 1987).

16. Tim Mason, 'Gli scioperi di Torino del marzo 1943', in Tosi, Grassi and Legnani (ed.) (above, note 7), pp. 399-422.

17. Paul Ginsborg, *A History of Contemporary Italy: Society and Politics 1943-1988* (Harmondsworth, 1990), p. 12.

18. The two opposing positions are exemplified by Claudio Pavone, 'Le tre guerre: Patiottica, civile e di classe', in Massimo Legnani and Feruccio Vendramini (ed.), *Guerra, guerra di liberazione, guerra civile* (Milan, 1990), pp. 25-36 which argues that what took place in northern Italy in 1943-45 was a civil war, the first time for some decades such a case had been put by an author associated with the far left rather than the far right, and Marco Palla, 'Guerra civile o collaborazionismo?' in ibid. p. 83-98 which contests the validity of this view. The articles, both scholarly and more popular, produced in the controversy unleased by Pavone are far too numerous to list in a general essay of this sort.

19. Ellwood (above, note 1), especially pp. 137-48.

20. Claudio Pavone, 'La continuità della stato: Istituzioni e uomini in Italia 1945-48', in *Le origini della repubblica* (Turin, 1974), pp. 137-289.

21. Lutz Klinkhammer, 'Le strategie tedesche di occupazione e la populazione civile' in Legnani and Vendramini (ed.) (above, note 18), pp. 99-115.

22. Ibid., p. 105 (translation Abse).

24. Ibid., p. 106 (translation Abse).

25. Maurizio Magri, 'Contro la guerra civile: La strategia del 'ponte' nel crepuscolo della RSI', in Legnani and Vendramini (ed.) (above, note 18), pp. 301-3.

26. Meir Michaelis, *Mussolini and the Jews: German-Italian Relations and the Jewish Question in Italy 1922-1945* (Oxford, 1978), pp. 291-341 provides the seminal account in English: Jonathan Steinberg, *All or Nothing: The Axis and the Holocaust* (London, 1990), pp. 50-134 gives us some further details.

27. Klinkhammer (above, note 21), p. 112.

28. Ibid.

29. Ibid., pp. 112-13.

30. Mafai (above, note 8), pp. 181-214.

31. Stuart Hood, *Carlino* (Manchester, 1985); Eric Newby, *Love and War in the Appenines* (London, 1971). Roger Absalom's views are stated most fully in *A Strange Alliance: Aspects of Escape and Survival in Italy 1943-45* (Florence, 1991).

32. Ginsborg (above, note 17), p. 22.

33. Ibid., p. 56.

34. A representative sample of recent work on this issue is provided by Bruna Bocchini Camaiani, 'Guerra civile, autorità, obbedienza: i richiami dei vescovi del centro-nord' in Legnani and Vendramini (ed.) (above, note 18), pp. 403-10, Silvio Tramontin, 'I documenti collettivi dei vescovi nella primavera-estate del 1944', in ibid., pp. 411-32 and Antonio Parisella, 'Cattolici, guerra civile, guerra di liberazione: orientamenti e problemi storiografici', in ibid., pp. 433-57.

8

THE NETHERLANDS

Bob Moore

As with all other European countries overrun by the Germans during the Second World War, the period of occupation has left a lasting impression on the minds of all Dutch men and women old enough to remember. Every individual and family has stories and recollections of what occupation meant, and these experiences have served to generate a large number of personal memoirs, biographies and local histories related to the occupation years. Although valuable in their own right, these writings highlight a serious problem for the historian attempting a survey of the 'home front' in the Netherlands, namely that experiences and conditions varied enormously. Major contrasts existed between one province and another, between city and rural life, and between rich and poor. Occupation, religious affiliation, and 'racial' origin also served to affect and vary the individual's experience of occupation. In addition, all these factors can be seen to have varied over time as the war situation altered and as the Germans made increasing ideological and economic demands on the country.

The problems of trying to encompass all these elements may help to explain the lack of a published social history of the period. For the most part, these issues have been dealt with by Dutch historians either as part of more general and extensive survey works on the history of the Netherlands during the Second World War,[1] or as monographs on individual subjects. The most extensive work on the subject is undoubtedly Louis de Jong's twenty-seven part history of the Netherlands and her colonies during the Second World War, yet the sheer size of the work makes a coherent overview of Dutch social history during the occupation problematic, as material is spread through many of the volumes. More importantly, the perspective adopted by the author tends to militate against an assessment of the changes in everyday life as the whole period is seen as something of a *caesura,* an isolated period in Dutch history unconnected with what went before or what came afterwards. Only recently has this perspective been altered. Historians such as Blom[2] and Hirschfeld[3] have not only prompted an investigation of concepts such as collaboration and resistance but have also encouraged a move away from a framework where the occupation period is seen in isolation to one where it is reintegrated into the study of longer-term trends in Dutch history. Debate now centres on the degree to which Dutch society was altered by the experience of the occupation and to what extent there were continuities in its structure and organisation between the pre-war and post-war periods. Inevitably therefore, this has prompted a further examination of the occupation of the Netherlands, and the way it affected different social, economic and even regional groups.

Any attempt to encompass even a small proportion of the published material on the wartime Netherlands involves the omission of many elements. For that reason, the experiences of Jews and other sections of Dutch society singled out for special treatment by the Germans have been left out of consideration. This is not because they do not merit consideration, but rather because they deserve separate and more detailed attention than space allows. The aim here is to outline the main phases of the occupation period and then to highlight the most salient features as they affected the majority of ordinary Dutch citizens. First of all, however, it is essential to look at Dutch society in the later 1930s, and the popular perception of what the war would mean for the Netherlands. Also important are some initial observations about the nature of German planning for the occupation and control of the Netherlands. As with the rest of occupied Europe, the character and execution of these plans to a large extent dictated the way in which German rule infringed on everyday life. This then provides the background for a general survey of the various phases of occupation before focussing on specific factors which had a major impact on everyday life such as the invasion itself, the nature of protest, food supply, employment, changes in public and family life and resistance activity. Finally, some attention has to be given to perhaps the most traumatic period of the occupation, and the one which left the deepest scars on Dutch society in the provinces of Holland, namely the so-called *hongerwinter* (hunger winter) when the Dutch cities of the west were deprived of food and fuel during the last six months of the war.[4] Yet even taken together, all these factors can do little more than give a brief insight into what life was like for the Dutch during their five years under German rule.

For the Dutch civilian population, the war and the period of occupation began almost simultaneously when German troops poured over the border early on the morning of 10 May 1940. In spite of the events in Europe over the previous nine months, the realisation that the war had reached their doorsteps undoubtedly came as a shock.[5] To understand this, one has to look briefly at the history of the country and the popular idea of the country's role in the world. The Netherlands had been at peace, at least in Europe, since the end of the war with Belgium in 1830. For the next 110 years, the country remained largely isolated from major European events. Her main concerns had been with internal matters and the security of her overseas empire in the East and West Indies. The outbreak of the First World War had necessitated a mobilisation of the armed forces to defend the country's traditional neutrality, and Dutch trading policy had created problems with several of the belligerent powers. Yet after the armistice, the Netherlands returned to its rather introverted existence apparently unscathed, and in the interwar period remained preoccupied with imperial matters, the health of the international economy and the country's trading relationship with important neighbours such as Germany.

This introversion, combined with the almost unversal belief in political and diplomatic neutrality as the only solution to the country's security problems in Europe made it difficult for the majority of the Dutch people in 1940 to come to terms with the failure of that policy and the fact that they were at war, and on the brink of defeat in a matter of days. In 1939, the publicly stated attitude of the government remained one of strict adherence to the principles of neutrality. The policy had served the country well in the previous world conflict and there was no reason to suppose that it would not do so again. In this way, it was possible for the population to go on believing what they wanted to believe, namely that the war which was coming to Europe would by-pass them a second time. In some quarters, the Dutch population's supposed 'moral and psychological' unpreparedness for war has been used as a criticism of Dutch government policy in the 1930s, yet it has been difficult for the critics to suggest what other courses of action might have been adopted.[6]

This is not to say that the Dutch government or population wilfully ignored events in Europe, either before or after the outbreak of war in September 1939. Even the maintenance of neutrality meant changes to the normal patterns of life. The pursuit of national security once again necessitated the mobilisation of the Dutch army and reservists, thereby taking men out of peacetime occupations and back into the forces. Moreover, the Dutch military plans to defend 'Fortress Holland' meant provision for the deliberate inundation of some areas to provide natural barriers and the rehousing of those people affected.[7] Finally, there was also the disruption to trade, the very life blood of the Dutch economy, and the readjustments which had to be made, with some enterprises finding it hard to continue normal operations and consumers finding some goods difficult or impossible to obtain in the shops. Yet with the exception of these inconveniences, everyday life went on much as usual until the invasion in May 1940.

Although the Germans had given some thought to the governance of the Low Countries, the actual form was more or less dictated by military necessity and ideological considerations.[8] In the case of Belgium, the strategic value of the country's coastline made it advisable to maintain a military government. In the case of the Netherlands, where the country was considered less strategically important, it was decided to install a German civilian Reich Commissioner to oversee the work of the Dutch bureaucracy. This policy was facilitated by the departure of the Dutch royal family and cabinet, and the continued existence of the civil service apparatus. The fact that the Dutch were considered as more 'aryan' even than the Germans, made it possible to contemplate the eventual incorporation of the country into the Reich, but this would have to be preceded by a period of education and nazification. Thus German policy during and immediately after the invasion was to treat the Dutch very correctly and very carefully. This would not only facilitate the carrying-out of the regime's ideological aims, but would also assist the German war effort.[9] If the Netherlands could be successfully administered and controlled with the minimum of German civilian and military personnel, manpower could be redeployed elsewhere to better and more constructive use.

If keeping the population quiet had proved to be the limit of German ambitions for the Netherlands, it is conceivable that the country might have remained a good deal more compliant than it did. In the event, the ideological and military imperatives of the Nazi war effort increasingly impinged on the initial relationship between the German occupiers and the Dutch, creating the basis for what has been characterised as a downward spiral of Dutch reaction and further German reprisals which continued from early 1941 until the liberation.[10] The main causes of Dutch protest can be grouped into three headings; the attempted ideological co-ordination of the Netherlands through policies of re-education, nazification and persecution of the Jews, the increasing economic exploitation of the country to meet the needs of the German war effort, and finally, the punitive and coercive measures used by the Germans against those who protested. This downward spiral can best be demonstrated by identifying distinct phases in the occupation period.

The immediate aftermath of the German invasion has been characterised as a 'honeymoon period'. The invading German troops were instructed to behave 'correctly' at all times in their dealings with Dutch civilians, and the German civilian administration was installed under Arthur Seyss-Inquart with the minimum of disruption to administrative and everyday life. Although most pre-war political life ceased relatively quickly, this was the heyday of adaptation, accommodation and attentism, and Dutch attempts to come to terms with the realities of the lost war and the need to rebuild a political structure which could function under German rule.[11] The honeymoon period lasted until February 1941 when attacks on the Jewish quarter of Amsterdam by Dutch Nazis were repelled by the inhabitants, prompting the Germans to take direct action against the Jews, which in turn prompted a short-lived general strike in the city and elsewhere on 25-26 of that month.[12]

The next phase, from February 1941 until early 1943, was marked by increasing German economic demands and the attempted nazification of Dutch institutions and organisations. These new impositions, together with the entry of the Soviet Union and the United States into the war, led to a general change in Dutch attitudes towards the Germans, characterised by the belief that the occupation need no longer be regarded as permanent. This period came to an end when the Germans attempted to re-intern the Dutch armed forces (with a view to employing them as labour in Germany), and prompted a second general strike in April and May 1943. It was at this stage that the Germans effectively abandoned any plans to nazify or incorporate the Netherlands. In the meantime, however, they had successfully managed to ghettoize and deport a large proportion of the Jewish community in the Netherlands without prompting any further major protests from the rest of the population.

The increasing conflict provoked by the suppression of the general strike in 1943, together with the demands for even more labour from the Netherlands to work in Germany and the deportation of the remaining Jews characterised the next period which lasted until the attempted allied breakthrough near Arnhem in September 1944 and the military stalemate which followed. By this stage, much of the country south of the main rivers had been liberated although fighting in the south-eastern province of Limburg continued through the following winter. This period also saw the growth of a more centrally organised resistance campaign against the Germans with various national bodies being set up to co-ordinate activities.[13] The last phase of the occupation relates only to the provinces north of the rivers which remained in German hands until the surrender on 5 May 1945. For the civilian population, this was without doubt the worst and most traumatic phase of the war. Resistance activity and the national railway strike in September 1944 carried out to assist the allied attacks around Arnhem led to German reprisals against the civilian population.[14]

The general picture is therefore one of gradually worsening conditions as the occupation continued, culminating in the total disruption of civilian life in the last eight months of the war. While some of the detrimental effects on Dutch society and economy were directly related to the economic and ideological impositions of the Germans, others came as a result of Dutch opposition to those measures and resultant German retaliation. This overview, although essential background, says very little about the ordinary civilian experience of occupation. To understand the main changes in day-to-day life, it is essential to begin by examining the months following the invasion, not least because they saw the establishment of many trends which were to become features of the whole occupation period.

Early on the morning of 10 May, the *Wehrmacht* attacked the Dutch frontier. Although it met with some stout resistance, the Dutch defensive plan involved conceding large amounts of territory to the German invaders and falling back rapidly to 'Fortress Holland', the north-western area of the country bordered by the rivers Lek, Waal, Maas and Ijssel. By all accounts, the Dutch fought hard, and even achieved some minor military successes, for example in thwarting the German paratroop attack on The Hague designed to capture the Dutch royal family. Ultimately however, with poor and outdated equipment, the Dutch proved no match for their German adversaries.[15] Nowhere was this more apparent than in the overwhelming air superiority of the Germans, which enabled them to bomb the city of Rotterdam with impunity. Faced with the threat of similar treatment for other cities, the Dutch supreme commander, Winkelman, decided to surrender his forces on 14 May. For the people of the Netherlands, the war had lasted a matter of five days.[16]

For the Dutch civilians in the eastern provinces of the country near the German border, their first intimation that the war had even started may well have been the arrival of enemy troops in their towns and villages. For those given more than a few hours to assess the situation, the choice for each individual and family was whether to take flight in front of the advancing Germans and become refugees, or to stay put and hope for the best. The decision to go or stay was subject to all manner of considerations. Personal circumstances and loyalties, assessments of the future under German rule, mobility, and the availability of transport were only a few of the more obvious factors involved. On the Dutch side of the lines, people were also moved out of their homes in the expectation of areas becoming war zones. Whether spontaneous or planned, there is no doubt that this flood of refugees assisted the German war effort by hindering Dutch military operations.[17]

On the day of the surrender, the airborne attacks and the broadcast of further German threats led the population to expect the arrival of a German army composed of 'wild, heavily armed bandits'.[18] This created a panic in many of the western cities and substantial increases in the numbers of attempted and succesful suicides.[19] Although the departure to England of the royal family and the government had taken place while the Dutch army was still fighting, many thousands of would-be refugees also made their way to the North Sea ports of Hoek van Holland

and Ijmuiden. A small number did manage to get away, but the congestion on the roads combined with German air attacks made any organised departure impossible. At least one group who had good cause to fear the German advance fell victim to this chaos. Jews whose departure from Ijmuiden had been planned in advance were prevented from reaching the port because the military authorities had received no orders to let them through.[20] Other refugees, both Jews and non-Jews also fled southwards in front of the advancing Germans, ultimately becoming trapped in France when hostilities there ceased in June.

For many Dutch men and women, the reality of the German arrival failed to match their fears. The *Wehrmacht's* explicit instructions for soldiers to behave correctly at all times and to establish good relations with the Dutch civilian population were almost uniformly obeyed.[21] Thus the expected 'bandits' turned out to be well-behaved and even polite representatives of the Third Reich. Moreover, with the important exception of Rotterdam, the material damage to the country had not been substantial, nor had civilian and military casualties been very high.[22] Within a matter of days, and in some cases hours, life in the Netherlands returned to a semblance of normality. Cafes and shops reopened, refugees returned to their homes, plans were made for clearing up the war damage and people went back to work. In some cases, bureaucrats and administrators began destroying books and records which might contain compromising material. Alternatively, they set about tasks which they *assumed* the Germans would ask them to perform. Yet everywhere there was an assumption of normality, even to the point of complaints when the public transport system did not run on time.[23] In the space of less than a week, the Dutch population had experienced the shock of war, the fears of warfare and occupation, and almost a sense of relief when the realities of the situation did not match those fears.

Initial changes were few. Wartime measures imposed by the Dutch government were continued by the Germans. There was, of course, a German military presence in the country, but this was kept to a minimum, not least because the war against Belgium and France was still to be won. The arrival of German civilian rulers under Arthur Seyss-Inquart meant changes and decisions for the higher ranking Dutch civil servants and police authorities, charged by the Queen with the task of continuing the administration of the country under German control. Knowing nothing of German plans they nevertheless realised that some form of *modus vivendi* was essential if the country were not to collapse into anarchy. At this stage, German rule appeared sufficiently benign not to give many bureaucrats sleepless nights over whether to continue with their jobs.[24] Others for whom the German occupation had some immediate consequences were the Dutch soldiers. They could not return immediately to civilian life as the Germans insisted on their internment. For the Jews, communists and social democrats, defeat and occupation contained a far more sinister and permanent threat, yet everyday life, even for these potentially vulnerable groups, did retain a semblance of normality.[25]

Initial Dutch reactions to the occupation were more varied than might have been expected. A small minority of the population, primarily supporters of the two national socialist movements (NSB and NSNAP) welcomed the Germans almost as liberators and certainly saw German rule as their passport to a better future. The vast majority, however, saw things in a different light. German military reports in May suggested that Dutch attitudes to the Germans varied from one area to another, with the eastern provinces being generally more well-disposed than those in the west.[26] While this may well have been wishful thinking,[27] the Germans also reported a certain amount of anti-Ally feeling as a result of military actions in Zeeland, Brabant, Amsterdam and Ijmuiden. More importantly, they noted a degree of popular disapproval towards the government and royal family for having left the country. The strength and extent of this anti-Orange feeling is impossible to measure, but it was to be reversed rapidly in the months which followed. Perhaps as a rationalisation for the rapidity of defeat, there was also widespread belief in the existence of a German 'fifth column' made up from the Dutch national socialists or from Germans living in the Netherlands.[28] While this belief was supported only by rumours, the activities and postures adopted by the Dutch national socialists seemed to give further credence to the story that the Netherlands had been betrayed from within. Other trends noted by the Germans were the hoarding of non-perishable food (and especially potatoes) by the Dutch peasantry, an action based on the belief that the Germans intended to take away all the available provisions and leave the country to starve in the coming winter. While the anti-Orange and anti-Ally feelings did not last for long, the implacable hatred for the NSB and members of other Dutch national socialist organisations did persist and indeed grew throughout the occupation period.[29]

In the period following the surrender, the Dutch were forced to adapt to the changed circumstances, yet even in these early weeks other lasting trends were to emerge which established the patterns for life under German occupation. Early German reports noted some limited protests against the occupying power. The Dutch resented 'loud' or 'arrogant' behaviour on the part of German military personnel in cafes and would endeavour to register their displeasure in some way. Although there were limits to protests of this nature against the military, civilians were more vulnerable and there were reports of physical attacks on German nationals in the street, and even on Dutch men and women who spoke German in the street or sang German songs.[30] For the most part, the German authorities allowed such infringements of the law to be dealt with by the police authorities and treated these protests as minor irritations which should not be allowed to detract from the main task of encouraging a passive and compliant Dutch population.

In this respect, the Germans had realised from the very beginning that the Dutch national socialists were going to become something of an embarrassment. Their marches through the streets, aggressive behaviour and attempts to lead the way on measures against the Jews did nothing to alter the hatred towards them felt by most of the Dutch population, both on ideological grounds and as a result of their assumed role in helping the Germans to overrun the country. NSB provocation of the civilian population only led to disorder and worked counter to the wishes of the German administration. Yet even the Germans were not immune from a tendency to take heavy-handed measures which prompted adverse reactions among the Dutch. Their taking of hostages from the Dutch population as a reprisal for the internment of Germans in the Netherlands East Indies was widely resented, as was the arrest of organ-grinders in Amsterdam for playing 'patriotic' tunes. If the tunes were so offensive to German ears, the occupying power should also perhaps have listened carefully to the church bells as the carillon in Amsterdam's *Westerkerk* went on playing the Dutch national anthem, the *Wilhelmus*, for some considerable time![31] It seems that in these early months, the Dutch were still trying to establish the parameters for life under German rule, testing out what was, and was not, permissible.

Initial uncertainties about the future were gradually overcome as the summer of 1940 progressed. On the one hand, the fall of France indicated that there was to be no rapid reversal of fortune and that German control of the country was likely to remain for the foreseeable future. In this context there was a move towards adaptation to the new conditions, and even some degree of accommodation with the occupying power.[32] On the other hand there was a refocussing of loyalty on the Queen-in-exile. Whatever ill feeling there may have been about her departure while the country fought on, this seems to have vanished and been replaced by a commitment to the House of Orange as a symbol of resistance. This renewed loyalty was given its first airing on Prince Bernhard's birthday, 29 June, when national and orange flags were displayed and people wore carnations (his favourite) or orange flowers. The German response to the so-called *Anjerdag* (carnation day) was to interpret such demonstrations as anti-German and to threaten reprisals if there was any repetition. Thus the protest was not repeated on the Queen's birthday in August but people found other ways of silent protest, by growing orange flowers or planting gardens with plants which would bloom in the national colours.[33] This restatement of loyalty to the Queen and to the idea of Dutch resistance was given a further boost after July 1940 when the BBC began daily fifteen minute broadcasts from London in Dutch.

On a more practical level, even in the first weeks of occupation, there were signs of trouble to come in the conduct of day-to-day life. For everyone, securing supplies of food and fuel were fundamental necessities. The Germans accused the Dutch of not having introduced rationing early enough. There were reports of hoarding and of the destruction of unsold food stocks in the markets, suggesting that prices were already reducing demand. Rationing only solved some of the problems. There was unrest in Amsterdam and the Hague when bread rationing was introduced. Rations were also cut rapidly and even staples such as cheese were soon restricted to 100 grammes per person per week. In some provinces meat became almost unobtainable.[34] On another level, there was widespread dismay at the rationing of two other Dutch staples, tea and coffee. In general, prices seem to have risen 15-20 per cent during the summer, making it impossible for some poorer sections of the community to afford even their rationed allowances.[35] It appears that, even in 1940, it was the poorer sections of the Dutch urban populations who suffered the greatest hardship. While those with money could afford to buy on the black market, those on the lowest wages or receiving state welfare benefits found it harder and harder to buy a sufficiency of food.

Apart from trying to find enough food to eat, the Dutch working class faced another threat. As soon as the new administration was established, the Germans attempted to extend what had been a policy of the pre-war Dutch government, namely to insist that unemployed Dutch workers should take up employment in Germany. Using the threat of withdrawing welfare benefits, workers were drafted, but even in the summer of 1940 there was widespread resistance and few were prepared to respond to the call. Some early returnees from an industrial plant in Salzgitter spoke of bad conditions and high prices.[36] Moreover, even if the work was reasonably paid, the Dutch worker had then to cover the costs of two households, one for himself at the place of work, and the other for his family in the Netherlands. While it is difficult to estimate how widely such information about work in Germany was disseminated, the reaction of those called up was clear. In July, only 60 men out of a total of 800 reported for one draft in Overijssel and while dole cuts were implemented against recalcitrants, they continued to be fed by sympathetic farmers and townspeople. Even workers who were allowed to remain on the dole in the Netherlands were heard to complain that 21 guilders per week was no longer enough to live on as prices had risen so much.[37]

While these factors were common throughout the country, any assessment of Dutch civilian life during the occupation has to take account of regional variations and the differences between conditions in urban and rural areas. City dwellers were bound to have far more contact with the Germans and the authorities than their rural counterparts. Indeed initially, the occupation of the country had very few visible consequences for many villages and rural communities. There was no German military or civilian presence, and administration, law and order were carried out by the same executive as before the war. As a result, new German laws and edicts often underwent some amelioration, with functionaries often turning a blind eye to transgressions, or even forewarning of measures to come. In the cities, however, such behaviour was far more difficult, and Dutch officials had to be far more careful as their conduct was under much closer scrutiny by the Germans.

City dwellers were also disadvantaged when it came to the supply of food and fuel. While staple foods were rationed from the very beginning of the occupation, people in rural areas were generally better off, having more opportunity to circumvent the rationing measures by buying direct from the producer (provided they had the money), and by growing food for subsistence themselves or poaching wildlife where they could find it. In the cities, people were almost entirely dependent on what the markets could supply, and also on the pricing of goods sold in this way. Regional and occupational variations also came to the fore in the first year of occupation. People living in the coalfield districts of Limburg or in wooded areas of the east were in a better position to provide themselves with fuel than their urban counterparts who were totally reliant on the adminstration and transport infrastructure to keep them supplied. Elsewhere, certain occupational groups found themselves immediately under threat from direct German measures. The Dutch fishermen found their livelihoods threatened by decrees which restricted their ability to put to sea, and additionally by allied mining of Dutch seaports. Later in the war, there were loud protests from the inhabitants of Dutch seaside towns when the Germans cleared or restricted coastal zones, not least because it ruined the holiday trade on which so many of them depended. Some ruefully observed that this was probably the Germans preparing for their last stand on the eastern front.[38]

All of these features were evident in the first nine months of the occupation period and can be seen to have set the pattern for what was to follow. Public life, family life, employment and the mere acquisition of basic necessities all underwent major changes in the months and years that followed. Normal public life did not continue for long in the occupied Netherlands. The Germans quickly subjected political parties, and anything of a party-based character, to restrictions and bans. This became especially severe, and problematic, in a country where the social structure was vertically integrated and the political and religious allegiances were organisationally linked to social, cultural and sporting activities.[39] Thus many of the links within the four major vertical 'pillars' of Dutch society were removed, or at least loosened. This represented a serious, albeit indirect assault on the secular life of much of the population, with many activities being restricted or curtailed altogether. While the Germans never made any attempt to restrict the practice of religion or the activities of purely religious organisations, the impact of these bans combined with the curfew and restrictions on travel conspired to reduce most peoples' effective participation in social and cultural life to a minimum. The one exception to the ban on political parties (other than those with a national socialist character) was the *Nederlandse Unie*. This was a mass political movement established in the summer of 1940 and based on the twin principles of accommodation with the realities of the German occupation, and viewing the changed circumstances as a chance for national regeneration.[40] The Germans at first tolerated the movement on the grounds that it might form the basis for more outward collaboration. Indeed, the leadership's stress on accommodation and adaptation to German hegemony and the alacrity with which so many Dutchmen joined the movement seemed to suggest that this belief might not be misplaced. For the first time in the Netherlands there was an organisation which transcended the traditional divisions within society. At its peak, the *Nederlandse Unie* had a membership of around 800,000, or about 9 per cent of the total population, but underlying this apparent strength were the seeds of the *Unie* downfall. While the Germans, and to an extent the *Unie* leadership, hoped that the organisation would become a vehicle for further accommodation and adaptation, the bulk of the rank and file members saw joining the *Unie* as a commitment to national revival and as a protest against continuing German rule and the activities of the NSB. As this divergence of interest between leadership and members became increasingly apparent in the course of 1941, even the leaders were forced to give greater stress to ideas of national regeneration. Once it became clear that the *Unie* would never be a vehicle for more permanent collaboration, the Germans had no hesitation in closing it down. As a result, the banning of the *Nederlandse Unie* in December 1941 ended the last vestiges of political life in the Netherlands outside national socialist circles, and reinforced the increasing fragmentation of Dutch society.[41]

The curtailing of public life, social, cultural and sporting activities, combined with the effects of blackout regulations, a curfew and shortages of fuel imposed major changes on the day-to-day lives of nearly all Dutch men and women. Most apparent was the fact that all these restrictions encouraged people to stay at home. Especially in the cities, social life now centred on the family even more so than it had done before the war, with card and board games undergoing a major renaissance. Reading also became a popular pastime although paper shortages rapidly made 'real' reading material hard to find. Shortages of clothing, shoes and every other type of household commodity turned mending and repair into an art form of its own.[42] The scarcity and later total absence of staples such as tea, coffee and tobacco led to all types of experimentation on whatever materials were available in order to try and make even a vaguely acceptable surrogate. Fuel shortages also encouraged people to visit nearby friends in order to save on this precious commodity. An extended family or group of friends spending an evening together in one room made good sense, as did the closing up of unnecessary or unused rooms in the house.

Another factor which contributed much to this trend was the limited availability of transport. In the bigger cities, the trams continued to run, although they stopped early in the evening at around 9.30 p.m. People still had their bicycles in the first years of occupation, but other forms of transport dwindled rapidly as petrol supplies were curtailed. Some taxis were modified to run on gas, instantly recognisable by the huge balloons attached to their roofs. All types of horse-drawn transport were also pressed into service, as were bicycles adapted to carry fare-paying passengers. While the bicycle taxis were banned in 1941 and the owners drafted for work in Germany, the other new forms of transport remained the prerogative of the rich, being able to charge more or less what they liked.[43] Yet even these entrepreneurs ultimately had their wings clipped. As the curfew hour was brought forward from midnight to 11 p.m. in early 1943 and to 8 p.m. in the autumn of 1944, so the Germans were able to exercise control via 'night permits'. These gave permission for individuals to be out after the curfew, but were denied to the taxi operators. This was a major blow, not least because they undoubtedly did most of their trade after the trams had stopped running. If the experience of Amsterdam is typical of life in the big cities, then it is clear that the occupation rapidly reduced the role of personal transport. In 1939, the Amsterdam trams carried 93 million fare-paying passengers. By 1943, this had risen to 200 million, and yet did not include the occupying Germans who travelled free anyway. While this was partly due to shortages of petrol-driven transport, the main cause was the German attempt to sequester bicycles during and after July of 1942 and convert the Dutch 'from a cycling nation to a walking nation'.[44] For so long a staple form of transport for many millions of Dutch men and women, bicycling had already been beset by an acute shortage of spare parts and the total lack of new tyres. Now the Germans mounted a sustained attack on this most prized possession. Bicycles were sequestered in the streets or through house-to-house searches. Many more were just stolen from bicycle stores at the stations. Even the German reports realised the damage they had done to relations with the Dutch people over this measure,[45] and this perhaps explains why only a few months later, the majority of bicycles not handed over were back on the streets. Workers who needed their bicycles to get to work were given special permits, and thus there was the opportunity for others to obtained forged permits. Even then, many hundreds of thousands of people continued to ride their bicycles 'illegally', and it appears that there were no immediate steps taken to enforce the permit laws.

The response to the sequestration of bicycles set a trend of disobedience to other measures. When the Germans realised that mere bans on listening to the BBC were insufficient and they attempted to confiscate all domestic radio sets, the Dutch handed in old sets or just casings - indeed anything rather than the real thing. On a more poignant note, the Germans also became worried about the ways in which racing pigeons might be used. They insisted that pigeon fanciers kill their birds and send in the feet as evidence. Rather than carry out this gruesome task, owners throughout the country contrived to amputate one foot from each bird, and by some judicious juggling of the figures, ensured the survival of their pets.

Other features of life under occupation were a tendency to buy and hoard goods of all sorts. In the main this was a response to fears about German plans for the economy and perhaps also the lack of trust in savings. As a result, most unrationed goods quickly became scarce as people converted their money into more tangible items. There was also a parallel trend into 'investment' in philately as collectable postage stamps were freely available and were likely to keep their value. A third feature of occupation life was the so-called 'flight into marriage'. While the Netherlands traditionally seems to have had a higher proportion of unmarried adults in the population than most other European states,[46] the war years seem to have encouraged many more people to marry. The reasons for this change are not hard to ascertain. When food and fuel were in short supply, it was clearly better for people to live together than apart, yet this alone cannot explain why so many people decided to make such an arrangement official. For an answer, we have to turn to changes in the Dutch taxation system which gave tax concessions to the married and discriminated against single individuals.

Yet however important these changes in social trends may have been, they were always subservient to the pursuit of food, fuel and employment during the occupation. In general terms, the amount of food and fuel in the country was gradually reduced as the Germans sequestered more and more foodstuffs, livestock and coal with each succeeding year. While it has been argued that the rationing system imposed actually made for a more equitable distribution of food, especially among the lower classes,[47] most people still had to buy more and more food on the black market in order to survive. German reports testify to the running down of wholesale markets as goods were withheld or hoarded by producers. The weather also played a part in reducing supplies to the western cities when the canals froze in winter and other forms of transport were restricted.

German reports chronicle the decreases in rations and increasing prices. During 1942, the meat ration was cut to 125 grammes per person per week, yet even at this low level supplies were often unavailable. Another indicator was the Alkmaar wholesale cheese market. The figures showed that by the end of 1943, the market had all but ceased to function as producers no longer wished to sell openly.[48] While the Germans believed that most of this food was ending up on the black market, there were other factors involved. Increasing German sequestration of foodstuffs and agricultural products had done much to aggravate the situation. Farmers had often abandoned dairy farming and stock-rearing on the grounds that animals were difficult to hide and easy for the Germans to remove. Instead, they were now growing crops. The net effect was to cut drastically the levels of milk and cheese production. Dairies closed as there was nothing left for them to sell, and prices continued to rise as shortages became acute. Meat and fish were rarely available and staples commanded unheard-of prices. During 1943, even the humble cauliflower was selling at more than three times its normal price. By April 1944, it was reported that a working-class family could only afford 70 per cent of their meagre ration allowances.[49]

The Germans continued to blame the black market for much of this and believed that 'well situated' people could still meet their needs in this way. Undoubtedly there was a huge shift from normal to black market trading, 1942-44. This took the form of direct transactions between producer and consumer, especially in the countryside, or via a middleman. There were fortunes to be made here, and the ingenuity of the black marketeers knew no bounds. German reports showed that these people were even using *Wehrmacht* trucks to transport merchandise as these were less likely to be stopped and searched.[50] For the ordinary consumer, this meant a different and more time-consuming method of buying necessities, and often having to bargain over each transaction. There seems little doubt that the lower paid suffered most from this trend. Rations became inadequate long before the *Hongerwinter* and reports in the summer of 1943 noted complaints from German civilians that rations in the Netherlands were much inferior to those in Germany, with the result that many of them ended up voting with their feet.[51] Shortages of agricultural products also had side effects. Brewing and distilling were reduced and the resultant scarcity of alcohol served to reduce drunkenness. Other consequences were more serious. There were outbreaks of dysentery, diphtheria and infantile paralysis reaching almost epidemic proportions in some towns and cities. Undoubtedly the food scarcity had a detrimental effect on the population as a whole and on children in particular.

Fuel supply was of equal importance during the winter months. Domestic consumers were in competition with industrial users for what coal supplies were available. Even in 1940, there were shortages in electricity and gas supply, petrol was unobtainable and wood and turf prohibitively expensive. Some order was brought to the situation in the cities by cutting electricity and gas supplies for certain hours during the day, but in the countryside where heating and cooking was done with wood coal or oil products, the situation remained critical and was never resolved. This lack of basic necessities gradually changed Dutch attitudes. While the Germans could be blamed for the shortages, separate *Wehrmacht* supplies of food and fuel were evident and even tantalisingly visible, but not available to the civilian population. The net result was a huge increase in thefts, especially from railway yards. In 1942 alone, some 4075 railway wagons were broken into, and a further 38,041 cases of theft from railway property were reported.[52] While some of this activity must have been attributable to the money which could be made from black market trading, many ordinary citizens also resorted to stealing in order to sustain themselves and their families. In this way, sections of the Dutch population which had started to become criminalised through disobeying German decrees on the surrender of bicycles and radios, now found themselves committing acts which were crimes and misdemeanours in any legal code. This increasing disregard for the law, born of the need to keep families warm and fed, turned a people who had traditionally been highly deferential to authority and essentially law-abiding, into a nation of law-breakers.

This disobedience to authority also extended into the world of work. From the very beginning of the war, the Dutch authorities had continued their policy of 'encouraging' the unemployed to take up work in Germany. This continued, using all types of pressure short of outright force until March 1942 when it became a legal obligation.[53] Initially, the main impact of the policy fell on the casual and unemployed workers who were rapidly called up for service. However, as time went on and the Dutch economy shrank, so more and more workers who had traditionally had stable employment found themselves made redundant and liable for work in the Reich. Even with the advantage of more Dutchmen being rendered unemployed by the changing circumstances, by 1942 the Germans were forced to resort to a degree of coercion in order to obtain the labour they required. Even people in employment were not wholly safe as the draft was extended to those who begged for a living, or who were 'of little social use'. Later it was more widely applied to encompass many other trades and professions deemed non-essential to the war effort. By the middle of 1944 it was estimated that 574,000 Dutch workers had been drafted, of whom 431,500 were still in Germany. More than 25% of Dutch miners, metal and construction workers were deported in this way.[54]

As in the early months of the occupation, there was widespread resistance to the draft and much public sympathy for its victims. Workers naturally preferred to stay in work at home in the Netherlands, but as factories and workshops closed, they were forced to seek public assistance and with it the certainty of being called up for labour service. Once drafted, there was a preference for being sent to work in other parts of the Netherlands, or even in other parts of occupied Europe. Anywhere other than Germany where in addition to poor conditions, workers were subjected to Allied bombing of industrial plants. The only other alternative was to try and avoid the draft altogether. Dutch doctors could often be persuaded to certify men as unfit for work. This ultimately necessitated the employment of national socialist doctors by the authorities to duplicate the work of their counterparts. In this way, some workers could continue to live at home and even receive state benefits, although their position became increasingly precarious. By 1944, any male between the ages of 16 and 60 out on the street was immediately suspect and in the autumn of that year, the Germans began indiscriminate round-ups of people from city streets.[55] By that stage, no one living openly in this way was safe.

The only other course of action was to go 'underground' in some way. By August 1943, it was estimated that only 60 per cent of men drafted for labour service in Germany actually registered, and only 20 per cent were still on the train by the time it reached the German frontier.[56] Sometimes employers conspired to keep their workforces together, often in 'grey factories' which had no official existence but which continued to function nonetheless, providing wages and sometimes a home for those workers who would otherwise have had to go to Germany. More likely the draftees would go into hiding, often in an area away from home. Hiding might mean concealment in an attic or perhaps masquerading as a farm labourer in another part of the country. Yet even with local assistance, life underground was difficult. With no valid papers or ration cards and food in short supply, the fugitive needed organised help. It came in the form of national organisations, the *Landelijke Organisatie voor hulp aan Onderduikers* (LO), and the *Landelijke Knokploegen* (LKP), which provided for the material needs of people in hiding and also arranged new refuges when required.[57] Lest it be thought that this was a relatively small scale operation, it has been estimated that by September 1944, there were about 350,000 people in hiding in the northern Netherlands alone. Included were members of the active resistance and also about 20,000 Jews, but the vast majority were trying to avoid the labour draft. In some areas during the last year of the occupation, the LO-LKP even assumed many of the functions formerly carried out by the local authorities.

If the main effect of the occupation between 1940 and 1942 had been to reinforce the Dutch traditions of family and communal living, after 1942 the effect of the labour draft was to put this process into reverse. As more and more breadwinners were deported to Germany or were forced to go underground, so their wives, mothers and grandparents had to cope on their own, dependent either on monies paid by the state for the work of an absent husband or son, or on the charitable activities of the LO. By 1944 there were more than 750,000, mainly male, workers displaced in this way out of a total population of around nine million.

Given that there were so many people in hiding, then it is reasonable to assume that there were also a large number of Dutch men and women implicated in helping them. This was another instance where the sense of justice overcame respect for German decrees and the rule of law. The help took all manner of forms: providing false documents, shelter or food, acting as a courier or providing information. These forms of illegal work undoubtedly involved large numbers of people and carried substantial risks. Those caught sheltering fugitives, Jews or, later in the war, enemy servicemen, were liable for arrest, imprisonment, deportation or even summary execution. Yet in spite of the risks for even this type of activity, there were some individuals and groups who were prepared to go still further and become part of the 'active resistance'.[58] The creation of resistance groups usually stemmed from former contacts established in military, Christian, left-wing or local circles, and involved a wide range of activities from information gathering and the hiding of agents to sabotage and assassination. While the range of resistance groups was varied, it should not be implied that the Netherlands contained a whole nation of resisters. In the early years of the war, the numbers involved were very small and, even at its height, this form of direct action probably involved no more than 45,000 people in all.[59]

In the summer of 1944, resistance groups were mobilised to assist the Allied advance as the southern Netherlands was liberated. This tactic was continued as Eisenhower's troops attempted to overcome the river barriers which straddled the country. The attempt to hold the bridgehead at Arnhem using paratroopers, was backed up by resistance groups which were given various tasks to perform. More importantly, the Dutch railways were paralysed by a strike designed to prevent the Germans moving in reinforcements. The failure of the Arnhem landings in September and the military stalemate which followed were to have serious consequences for the Dutch population of the unliberated north. As a punitive measure, the Germans made no attempt to restore normal railway services, merely bringing in their own personnel to keep military trains running. With the onset of winter and the freezing of the canal system, very little food and fuel reached the cities of the west, beginning what came to be known as the *Hongerwinter*. Prices of even the most basic of items reached astronomic proportions. A pound of butter had cost 80 cents in August 1939. By August 1944 it had gone up to 38 guilders on the black market, and by April 1945, 140 guilders. Over the same period, a pound of tea had also increased in price, from 1.50 guilders before the war to a thousand guilders in 1945.[60] By this stage, such purchases were only for the very rich. Central kitchens were set up in Amsterdam and elsewhere to try and offset the problems of near starvation among the poorer sections of the community, but even these were hard hit by shortages and in the end only opened one day in two. The hunger and winter cold took their toll. Mortality rates in Amsterdam increased fourfold, with children and the aged being the worst affected.[61] From being the most important thing, the acquisition of food and fuel became the only thing that mattered.

When the shops could no longer provide and the black market became to expensive, people reverted to the few unrationed goods. Tulip bulbs made a comeback. Having been tried in the early years of the war, they now became almost a staple in some areas, but over time they also became expensive as demand increased. For many people, the only alternative when the food ran out was to trek into the countryside in search of supplies. The starving citizens of Amsterdam, Rotterdam and The Hague travelled miles on bicycles or with carts to try and barter with the farmers.[62] This led to accusations by both sides; of farmers charging outrageous prices and of city dwellers stealing food or reselling it on the black market. In the depths of winter, fuel also became unobtainable at reasonable prices. People resorted to burning their furniture, doors and even floorboards in order to try and keep warm. Squads of illicit woodcutters raided public parks under cover of darkness, removing trees and anything else that would burn. Other resorted to digging up the streets to remove wooden sleepers from the tramlines.[63]

As spring arrived, so fuel for heating purposes became less of a problem, but by this stage food was almost non-existent. Some supplies from the Swedish Red Cross did get through, but it was only in the final days of the war that the Allies began their famous air-drops of food to beleaguered Dutch cities.[64] On 5 May, three days before the final German capitulation, the *Wehrmacht* commander in the western Netherlands surrendered his forces without a fight. For the people of the western cities, the traumas of malnutrition and cold during the last eight months of the war were to provide the most enduring memory of the occupation period. Elsewhere, the Dutch had different experiences of liberation. There had been little fighting in the southern Netherlands in the summer of 1944, but Limburg in the south-east experienced continued warfare through the winter with some towns changing hands more than once. The destruction was considerable. In the east and north east, liberation came during April. As a food-producing area, there had been fewer problems of supply, but greater dangers to civilians from an increasingly nervous German soldiery, especially in the final days before the surrender.

In surveying the occupation of the Netherlands, it is possible to identify a number of trends. The first of these is the apparent ease with which the Dutch population adapted to the changed conditions after the shock of invasion and occupation, and attempted to return to normal – or as near normal as possible – as soon as was practical. Yet, this return to normality is perhaps not so surprising if one considers what the alternatives might have been. The arrival of the Germans did not alter the fundamental need to provide for material necesities, and returning to everyday pursuits was perhaps the most natural and the most logical thing to do.

Although judging the popular mood in the Netherlands is difficult, some general observations can be made. After a short period of uncertainty during the first months of German rule, most of the country rapidly refocussed its loyalty to the Queen and government-in-exile, and put its faith in the eventual victory of the Allied cause. The short-term success of the *Nederlandse Unie* was more a result of its function in unifying a previously segmented pre-war society than a desire to collaborate with the Germans. Indeed, a feature of Dutch public opinion was the hatred and loathing shown by the rest of the population to the NSB and members of other Dutch national socialist organisations. These Dutch 'traitors' were universally despised as collaborators and, in the early years of occupation, attracted even greater opprobrium than the Germans themselves. Only later, when the Germans stepped up their ideological and economic demands on the country, did such differentiation disappear.

The motivation behind the protest and strike actions of 1941, 1942 and 1944 have been well documented, but arriving at a more detailed assessment of the public mood remains difficult. One rather unusual indicator of public optimism involves the juxtaposing of birth-rate figures - or rather the conception figures – against the major events of the period. The statistics do show a general upward trend with peaks after the German defeat at Stalingrad, the D-Day landings and the liberation, and troughs after the *Februaristaking*, the loss of the East Indies, and during the *hongerwinter*.[65] Perhaps surprisingly, except for the last six months of occupation, this indicator of optimism seems to be unaffected by the gradually worsening material conditions in the country as a whole.

Another feature of the period is undoubtedly the impact of wartime shortages and German decrees in increasing the centrality of family life in the first two years of the occupation, only for this to be put into reverse during and after 1942. German attempts to call up a large proportion of the Dutch labour force for service abroad led to widespread displacement of breadwinners as they either complied or went underground. Families became fragmented and, as conditions deteriorated, so life became increasingly difficult for the dependents left to fend partially for themselves. In itself, the avoidance of the labour draft by large numbers of Dutch workers demonstrates another important trend, namely the criminalisation of an otherwise law-abiding people. From being a nation conditioned to a highly deferential attitude towards authority, the Dutch found themselves increasingly at odds with the law as it diverged more and more from their concepts of norms and natural justice. Decrees which threatened private property or liberty were evaded on a large scale. People hid bicycles and radios, and helped those who went underground to avoid the labour draft. Finally, some were driven to steal food and fuel, not for profit, but merely in order to survive, and this perhaps highlights the most enduring memory of the occupation for those north of the rivers, namely the privations experienced during the last six months of the war. As supplies of food and fuel ran out, so for many city dwellers each day turned into a struggle just to stay alive.

NOTES

1. The most notable of these are: L. de Jong, *Het Koninkrijk der Nederlanden in de Tweede Wereldoorlog* (13 vols, The Hague, 1969-89); J.J. van Bolhuis, *et al.* (ed.), *Onderdrukking en Verzet: Nederland in Oorlogstijd* (4 vols, Amsterdam/Arnhem, 1948-53) and W. Warmbrunn, *The Dutch under German Occupation, 1940-45* (Stanford/London, 1963).
2. For an examination of these issues see: J.C.H.Blom, *Crisis,Bezetting en Herstel: Tien Studies over Nederland, 1930-1950* (Rotterdam/The Hague, 1989), especially pp.102-20, and id., 'The Second World War and Dutch Society: Continuity and Change' in A.C.Duke and C.A.Tamse (ed.) *Britain and the Netherlands*, Volume VI: War and Society (The Hague, 1977), pp. 224-48.
3. G.Hirschfeld, *Nazi Rule and Dutch Collaboration: The Netherlands under German Occupation, 1940-45* (Oxford, 1988); id., 'Collaboration and Attentism in the Netherlands, 1940-41' *Journal of Contemporary History*, 16 (1981), pp. 467-86.
4. H.van der Zee, *De Hongerwinter, 1940-45* (Amsterdam, 1979) reprinted as *The Hunger Winter: Occupied Holland, 1944-45* (London, 1982).

5. The psychological 'shock' of invasion forms the basis for a bibliographical essay by H.von der Dunk, 'The Shock of 1940', *Journal of Contemporary History*, 2, (1967), pp. 169-82 but is widely quoted as a reaction to the events of May 1940. See also, Blom, *Crisis* (above, note 2), pp. 61-2.

6. H.von der Dunk, 'Neutralisme en Defensie: het dilemma in de jaren dertig' and J.C.H.Blom,'"Durch kamen sie doch":Het Nederlands defensie beleid in de jaren dertig opnieuw beschouwd', in G.Teitler (ed.), *Tussen Crisis en Oorlog* (Diemen, 1984), pp. 5-23, 116-29.

7. de Jong (above, note 1), III, pp. 124-5, 176-80.

8. Hirschfeld, *Nazi Rule* (above, note 3), pp. 16-19.

9. Ibid., p.19; Blom, *Crisis* (above, note 2), p. 65.

10. A detailed assesment of the phase of occupation can be found in Blom, *Crisis* (above, note 2), p. 58, and Warmbrunn (above, note 1), p. 100.

11. Attentism (fr. *attentisme*), literally wait-and-see, has been used to explain the attitudes of certain groups and individuals to the first years of German occupation: G. Hirschfeld, 'Collaboration and Attentism'. Foremost among these attempts at accommodation with the new order was the establishment of the *Nederlandse Unie* in July 1940. See Hirschfeld, *Nazi Rule* (above, note 3), pp. 66-90 and M.Smith, 'Neither Resistance nor Collaboration: Historians and the Problem of the *Nederlandse Unie*' *History*, 72 (1987), pp. 251-78.

12. For a comprehensive survey of the strike and the debates which surround it, see B.A.Sijes, *De Februaristaking, 22-26 Februari 1941* (The Hague, 1954).

13. For a basic outline of Dutch resistance movements, see R.Roegholt and J.Zwaan, *Het Verzet 1940-45* (Weesp, 1985).

14. de Jong (above, note 1), *Het Laatste Jaar*.

15. Ibid., III, pp. 498-522; Warmbrunn (above, note 1), pp. 9-10.

16. de Jong (above, note 1), III, pp. 400-4. Warmbrunn (above, note 1), pp. 9-10.

17. de Jong (above, note 1), III, pp. 105-11, 341-2.

18. Warmbrunn (above, note 1), p. 103. Blom, *Crisis* (above, note 2), p. 61; A.Herzberg, *Kroniek der Jodenvervolging* (2nd edn., Amsterdam, 1985), p. 14.

19. Blom, *Crisis* (above, note 2), p. 61; *Rijksinstituut voor Oorlogsdocumentatie* (RIOD), *Archives of the Generalkommissariat zur Besonderen Verwendung* (61), Box 73, *Stimmungsberichte* 40044-52 (June 1940).

20. de Jong (above, note 1), III, pp. 443-6.

21. Warmbrunn (above, note 1), p. 103; M.J. Adriani Engels and G.H. Wallagh, *Nacht over Nederland* (Amsterdam, 1946), p. 15.

22. de Jong (above, note 1), III, p. 461; Warmbrunn (above, note 1), p. 10. The bombing of Rotterdam destroyed an eighth of the city and caused 800 civilian casualties. The total Dutch deathtoll for the invasion was 2,193 military and 2,159 civilian fatalities.

23. Warmbrunn (above, note 1), p.103. P.J.Margry *et al.*, (ed.) *Van Camere vander Rekeninghen to Algemeen Rekenkamer* (The Hague, 1989), pp. 273-4.
24. Hirschfeld, *Nazi Rule* (above, note 3), ch. 4.
25. RIOD 61/73 *Stimmungsberichte*, 40115 (August. 1940), KR537 (n.d.). RIOD 1-12/26 *WBN Archief* 4g *Schlussbericht* 16-29 May 1940.
26. Hirschfeld, *Nazi Rule* (above, note 3), p. 16. RIOD 61/73 *Stimmungsberichte* 40058-40073 (4 July 1940).
27. There remains some debate on the popular attitude to the Germans during the occupation. Many would argue that hatred of the Germans was a consistent feature, but more recent, but as yet unpublished, research suggests that this is not entirely accurate.
28. de Jong (above, note 1), III, pp. 103-14, 169-80, 464-8; Blom, *Crisis* (above, note 2), p. 61. For a more detailed investigation of the fifth column, see Louis de Jong, *De Duitse Vijfde Colonne in de Tweede Wereldoorlog* (3rd edn., Amsterdam, 1977).
29. RIOD HSSpF Archive 15/28-29. RIOD 61/73; *Stimmungbericht* KR537. The Germans were well aware of popular hatred for the indigenous national socialists and did their best to avoid direct association with the NSB.
30. RIOD 61/73 *Stimmungsbericht*, 40261 (30 October 1940).
31. Ibid.; Adriani Engels and Wallagh (above, note 21), p. 122.
32. For a detailed discussion of this, see Hirschfeld, *Nazi Rule* (above, note 3), and 'Collaboration and Attentism' (above, note 3).
33. Warmbrunn (above, note 3), pp. 42, 104-5.
34. RIOD 61/73 Stimmungsbericht 40249 (30 October 1940); RIOD HSSpF 15/28-29 *Meldungen aus den Niederlanden*, No.3 (30 July 1940), p. 59.
35. RIOD 61/73 *Stimmungsbericht* 40249 (30 October 1940). For the debate on food supply during the occupation, se G.M.T.Trienekens, *Tussen ons volk en de honger: De Voedselvoorziening, 1940-45* (Amsterdam, 1988), especially pp. 409-21.
36. RIOD HSSpF 15/28-29 *Meldungen aus den Niederlanden*, No.3, p. 27
37. RIOD 61/73 *Stimmungsberichte* 40132-40134 (6 September 1940), 40261 (30 October 1940).
38. RIOD 1-12/26 *WBN Archief* 4g *Berichte* (20 May 1942, July 1942).
39. The four main pillars were Calvinist (protestant), Catholic, Socialist (social-democratic) and Liberal with the last being the least cohesive of the four. There is now a substantial body of literature on this in Dutch, but for an explanation in English of the Netherlands as a vertically integrated (*verzuild*) society, see A.Lijphart, *The Politics of Accommodation. Pluralism and Democracy in the Netherlands* (Los Angeles, 1968).
40. See Hirschfeld, 'Collaboration and Attentism (above, note 3)', and Smith (above, note 11).

41. Blom, *Crisis* (above, note 2), pp. 71-2.
42. Adriani Engels and Wallagh (above, note 21), p. 34.
43. Ibid., p. 36.
44. Ibid., p. 230.
45. RIOD 1-12/26 WBN Archief 2g Berichte (13-19, 20-26 July 1942).
46. Adriani Engels and Wallagh (above, note 21), p. 37. Warmbrunn (above, note 3), p. 101.
47. Trienekens (above, note 35), pp. 409-21.
48. RIOD 1-12/26 WBN Archief, Bericht (December 1943).
49. Ibid.(April 1944). This report also mentions people having starved to death in unheated houses.
50. Ibid. (July 1942).
51. Ibid. (April 1943, May 1943).
52. Adriani Engels and Wallagh (above, note 21), p. 34.
53. Hirschfeld, *Nazi Rule* (above, note 3), pp. 221-2.
54. Ibid., p.221. See also Hirschfeld, 'Der "freiwillige" Arbeitseinsatz niederländischer Fremdarbeiter während des Zweiten Weltkrieges als Krisenstrategie einer nicht-nationalsozialistischen Verwaltung' in H.Mommsen and W. Schulze (ed.), *Vom Elend der Handarbeit* (Stuttgart, 1981), p. 512.
55. For a survey of the most famous of these raids where around 50,000 workers were seized, see B.A.Sijes, *De Razzia van Rotterdam* (2nd edn., Amsterdam, 1984).
56. RIOD 1-12/26 *WBN Archief, Bericht* (August 1943).
57. For more detail on these organisations, see Warmbrunn (above, note 1), pp. 187-98.
58. For a brief summary of resistance activity, see Roegholt and Zwaan (above, note 13).
59. Blom, *Crisis* (above, note 2), p. 88; de Jong (above, note 1), Xb,I, p. 746.
60. Adriani Engels and Wallagh (above, note 21), pp. 186-7.
61. Ibid., pp. 284-5. For a more detailed breakdown of mortality in the whole of the Netherlands, see Trienekens (above, note 35), p. 476.
62. For an account of one such journey, see H.J.Oolbekink, *Met Lege Handen, Een Hongertocht in Februari 1945* (Zwolle, 1979).
63. RIOD 1-12/26 *WBN Archief, Bericht* (October 1944), p. 3.
64. van der Zee (above, note 4), pp. 201-9.
65. Blom, *Crisis* (above, note 35), p. 60.

9

POLAND

Joanna Hanson

General Tadeusz Bor-Komorowski, the commander of the Polish Home Army (the AK) from June 1943 to October 1944 during the latter half of the Second World War, has written of the occupation of Poland during the Second World War: 'Both invaders drew up similar aims for themselves – to annihilate the Poles. Their methods, however, differed. The Germans quite simply tried to exterminate us. The Bolsheviks were not interested in the physical destruction of the Poles, but in breaking and enslaving the national spirit, which had been born and raised in traditions of freedom.' [1] *Both* invaders, *both* occupiers: that is the German and the Soviet. Occupied Poland during the Second World War is usually understood as the German occupation. Few remember that the eastern territories of Poland were occupied by the Soviets for nearly two years at the beginning of the war, and very few have any idea as to what that occupation meant for those peoples living there. Little attention has been paid to this problem by western historians and it has only been with the changes in Poland after 1980 and Gorbachev's policy of 'Glasnost' in the Soviet Union that the real stimulus has come to research that tragic chapter of Polish history, a chapter so alike and yet so different to that of the German occupation.

A word or two here should be said about the materials on which this study can be based. Polish historiography has not produced many monographs on the German occupation. This is partly due to research directions and lack of access to materials for whatever reasons. German historians with ready access to materials have done little to make up for this. In the 1940s memoirs and reports were compiled by the Polish authorities in exile from survivors of the Soviet occupation and deportations on their experiences. The Sikorski Institute in London and the Hoover Institute in Stanford hold these very valuable collections. Naturally. however, they mainly deal with the earlier period of the Soviet occupation. Emigré publishers have published memoirs and diaries. The subject has been virtually taboo in Poland for the last 45 years and it is only now, and with a vengeance, that the Poles in Poland are making up for lost time, but again mainly memoirs are being published. Jan Gross has made an invaluable contribution to our knowledge on both the occupations.[2]

Poland before the outbreak of the war was a country which had only been an independent state since 1918. It had a population of more than 35,000,000, predominantly agricultural. That population was far from monolithic, there being large German, Belorussian, Ukrainian and Jewish minorities.

On 20 August 1939 Molotov and Ribbentrop signed their famous Pact whose secret clause agreed a new partitioning of Poland. On 1 September 1939 German forces invaded Poland. Poles had feared an attack from their German neighbours after Jozef Beck, the Polish Foreign Minister, had rejected Hitler's claims to Gdansk in May 1939, stating that Poles did not regard peace as being desirable at any cost. A few days earlier Hitler had renounced the 1934 Polish-German Non-Agression Pact. On 17 September, the Red Army invaded Poland from the east. This 'stab in the back' was quite unexpected, and left the Polish nation stunned. No declaration of war was made. Stalin had not renounced his Non-Agression Pact of 1932 with the Poles and gave a defence of the minorities as an explanation of his action. The communiqué handed to the Polish Ambassador at 3 a.m. on 17 September referred to the Polish state and government having ceased to exist and the Soviet government's inability to remain indifferent to the fate of their Ukranian and Belorussian brothers living on Polish territories. It also renounced all existing treaties between Poland and the USSR.[3]

Occupied Poland was thus a double occupation, at least until 21 June 1941, and the country was divided into three. The Germans annexed part of the Polish territories – Polish Pomerania, Upper Silesia, the Dabrowa Basin, part of the Lodz and Cracow provinces and the Suwalki district – which were included in the Third Reich. This area was 91,974 km^2, a quarter of the area of the Polish state, and its prewar population numbered 10,139,000 inhabitants, of which 8,905,000 were Poles, 603,000 Jews and 600,000 Germans. The remainder of the Polish lands occupied by the Germans were formed into the *Generalgouvernement* (not a buffer state as once planned) and formed a reserve of Poles and Jews administered by the Germans. Up until the summer of 1941, this was an area of about 95,000 km^2, with a population of c.12,300,000, and after then when the district of Galacia was added, 142,000 km^2, bringing the population up to 16,000,000.[4] The *Generalgouvernement* was divided up into four districts: Cracow, Lublin, Radom and Warsaw. On 12 October, Hitler appointed the leading Nazi lawyer, Hans Frank, as Governor

General. His administration was almost entirely made up of Germans although Poles were employed at lower regional levels.[5]

These eastern frontiers between Soviet-occupied Poland and German-occupied Poland were the result not only of the Molotov-Ribbentrop Pact but of important modifications made to it. The German-Soviet Boundary and Friendship Treaty of September 28 conformed to new demands by Stalin and gave him nationalistically a more consolidated area. This also included a secret protocol stating:

> Neither party will permit on its territories any Polish agitation which affects the territories of the other party. They will suppress in their territories all beginnings of such agitation and inform each other concerning suitable measures for this purpose.[6]

The Germans had originally captured some of these territories only to hand them over to the Soviets. They covered an area of c.200.000 km^2, inhabited by about 13 million people.[7] The Poles made up about one third of the population, the Ukranians another third and the Jews and Belorussians the rest. Part of this Polish territory, including Wilno, was handed by Stalin to the Lithuanians, until June 1940 when he incorporated the Baltic states into the Soviet Union.

Administratively, the Soviet-occupied area became an integral part of the Soviet Union. Many Polish or former Polish state employees initially remained in their posts, otherwise the posts were taken over by other Poles for purely careerist or opportunistic reasons, or were given to Poles regarded as being politically safe, or to representatives of other nationalities. Russian officials and other Soviet citzens were also brought in. Posts in Soviet-occupied territory were much sought after by Soviet citizens.

The average Pole who survived the German occupation would probably describe it in three words: terror, hunger and destitution. In the Soviet occupation the words would be: Communist indoctrination, terror and hunger. Two further adjectives should also be added: insecurity and humiliation. The treatment of Poles as *Untermenschen* in the sublime form of German chauvinism, struck at the most sensitive place of the Polish character, their national pride and dignity. At times it was more difficult to sustain this national humiliation than the brutality and cruelty. But terror was the common denominator of both occupations, ever present, ever visible, and virtually inescapable. To understand this terror one must first look at the attitude of the two respective occupiers towards the Poles.

Hitler's attitude to Poland and his aspirations for *Lebensraum* in the east are well known. His policy was a racist one *par excellance* and he had, albeit not always precise and constant, long-term objectives for the territories involved. Poland was to cease to exist, its population was to be gradually destroyed, and that which remained was to form a labour supply and reserve for the Third Reich. The lands were to be gradually colonised by German settlers. This policy was to be realised by systematic extermination policies, especially in relation to the Jews, by the removal and transfer of population and forced labour, by depriving the Poles of the necessary means of livelihood, and thus biologically weakening and destroying them, and by intellectually depriving them of all necessary schooling and education, bar a minimum required by their German employers.

However, life in the annexed territories and the *Generalgouvernement* varied. In the annexed territories not a single Polish school or library was left, and the use of the Polish language resulted in persecution. Here the principle that Poles were only a work force was fully implemented and they were shown in the most brutal manner that the Germans were their masters and the Poles mere slaves. Here the stereotype of *Übermenschen* and *Untermenschen* was cultivated and all the Polish leaders, patriotic acts and symbols, or acts of self-defence cruelly suppressed. In the *Generalgouvernement*, however, in spite of the appalling living conditions, especially for the intelligentsia and the working class in the towns, and in spite of the terror and preparations being made to absorb these territories into the Third Reich, Polish employers were allowed to exist, primary and vocational schools teaching in Polish functioned and, to quote a Polish specialist, 'They were allowed to be Poles', although this must be understood in a relative sense. [8]

Stalin's attitude to the Polish territories he had obtained is not so straightforward, although it would be a mistake to look for deep and complicated motivations. He had regained lands Russia felt she had lost at the Treaty of Riga in 1921 and he had agreed to Molotov signing a pact with Ribbentrop for specific reasons, which are not important here, but the primary aim was probably not the regaining of those territories. It is argued he was playing for time, but having gained the territories he incorporated them into the Soviet Union on a permanent basis and introduced similar changes to those which had been introduced in the USSR since the Revolution. His approach was surely part of his universal policy and not a specific one to Poland. His treatment of the populations there is comparable and often identical to that of other populations in the Soviet empire. It carried in its wake all the negative aspects, horrors and terror of the Bolshevik Revolution. One of his main tasks was to put Poland on an equal footing with the rest of his Union of Soviets, to level it down to their level and erase the glaring differences between the standards and styles of life. His Poland, 'the bastard of Versailles', and its independence, was to cease to exist, the independence of its citizens likewise, and their total dependence on the Soviet state to be initiated. This was not a racist policy, although there may have been traits of national complexes in it; it was a Marxist and class policy. It was to be the end of reactionary Poland.

The oubreak of the war immediately brought heavy civilian losses and suffering. Refugees and people escaping to the east were indiscriminately attacked and shot at from the air; hospitals were bombed. The German terror began straight away. *Einsatzgruppen* of the *Sicherheitspolitzei* (Sipo), which had been created before the outbreak of the war, were attached to each of the five German armies involved in the invasion of Poland. They were to operate in the rear, were commanded by an SS Brigade Commander and were the responsibility of Reinhard Heydrich, the head of the *Reichssicherheitshauptamt*, and their ranks contained SS men and police. Hitler's orders to shoot all Poles offering resistance were applied very liberally and even led to conflicts with the *Wehrmacht*, although the latter were not guiltless. It is estimated that more than 16,000 Poles were executed in the first ten days of the war.[9]

The Nazi terror took on specific forms. Imprisonment, often accompanied by brutal torture and death, and executions or transportations to concentration camps or to the Third Reich as forced labour, were the most common. This mainly affected the Polish intelligentsia and public and politically prominent individuals, who could be considered to be a possible centre for any opposition. The Germans thereby attempted to deprive the Poles of their elite. Hitler had ordered that the Polish 'gentry, clergy and Jews' be liquidated. It was amongst these sections that widespread arrests were carried out from the very outset, lists of undesirables often having been compiled before the outbreak of the war. These were far more extensive for the western territories where according to Heydrich at the end of September at the most only 3 per cent of the political leaders remained. Examples of this policy of terror can be found from the very first months of the occupation : on 6 November 1939 in a 'Sonderaktion' in Cracow, 183 Jagiellonian University professors and academics were arrested and sent to Sachsenhausen; on 9 November, the first mass arrests of the intelligentsia in Lublin and Czestochowa began.[10]

Mass arrests were carried out within the Polish underground movement and this affected not only the military underground but also the civilian and government underground bodies. Poles could also be arrested for a whole series of petty offences under the Nazi occupation, such as smuggling food, black marketing, failure to raise their hats to the Germans in the annexed territories, breaking curfews, entering *Nur fur Deutsche* areas, etc., apart from normally accepted petty and common law crimes.[11]

Another form of terror was the German policy of expulsions, resettlement and deportation. This mainly affected the annexed territories, although later, when the Nazis started to implement their resettlement policy – which, however, never really got off the ground – it was also carried out in the *Generalgouvernement*, particularly the *Wehrwolf* operation in the Zamosc area. About 1.5 million people were resettled into the *Generalgouvernement* from the annexed territories. Poles were transported to the Third Reich as forced labour. Throughout the entire war between 1.3 and 1.5 million workers were deported from the *Generalgouvernement* and 645,000 from the annexed territories to the Third Reich.[12]

It is worth saying a word or two more here about the forced resettlement of Poles from the annexed territories to the *Generalgouvernement*. The criteria applied in selecting Poles to be deported were somewhat fluid. Initially, the most important were their political past, their role in the community and ability to command respect, the size of their properties and local animosities between Poles and *Volksdeutsche*. Himmler had instructed that all Poles who had moved into these areas after 1918 were to be removed as a priority, but, as these were mainly small farmers or farm labourers, the instructions were impractical. The Germans wanted large estates and properties. All Jews were to be evacuated from the annexed territories. Numerically, the German plans were to prove to be unrealisable and the original numbers of transports planned were never to be realised.[13] These dispossessed Poles were often transported in the most foul and inhumane conditions, journeys lasting several days in below freezing temperatures. The following is a description of the arrival of such a train somewhere in the *Generalgouvernement*:

All six carriages were opened at the same time and out of them people wrapped in rags and blankets, white, covered in frost, started to fall. Some fell on their knees straight away and started to eat the snow. They were not allowed to leave. Many of the women were clutching dead children under scarves. With kicks and beatings they were made to pile the corpses up in one of the carriages. Next the men were told to clear out the remaining carriages. First of all suitcases and bundles were thrown out, and only then the stiff and twisted corpses, which had to be piled up. The women and children stood there stupified and resigned, looking at the bodies, where they could also see their nearest and dearest. When one of the women tore herself away from the group, a shot was heard. Another corpse was added. After emptying the carriages the men were given spades and told to clean the floor. This seemed to take an eternity. The frozen dirt stuck hard and the frozen and starving people had no strength. Shouting and beatings by SS men speeded up the work somewhat. When the carriages were regarded as being clean enough, they were ordered to put the bodies into one of them, whose doors were then closed ... When the train had been 'unloaded' and cleaned, a whistle was blown and in a moment the whole company had formed into ranks. The commanding officer accepted a report, made some sort of command and the unit marched off. A second later a locomotive drew up and the ghost train left. The groups of people left on the railway tracks didn't move. The sudden departure of the SS hadn't made the slightest impression on them. They couldn't understand they were free to leave ... it was dusk before the locals ventured to approach this phantom of people.[14]

Random round-ups were one of the forms of terror most practised by the Germans. Houses, blocks of flats, streets or specific areas were suddenly sealed off and the inhabitants or anyone there at the time rounded up. These people were usually deported for forced labour or to concentration camps, or taken as hostages or victims in the German policy of applying collective responsibility for attacks of whatever kind on Germans. For example in Wawer, a suburb of Warsaw, 107 innocent Poles were dragged from their beds and shot in retaliation for the murder of two German NCOs in a bar by local criminals.[15] Their only offence was that they happened to be in the area covered by the raid. This was probably the greatest fear for the Poles, the perpetual fear of going out and being caught in a street round up, lined up against the wall and shot just because you were there, just because you were Polish. 'After all, it made no difference whether your papers were in order or not, whether you were guilty or innocent. The German terror was incalculable and the fact of being a Pole a deadly sin in itself – so you left it at that.'[16]

Polish families also lost children, who were removed by the Germans to be Germanised. Between 160,000 and 200,000 Polish children were sent to the Third Reich from German-occupied Poland by the Nazis during the war.[17] In the annexed territories all Polish men born between 1910 and 1945 were registered as *Volksdeutsch* and forcibly drafted into the German army.

It would require a separate paper to deal with the question of terror in relation to the Polish Jews. who were herded into ghettos, overcrowded and cut off, where the death rate soared due to starvation and disease. German policy towards the Jews was straightforward, extermination. 2,600,000 Polish Jews perished under the German occupation out of a pre-war population of about 3,000,000.[18]

In Soviet-occupied Poland the terror also started on the first day. But this was of a slightly different nature in so far as the invading Red Army allowed the local populations to settle long-outstanding political, nationalistic and personal accounts; 'a period of lawlessness was decreed'. From the very outset in leaflets and propaganda the Poles were referred to as a nation of 'exploiters and landlords' and local populations were encouraged to take their vengeance on them. People took justice into their own hands and a bloodbath of indescribable cruelty and sadism followed. I quote just one example from the Polesie area:

> They took away my 68 year old father and a cousin, all the neighbours who didn't get away in time, and a few officers caught on the road. All were brought to the schoolhouse. A Soviet commissar came by and shot one lawyer who admitted he had prosecuted in some communist trials; the rest he left for the hoodlums to do with as they pleased.

Or in a parish in the Nowogrod voivodship its governor, some policemen and some settlers were brought in, sentenced to death and killed with axes. In Karczowka in the Wolyn area, 24 Polish settlers were tied up with barbed wire, and then shot or drowned by Ukranian peasants.[20] The examples are legion. It would appear that the Poles had no protection or redress from this violence as often its perpetrators were agents of the new authority being established in an area. Peasant groups on the rampage were often appointed to be the new authority in an area by a passing Soviet commander or commissar.

As life in the Soviet-occupied territories became more stable and organised following the invasion, a mass wave of organised and systematic arrests began. They became such a fact of life that they brought daily fear to virtually everyone, and some even felt relief when their eventual arrest materialised. To begin with, it was the elites, the social and political activists, the police, professors, priests, landowners, and industrialists, who were arrested but later the arrests embraced far wider sections of society. They were usually made on the basis of lists. There were also spontaneous random arrests, street round-ups (but less frequently than in German-occupied Poland) and individual arrests.[21] The Soviet authorities were far better informed about the residents of the territories they occupied than the Germans were. This is partly due to the fact that records fell into their hands and because by various devious means they drew up lists (e.g. for elections, or of people wishing to return to occupied Germany etc.). Furthermore, Poles could be arrested for far more trivial things than in the German-occupied territories e.g. for being late to work, having overdue taxes, selling off their own goods.[22] Many were arrested trying to cross the border. Prisons were inhumanely overcrowded and new and totally unsuitable premises were sought.[23]

Arrest and deportation were often synonymous in the Soviet-occupied territories. No one was safe from them as the net drew in both 'reactionaries' and people known for their leftist views. These were the worst fears, the fear that the whole family would be uprooted, removed and deported deep into the Soviet Union, in the most awful conditions, never to return. There were four waves of deportations: the first in February 1940, the second and third in April and June of that year, and the fourth in June 1941 just before the outbreak of the Russo-Soviet War. The deportations embraced everyone, although each one had a specific character. The first deportations removed Polish 'military settlers' and forestry employees, police and officials – about 220,000 people were deported in this wave. The second deportation embraced the families of previous deportees or arrested persons, POWs or internees, farmers, teachers, workers, landowners, merchants, Jews, Ukranians and Belorussians: about 320,000 people were deported. In the third deportation mainly Jews were affected. In total during these three deportations c.780,000 people were deported. The final deportation in 1941 removed 200-300,000 people, mainly from the areas incorporated into Lithuania, including many children and orphans. Thus in all about 1,100,000 people were deported, i.e. about 7-8 per cent of the population (of which 50 per cent were peasants, 24 per cent workers and 17 per cent intelligentsia).[24] To these figures should be added about 210,000 men forcibly conscripted into the Red Army.[25]

This is a comparable record to the German one and the deportees were transported in equally awful conditions, the journeys often lasting far longer. The worst was probably the February deportation which took place in below freezing temperatures. Deportees were given between 15 minutes and two hours to pack their possessions and leave. Such was the deportation mentality, however, that some already had bags ready.[26] Another policy which was common to both occupiers was that of forcing Poles to vacate their homes and even villages, in favour of Germans or others. In the territories annexed to the Third Reich this policy usually resulted in deportation to the *Generalgouvernement* or the Third Reich as forced labour. In German-occupied territories Poles were also forced to vacate their homes in areas where ghettoes were organised.

These were the direct methods of terror and extermination, but the specific policies of both occupiers went far further directly or indirectly in destroying, enfeebling or humiliating the nation they had chosen to subdue. This was particularly evident in specific aspects of life such as education, culture, religious life, health, accommodation and feeding.

In all the areas of Poland annexed to the Third Reich Polish schools were closed. Polish children were mainly taught only their three 'R's , in German, so as to be able to communicate with and work for German employers later on. The school day and length of compulsory education was shortened. Poles were not allowed to attend vocational schools. In the *Generalgouvernement*, however, compulsory schooling lasting seven years was maintained, although classes tended to be much larger, and the staff more elderly. In the middle of 1944 there were on average 90 children per teacher. The teaching of Polish history, geography and literature was forbidden. Instruction was in Polish. Vocational schools were permitted. The result of this was the formation of a secret underground educational organisation, TON, some illegal classes even being held in legal schools. Secret schooling and also secret university lectures and seminars (as all Polish universities in the German-occupied areas were closed) became a specific part of the Polish civilian resistance movement. This was the result of the exceptional restrictions on schooling introduced in occupied Poland, comparable only with the occupied part of the Soviet Union, as well as the belief of the Polish teaching profession in a better future, for which young people would be needed.[27]

Secret schools were also created in the Soviet-occupied territories; we know of ones in Lwow and Wilno, although no studies have been made of them. In the Soviet-occupied territories schools were reformed to fall in line with the Soviet system of education and this was done very swiftly. Schools were secularised and depolonised. The teaching of religion, history, Latin (if taught), and, in some, Polish was banned. Marxism and atheism were added to the curriculum. One of the biggest struggles in schools was over the crucifixes, which were forcibly taken down as were portraits of Polish statesmen. Parents were usually given the choice of the language of instruction of their children's schools, but frequently in practice there was no choice. Teachers were speedily and badly trained in these new languages. An attempt was also made to make children attend school on Sundays, but this failed due to the opposition it encountered. The Polish universities of Lwow and Wilno were not closed down, but departments of Marxism and Leninism opened and the old faculties of law, philosophy and history disbanded. New staff were brought in. Ironically, the Soviet occupation resulted in more schools, more opportunities for higher and vocational training, and more instruction in the native language of the minorities.[28]

As Poland is an overwhelmingly Catholic nation and the Polish Church played a very important role in Polish life, the attitude of the occupiers to that institution and to religion was important not only as an instrument of their policies but also because of the reaction it generated. German policy to the church was obviously an integral part of its policy to destroy the Polish nation. In the territories annexed to the Third Reich the Polish Church was to be destroyed. Polish Roman Catholic churches were closed down, some blown up or destroyed, plundered of their treasures, transformed into stores, garages, stables and the like, or handed over to the Evangelical Church. Polish priests were removed, imprisoned or sent to concentration camps, replaced by German ones or put on the *Volksdeutsche* list. The use of the Polish language was forbidden in churches. In some cemeteries Polish headstones were removed or inscriptions replaced by ones in German. Roadside crosses, altars and chapels were removed; round-ups were organised of peasants leaving churches on Sundays. In the Warta area, where these policies were probably applied most severely, of 2,500 pre-war Polish priests, 752 died, and approximately another 800 ended up in prisons or concentration camps; in the Poznan diocese of the 800 pre-war Polish priests there were only 34 left in 1943 and 30 of the 841 Polish churches.[29]

In the *Generalgouvernement* the policy was more moderate and there was no real fight as such with the Church and religion, as it was felt that it would be possible to persuade the clergy to preach according to the desires of the Third Reich, and any resistance to this would be quickly dealt with. The taking over of churches was a sporadic practice. But the losses amongst the Polish clergy and monastic orders were high. Hundreds died and far more were arrested. Poland was the only country where bishops were arrested, some later to die in concentration camps. There were no real financial burdens placed on the Church by the German occupier.[30]

In the Soviet-occupied territories, however, the Church was obviously the victim of Communist secularisation of life. Heavy taxes were imposed on it. Stalin was now to be the Poles' God. Polish children had chains with religious emblems removed and replaced by ones with Stalin's picture. One small boy from Baranowicze recalls how two holes were drilled in the ceiling of his class room and:

> To one hole the (teacher) said, God, O Lord, give us some dumplings, and nothing happened. To the other he said, Soviet, Soviet give us some sweets, and the sweets came pouring down.[31]

All evidence points to an increase in church attendance under both occupations. The pattern was to be the same with cultural life under the occupation. In the Soviet occupied territories Communist policies were applied, which excluded all patriotic, nationalist and bourgeois elements from the cultural life of those territories. People were forced to attend propaganda meetings both in their places of work and homes. These were frequent and absorbed a great deal of time in the difficult and daily lives of the people.[32] This was a totally new factor for them. Polish writers and artists were allowed to work as long as their work conformed to the Marxist guidelines; many did conform, especially those who could find an ideological (albeit at times, opportunist) justification for it. This did not always spare them later from imprisonment or deportation.[33]

In German-occupied Poland there were no possibilities of participating in any cultural life except as blatant collaborationists. The only exceptions were probably one or two actors, who performed in variety theatre, which was permitted for Poles. Cinemas were open to Poles but the films shown were of an undesirable quality. A slogan was developed by the Polish underground; 'Tylko swienia siedza w kinie' – only pigs go to the flicks ! But people did go to the cinema because they had nothing else to do. All Polish libraries were closed down as were sports facilities. An underground theatre network slowly developed, where actors and artists would perform or give recitals to very small groups of people in private flats. Concerts were held in coffee shops. Books were published by the underground; new novels and beautiful poetry were written and clandestinely published. Books were circulated secretly. Bridge became extremely popular, if only to pass away the curfew hours.[34]

Here was a nation terrorised, nationally, intellectually and culturally humiliated by its occupiers, and, at the same time, physically enfeebled by the living conditions it was forced to live in. The information available for the German-occupied territories is very detailed and well sourced, whereas for the Soviet-occupied areas it is fragmentary so no real picture can be drawn up for those areas.

The war and new administrative divisions resulting therefrom totally broke up the economic organisation of Poland. Polish towns and cities were cut off from their normal supplies of food. In addition to this, Poland was to be a source of food for the Third Reich and the German army. No food was permitted to be imported from the Third Reich into the *Generalgouvernement*. The result of this was well summed up by a Polish undergound emissary on his return to London:

> The standard of living became primitive in the extreme. The diet of those who fared
> the worst consisted exclusively of black bread mixed with sawdust. A plate of cereal a
> day was considered a luxury. During all of 1942 I never tasted butter or sugar ... we
> were all hungry nearly all of the time...[35]

Rationing was introduced, though not for everyone, and the calorific value of the rations was very different for Germans, Poles or Jews. In 1941, the German daily ration was about 2,600 calories, whereas that for the Poles and Jews was 669 and 184 respectively. The Poles and Jews had obviously, therefore, to make up the difference by buying on the free market where prices were very high. It was this black market that bridged the gap between survival and starvation. The people who smuggled in goods did so at very great expense because of the high cost of train fares and the bribes often involved, and the risk of confiscation, being sent to a concentration camp or even death. The Germans were always on the look out for smugglers. They would set up road blocks and search trains, they would raid markets. But the traders soon came back, although a successful raid by the Germans could result in a quick rise in prices, often by as much as 30 to 50 per cent.[36]

For many people survival was found in their contacts with the villages and countryside; help came from families there, who might have farms or land on which extra food could be grown. For others, especially workers, who worked in factories for the *Wehrmacht* or occupation authorities, there was a meal, usually only a bowl of soup, in the factory canteen.[37] The Poles also dug for victory as Jozef Retinger, a Polish emissary, wrote after his visit to Warsaw in 1944:

> ... the aspect of the city amazed me; it had changed so much. The inner courtyards of
> all the bigger houses and buildings have been turned into vegetable gardens. The grass
> strips down the centre of the broad avenues have been dug up and made into allotments
> ... vegetables were everywhere.[38]

The situation was alleviated also by self-help organisations which set up soup kitchens, and also provided clothing, financial help, care for children, orphans, refugees, families of POWs and prisoners. This work was carried out and organised by the Poles, but with the agreement of the Germans.[39]

A brief look at prices will explain why feeding was such a problem. In 1938 the average cost of feeding a worker's family of four was 61.27 *zloty* per month, by June 1941 it was 1,568 zl. A worker in an average non-heavy industry enterprise in June 1941 earned between 120 and 300 zl. a month, white collar workers between 100 and 250 *zloty*. By the turn of 1943/44 the wages of a Polish worker represented about 8 per cent of the real value of pre-war wages.[40] Where then did people get the extra money from to buy food ? Those who could sold or bartered possessions; people rented out rooms or found extra employment; many were involved in the Polish underground and were paid for that; others black marketed; some moonlighted; other stole from work and sold what they could. Many women had to start working; some were even forced into prostitution. In some enterprises workers were even sold goods at normal prices or given bonuses in kind, e.g. cigarettes and vodka which they were later able to sell on the black market.[41] A result of this was something called *Bumelanctwo*, which literally means shirking from work, but during the occupation it was a manifestation of Polish workers' total disrespect for the work they had to do and the fact that they could earn considerably more by other means in the same time. The occupier tried to fight these practices by removing ration cards, even police intervention, and in one factory in Stalowa Wola an *Erziehungslager* was started with re-education courses lasting eight to fourteen days. But these policies were obviously unsuccessful as, by the end of 1941, the shirking rate fluctuated between 6 per cent and 20 per cent of the workforce. In Warsaw, in 1943, 30 per cent of the work force were not turning up for work and it was quite normal for a worker to work only four days a week.[42] Polish workers also went on strike.[43] This would never have been possible in the Soviet-occupied territories, where even arriving late for work resulted in imprisonment.[44]

The effects of this on the general health of the Polish population probably do not need to be explained. There was an increase in the number of cases of typhoid, tuberculosis, scarlet fever, diphtheria, rickets etc. Hospital space was limited for the Poles, but they were treated by their own doctors. There was a terrible shortage of vaccines, medicines and dressings etc.[45]

The Poles did, however, have information about what was happening in the rest of Europe and the outside world at the time. The news and propaganda fed to them was supplemented by what they could gain themselves from reading the underground press and from listening to the radio, particularly the BBC, illegally. In German-occupied Poland it was illegal to possess a radio, whereas in the Soviet-occupied territories it was only illegal to listen to foreign broadcasts. The author has come across recollections there of people listening to both French and British stations. The Polish underground press, which was very voluminous in the *Generalgouvernement*, used to publish monitored broadcasts. It is impossible to say how wide the circulation was of these papers, although in the urban communities they were quite widely read and many different ones were published. People obviously also read the German papers.[46] I have not been able to find such references to underground papers in the Soviet-occupied territories although some were published, and even brought in from German-occupied areas. They also existed in the annexed territories, but to a far lesser degree. Resistance and underground work were far more difficult there. Correspondence from abroad also contained information.[47]

The Poles did not succumb to the occupation and the policy of the German invader. Their resistance was both active and passive, both physical and psychological. They believed that a better future had to be envisaged, that humanism must overcome the awful inhumanity which they daily witnessed, and that national dignity had to be sustained. At the same time, they lived in the fear that they were next in line for the same fate as the Jews. The organisation of the Polish military underground and the underground part of the Polish Government in London are not the subject of this paper, but their presence and the overwhelming support they commanded amongst the Polish population must be emphasised and remembered.

A separate and organised civil resistance was also formed, and there were also many cases of spontaneous individual defiance and unorganised actions under both occupations. It must, however, be stressed here that, due to the greater difficulties of organisation in the Soviet-occupied territories and the fact that the occupation there lasted less than two years, no real civil resistance was established, although we have evidence of numerous individual acts.

In April 1940 a *Kierownictwo Walki Cywilnej* (the KWC), the Directorate for Civilian Resistance, was established by the Polish Government in the *Generalgouvernement*. Later in 1943 it amalgamated with its military counterpart and was renamed the Directorate of Underground Resistance. The KWC was responsible for watching over the morale of the community and for maintaining an inflexible attitude towards the Nazi occupier. It set up a code of behaviour for the Poles based on three principles: a universal boycott of all German orders and measures which were socially harmful or damaging to the national substance; engaging in any sabotage causing material and moral losses to the Germans; obedience to the Polish underground authorities. Instructions were issued either by the underground press or on the SWIT (the Polish government's underground radio station in London), broadcasting from London to Poland on a whole array of issues including: a ban on registering as *Volksdeutsch*; the boycott of forced labour in the Reich; the ban on maintaining any kind of relations with the Germans, buying German lottery tickets, going to the cinema, casinos, theatres or concerts performed by Germans; the sabotage of delivery quotas imposed by the German occupier on Polish farmers and peasants; sabotage at work. In addition doctors were instructed to issue false medical certificates to help people avoid being taken as forced labour, priests were instructed to falsify baptism certificates for Jews, and judges were forbidden to transfer cases from Polish to German courts. They would also warn the Polish population of impending events, e.g. round-ups. They called on the Poles to help their fellow Jews and Hungarian, Italian, Romanian or Slovak deserters.[48]

Underground courts were set up by the KWC dealing with transgressions of a civil nature. Sentences were published in the underground press, on SWIT, or even posted up on posters. They could pass the death sentence. Smaller court commissions dealing with lesser cases were also established. They issued sentences of infamy or censure, or just a reprimand, and even head-shaving or flogging.[49]

At the end of 1940, the KWC also set up a small sabotage organisation, the *Wawer* organisation, which was a scouting organisation personifying the aims of the KWC and making its activities openly visible. These were the young men and women, often boys and girls, who tore down German posters, put up Polish ones, painted nationalistic symbols or slogans on walls, set up various what to-day would be called 'happenings' etc. For example on 27 June 1943 a group of *Wawer* members clambered up the ruined tower which still stood following the destruction of the Royal Castle in Warsaw in 1939, and hung up the Polish flag, which was to remain there for several hours, to the great satisfaction of the Varsovians. Similar actions were also performed in other parts of the *Generalgovernement*, many quite spontaneously.[50]

Likewise, in the Soviet-occupied territories there were also many examples of civilian defiance and resistance. They have in no way been catalogued and it is not possible yet to quantify them nor put some kind of structure on them. Most of them were uncoordinated and spontaneous actions, perhaps more so than in the *Generalgouvernement*, many were scout-inspired. The author has found one mention of scouts being sent from Warsaw to Lwow to set up a sabotage organisation there. The Soviets, when they entered the town of Lomza were met by demonstating Poles dressed in black. The reception for the Red Army varied from great enthusiasm to hostility and indifference. In Suwalki an 18-year-old girl stepped forward to greet the entering Red Army commander with a bunch of flowers, in which she had hidden a gun, with which she shot him. It is interesting to note that there was an identical scene in Silesia, hundreds of miles to the west, when the Germans entered there. On 11 November 1939, Poland's Independence Day, there were patriotic demonstrations in Bialystok and Lomza. A few days earlier, on 7 November, Poles in Nowogrod had turned up in mourning for compulsory October Revolution celebrations. Polish youth pulled down Soviet propaganda and slogans, and wrote up their own. Poles attending compulsory meetings would often in defiance stamp their feet, shuffle their chairs, cough and whistle. In Grodno, at a public meeting, Poles sang their national anthem. At one such meeting in Lwow in 1939 one of the participants remembers the audience defiantly singing the Polish patriotic song, 'We want God', in competition with the voices of the organisers on the stage singing the 'International' with clenched fists.[51] The battle to remove crucifixes in schools only resulted in Polish school children making their own and putting them up. Soviet attempts to close down Polish churches were sometimes thwarted due to the resistance of local populations. The Huculi, a mountain and rural population in the border areas with Romania, put up an unbelievable fight against the Soviet policy of depopulating the border areas.[52] In Wilno, in 1941, one of the priests preached a very strong sermon, condemning the Polish youth who had taken part in the May Day celebrations there, accusing them of succumbing to the occupier, when those were issues over which blood should be spilt.[53]

Here one more example of civilian defiance in Soviet-occupied Poland must be cited. In Augustow a monument to Stalin had been erected and so designed that he had one of his hands stretched out. On to this hand, one night, a chamber pot was cemented, and then a few days later a bucket of excreta. The Soviets, therefore, had to put a guard on the monument. After a time it was removed, and then one night Stalin's head was unscrewed and placed between his legs![54]

The Soviets had hardly entered the Polish territories when they started to organise elections to the assemblies in part of them, in the Western Ukraine and Western Belorussia.[55] The elections were announced by the Military Councils on 4 October for 22 October and were held according to the well-known principles of Soviet democracy. The whole area was gripped by an election fever, in which the local electorate felt totally lost and terrorised. Electoral lists were drawn up, later to be very useful for the deportations, and electoral meetings were organised in factories, offices, schools and places of residence. Landlords marched their tennants to meetings in compact groups, hamlets were marched to meetings singing, in factories gates were locked and people could not go home but had to attend meetings. People not attending meetings were regarded as enemies of the state and often arrested.

People were forced to vote. They were tempted to the polling stations by stalls with free white bread and sweets. They were dragged out of their homes by the militia to vote, often with the help of rifle butts. Bands played music at polling stations. For those who were sick, old or forgetful, and had not turned up by the evening, the ballot box was brought, for their convenience, to their homes or to hospitals. In one town the ballot box was taken to Jews praying in the synagogue. Landlords had to take their tenants; villages voted en bloc and people at work came together. People tried to spoil their ballot papers, crossed or marked them with obscenities or patriotic slogans, rubbing the Polish eagle from a coin on bits of paper which were dropped into the ballot box. Many escaped to the forests so as not to vote. In some mountain villages, where there were no pens and the peasants were illiterate, they brought cow or horse manure, and put that in with their ballot. These were actions carried out by Poles representing both the intelligentsia and peasants. In a few areas there had to be a second round of voting. But true to the falsity of the elections the turn out was reported to have been between 93 and 97 per cent and about 91 per cent voted for the official candidates. In the Postawy constituency 103 per cent of the electorate voted yes! The outcome of these elections was that the Western Ukraine and Belorussia were included into the Soviet Union. There is no doubt that Poles felt shame and distress.

Finally a word must be said about the Polish peasant population, which represented about 60 per cent of the Polish population. The question of compulsory delivery quotas, however, is the key to understanding the peasant during the war; and they were being collected alongside the requisitions, round-ups and terror in the countryside, which were often far worse than in the towns. For example, in the towns if someone did not turn up for forced labour, the whole family was not made responsible as was the case in the countryside. Failure to hand over a quota could mean death or the destruction of a peasant's property. The size of the quotas increased as the war went on, becoming an increasing and often impossible burden for the peasants. Although landowners and peasants with larger farms undoubtedly gained from the occupation, if only because they could trade and speculate, the plight of the poorer peasants was very different. They might even have to buy supplies to be able to hand over quotas or feed their families; they had no money to pay bribes. However, generally speaking if these rural people were able to trade illegally, they were better off than before the war, especially in areas near large towns. In the *Generalgouvernement* the first two years of the war resulted in a more favourable economic situation in the countryside than before the war.[56]

In the annexed territories Poles were no longer allowed to own land and were therefore, reduced to the role of labourers for their German masters. In the Soviet-occupied territories the situation was worse and there seems to have been no gain for anyone. There was a deterioration and fall in production. The peasant lacked confidence in the new authorities and had little motivation to produce for the market. Many peasants had lost large stocks, including grain for sowing, as a result of Red Army requisitions in 1939. Compulsory quotas were also a disincentive. Unrealistic official prices in comparison to market prices meant that any money a peasant might earn had virtually no purchasing power. Peasants were as much a victim of the deportations as any group, and in fact made up 50 per cent of those deported. Land was redistributed; the landowners, colonists and better-off peasants were forced off their property. Many peasants, sometimes entire villages, refused to take part in the land distribution. The final nail in the coffin for peasant attitudes was, however, the forced collectivisations which were started in 1940.[57]

What conclusions can thus be drawn, what impressions gained? Overwhelmingly and immediately, one of terrible human loss and destruction. Out of a population of 35,000,000, 6,028,000 had perished (only 664,000 as a result of military operations), 2,600,000 of whom were Polish Jews. Over one million had been deported into the Soviet Union, of whom probably 400,000 had died, including POWs and military internees, but not the Katyn victims. The intelligentsia had been devastated. Poland had lost 30 per cent of her academics, 57 per cent of her lawyers, 21.5 per cent of her judges and prosecutors, 39 per cent of her doctors, 15 per cent of her teachers, 50 per cent of her qualified engineers and 18 per cent of the clergy. Five million Poles were scattered around the world. About one third of the Poles in the Polish lands included in the Soviet Union were never to return to Poland.[58] Thousands more were in refugee and displaced persons' camps. Many Poles were still to die or to be permanently physically or mentally handicapped as a result of their experiences. Families had been irretrievably broken up. Up until today there are still thousands of untraced Poles and the searches still go on. Poland's capital Warsaw had been totally destroyed.

Generally amongst the Poles there was a determination to defy the occupier and to survive the war and a belief in a better future. There was support for civil resistance and many in their own ways – not only by participation in underground work, but by such actions as secret schooling, concerts in cafes, public demonstrations – manifested this. Of course there were some also who did not abide by the rules of accepted civic behaviour; Polish society was not totally uniform, but these were not frequent examples and were usually done for material gain. In the Soviet-occupied territories this was more complicated because of ideological and nationalistic factors. Here the Soviets were not always seen as the enemy in the same way as the Germans were. However, people to a certain extent came to terms with life and had to adapt, as this example of a Polish diarist shows:

25 November 1943. Round-ups again on the electric train line, four people were apparently shot when they jumped off the tram at the sight of the Germans ... If generally fear, depression and concern is the overriding mood – on the other hands the Varsovians have virtually adapted themselves to this: no longer do trams empty at the news of a round-up. People who have to go out and move on the streets, are resigned to doing so, not paying much attention to the dangers, which they have started to get used to.[59]

The Nazi methods produced negative results as far as the Germans were concerned. Where they had hoped to divide they had united. The more vicious the terror became and the more intolerable the conditions, the more the Polish community became strengthened, unified, solidified, and the stronger the desire for revenge. German propaganda attempts at possible Polish-German cooperation in fighting the Communists found no resonance, and to quote one source: 'Class and party differences have disappeared. Everyone feels themselves to be above all Poles.'[60] In a memorandum to Hitler in 1943 Hans Frank wrote:

> The paralysing of schooling and the considerable restriction on cultural activity results with increasing momentum in the strengthening of Polish national unity under the leadership of the Polish intelligentsia conspiring against the Germans. What had not been possible during the course of Polish history and during the first years of Polish rule, namely the creation of national unity having a common aim and internally linked in life and death, is at present as a result of German action slowly and surely becoming a reality.[61]

The intelligentsia during the occupation was to come into closer contact with other social groups, with whom they shared poverty and humiliation, and this was to have an important influence on their political and social outlook. Social origins and education were no guarantee of a greater chance of survival or better income.

To what extent this was true in the eastern territories is much more difficult to say; the occupation was shorter there. Different social and nationality structures complicate an assessment. Sources are very inadequate. General Bor-Komorowski, however, has written that Soviet methods managed to weaken and divide the nation, where German ones had solidified and strengthened it.[62] The intelligentsia were probably more wavering in their attitudes in Soviet-occupied Poland. One factor which, however, is often mentioned is that Soviet policies actually brought the various minorities closer together with the Poles and they adopted a more sympathetic attitude to the Poles. One example is in a report sent by the Polish underground from the Wilno area to London, dated 28 August 1940:

> The Belorussian people desire Polish governments as they never did when we ruled those territories. No activities of theirs can be counted on, however, due to the deportation of the most active elements... Fear of deportation to Kazakhstan and the far

north is having an extremely depressing effect, particularly on the intelligentsia, where morale is the worse. Hence a large section of the intelligentsia would like to move into German-occupied territories.[63]

But these were probably only transitory changes as later events do not always confirm them.

From other information it would also seem that the German occupation was regarded, especially by the intelligentsia, as a lesser evil. There were even Jews who tried to leave the awful conditions in the Soviet-occupied territories and return to the German side. Perhaps here it should be mentioned that the German attack on the Soviet Union was in a way received with relief, relief from the prospect of deportation and a manifestation of the belief that Soviet-German conflict could only hasten the end of the war and a return to peace. This is also a reason given for the support shown by certain sections of the Polish intelligentsia for the communist occupier. They saw the inevitability of a German-Soviet conflict and its long-term implications.

The war and occupations shattered the accepted values of Polish life. Pre-war values of honesty, decency and openness had to be put into cold storage, although many were slow to realise this. Respect for work disappeared; behaviour such as stealing, pilfering, lying, black marketing, previously unacceptable, was approved and commended. Women had to play a far more predominant role in society than before the war and children often had to take on a more important role in family life. They were involved in street trading (usually cigarettes); they hawked papers, and matured earlier, often having to carry secrets and turn a blind eye to many activities. Polish society became atomised.

Poland by the end of the war was decimated, exhausted and enfeebled, and this coupled with the political and international problems helped to facilitate a new occupation of the entire country by the Red Army and NKWD, aided and abetted by their Polish Communist fellow travellers.

NOTES

1. T. Bor-Komorowski, *Armia Podziemna* (English version *The Secret Army*) (London, 1950), pp. 33-4.
2. The best works in English on the subject are: J.T. Gross, *Polish Society under German Occupation – The Generalgouvernement, 1939-1944* (Princeton, 1979) and id., *Revolution from Abroad – The Soviet Conquest of Poland's Western Ukraine and Western Belorussia* (Princeton, 1988);

S. Korbonski, *The Polish Underground State — A Guide to the Underground 1939-1945* (Columbia, 1978).

3. Gross, *Revolution* (above, note 2), p. 12.
4. E. Duraczynski, *Wojna i okupacja wrzesien 1939 - kwiecien 1943* (War and occupation September 1939 – April 1943) (Warsaw, 1974), pp. 39, 50.
5. C. Madajczyk, *Polityka III Rzeszy w okupowanej Polsce* (Third Reich policy in occupied Poland) (Warsaw, 1970), vol. I, pp. 118ff.
6. Gross, *Revolution* (above, note 2), p. 13
7. Ibid., p. 3.
8. Madajczyk (above, note 5), vol. I, p. 137.
9. Ibid., p. 38.
10. Ibid., pp. 102ff.
11. J. Hanson, *The Civilian Population and the Warsaw Uprising of 1944* (Cambridge, 1982), p. 14.
12. Gross, *Polish Society* (above, note 2), pp. 72 and 78; Madajczyk (above, note 5), vol. I, p. 252.
13. Ibid., pp. 309-24.
14. Ibid., p. 309.
15. W. Bartoszewski, *The Warsaw Death Ring 1939-1945* (Warsaw, 1968), p. 29.
16. A. Pomian, *Jozef Retinger: memoirs of an eminence grise* (London, 1972), p.159.
17. Madajczyk, (above, note 5), vol. I, p. 260.
18. The fate of the Polish Jews has been the subject of many publications in English. The following are some of the main ones: A. Adelson and R. Lapides, *Lodz Ghetto; Inside a Community under Siege*, (New York, 1989); R. Hilberg, S. Staron and J. Kermish (ed.) *The Warsaw Diary of Adam Czerniakow: Prelude to Doom* (New York, 1979); A. Polonsky (ed.), A. Lewin, *A Cup of Tears: A Diary of the Warsaw Ghetto* (London, 1988); L. Dobroszycki (ed.), *The Chronicle of the Lodz Ghetto 1941-1944* (London, 1984); M. Gilbert, *The Holocaust: The Jewish Tragedy* (London, 1986); Y. Gutman, *The Jews of Warsaw, 1939-1943. Ghetto, Underground, Revolt* (London, 1982); J. Kermish (ed.), *To Live with Honour and Die with Honour: Selected Documents from the Warsaw Ghetto Underground Archives* (Jerusalem, 1986).
19. Gross, *Revolution* (above, note 2), p. 37.
20. Ibid.
21. Ibid., p. 147.
22. Ibid., p. 148.
23. Ibid., p. 151.

24. Ibid., p. 194; *Deportacje i przemieszczenia ludnosci polskiej w glab ZSRR 1939-1945* (The deportations and resettlement of the Polish population in the USSR) (Warsaw, 1989), p. 154.
25. *Deportacje* (above, note 24), p. 154.
26. J.Malanowski, 'Sociological Aspects of the Annexation of Poland's Eastern Borderland to the USSR in 1939-1941' (unpublished paper), p. 10.
27. Madajczyk (above, note 2), vol. II, pp. 142ff.
28. General Sikorski Historical Institute (hereafter cited as GSI), A.9.III.2a/30ai; Madajczyk (above, note 5), vol. I, p. 157; Gross, *Revolution* (above, note 2), p. 141.
29. Madajczyk (above, note 5), vol. I, p. 178ff.
30. Ibid., pp. 19ff.
31. Gross, *Revolution* (above, note 2), p. 131.
32. GSI. Kol.138/253.
33. Bor-Komorowski (above, note 1), p. 49
34. Korbonski (above, note 2), p. 71; T. Szarota, *Okupowanej Warszawy dzien powszedni* (Daily Life in Occupied Warsaw) (Warsaw, 1978), pp. 347-52 and 365-6.
35. J.Karski, *Story of a Secret State* (London, 1945), pp. 205-6.
36. Madajczyk (above, note 5), vol. I, pp. 596-9 and vol. II, pp. 45ff and p. 71.
37. Ibid., vol. II, p. 74.
38. Pomian (above, note 16), p. 162.
39. See B.Kroll, *Rada Glowna Opiekuncza 1939-1945* (The Main Welfare Council 1939-1945) (Warsaw, 1985) for detailed information on this subject.
40. Madajczyk (above, note 5), vol. I, pp. 69-71
41. Ibid.; Szarota (above, note 34), p. 251.
42. Madajczyk (above, note 5), vol. I, p. 68.
43. Hanson (above, note 11), p. 22.
44. IGS. A.9.III.2a/30 ai.
45. Hanson (above, note 11), pp. 30-2.
46. Korbonski (above, note 30), pp. 117ff.
47. Hanson (above, note 11), p. 38.
48. Korbonski (above, note 2), pp. 71ff.
49. Ibid., p. 74.
50. W.Bartoszewski, *859 dni Warszawy* (859 Warsaw Days) (Cracow, 1974), pp. 167 and 409; K.Gorzkowski, *Kronika Andrzeja, Zapiski z podziemia 1939-1941* (The chronicles of Andrzej, notes from the underground 1939-1941) (Warsaw, 1989), pp. 11-13.

The Civilian in War

51. Gross, *Revolution* (above, note 2), p.140; IGS.A.9.III.2a/30ai, 2a/30i, Kol.138/253, Kol.138/167B;
52. Gross, *Revolution* (above, note 2).
53. Ibid.
54. Ibid.
55. Ibid., pp. 71-113 for all information on the elections.
56. Madajczyk (above, note 2), vol. I, pp. 93ff; cf. Gross, *Polish Society* (above, note 2), pp. 103-5.
57. IGS. A.9.III.2a/30ai; K.Sword, 'Soviet Economic Policy in the Occupied Polish Territories 1939-1941' (unpublished paper).
58. K.Kersten, *Narodziny systemu wladzy, Polska 1943-1948* (The birth of a system of government, Poland 1943-1948) (Paris, 1986), pp. 131-3; id., 'Ludzie na drogach: O przesiedleniach ludnosci w Polsce 1939-1948' (People on the move: the resettling of the Polish population 1939-1948), *Res Publica*, 4 (1987), pp. 54-7.
59. Bartoszewski (above, note 50), p. 476.
60. GSI. A.9.III.2a/31.
61. *Dziennik Hansa Franka* (The diary of Hans Frank) (Warsaw,1970), p. 353.
62. Bor-Komorowski (above, note 1), p. 49.
63. *Armia Krajowa w dokumentach 1939-1945* (The Home Army in documents) (London, 1970), vol. I, p. 283.

10

FRANCE

J.C. Simmonds and H. Footitt

Introduction

A strictly defined 'home front' in France existed for only a very short period between 3 September 1939 and the armistice on 22 June 1940. The creation of a home front during this short period of war with Germany (and later Italy) was a feeble thing at best. The contrast between Daladier's enthusiastic pursuit of French Communists (after the Germano-Soviet pact) and his dilatory attitude towards the enemy has been frequently noted, but at the same time little was done to create a home front.[1] So patently lacking in urgency was this policy that the peasant fascist leader – Dorgères – nicknamed it the 'drôle de guerre' or 'funny old war'. Reynaud, Prime Minister from March 1940, was clearly more active in prosecuting the war, but the emergency decree powers of the government, granted in September 1939 and needed to carry through a firm policy, were constantly being challenged in the Assembly and there was continuing difficulty in constructing a home front. The problem, says Henri Michel, was that there was 'no civil unity or gathering of national morale, because there was no agreement on who was the enemy: Nazism or the eternal enemy, Germany'.[2] Shamir has pointed out that this unwillingness to contemplate war was given support by some political parties, the press, the unions, the churches, associations and other central groupings in French society.[3] Many felt that the longer war could be avoided, the more hope there was that it would never happen. This feeling, backed by official confidence in the efficacy of the Maginot Line, made people even less willing to countenance war and thus prepare for it at home. France then, during the war with Germany and Italy, had only a makeshift concept of a home front and the fighting of May-June 1940 was of such short duration that a home front, as contrasted to a fighting front, never had time to develop. The defeat, the exodus, German occupation of the north, the new regime in the south, the disruptions of annexation, demarcation lines and the collapse of infra-structures, meant that there was hardly even the social coherence and community base upon which to build a home front after June 1940.

But the Resistance – although slow to develop in the south – did begin to establish the idea of an internal fighting front against the occupier and Vichy by the end of 1940. Along with this came the concept of a 'home front' for the Resistance, often intermixed with the fighting front and confused with it, but existing nevertheless. Some organisations like the *Musée de L'Homme* group took up the task of defending French culture against the invasion of German ideas, others like Texier hoped to stimulate a climate of non-cooperation and the Père Chaillet, in founding *Témoignage Chrétien,* sought to build a popular moral resistance on the basis of liberal Catholic theology.[4] Such initiatives were prototypes of home front organisations and mentality, created to oppose the enemy by groups who saw it as their primary task. Other movements and groups built home front organisations to support their direct actions, but it must be remembered that, even at its height, the Resistance was only a small section of the French population and that the majority either supported Vichy, waited hopefully, retreated into their family, or collaborated. Thus the Resistance was a small society in revolt against the societal norms of its time, but existing within the normal structures of France. Claude Bourdet in his memoirs, *L'Aventure Incertaine,* declared that 'La Résistance a fait de nous tous des contest-ataires dans tous les sens du terme, vis-à-vis des hommes, comme vis-à-vis du système social' ['The Resistance made combatants of us all in every sense of the word, against individuals as well as against the social order']; a sentiment which is repeated time and again in the memoirs and literature of the Resistance.[5] Individuals, cells, small armed groups and larger chains all needed aid and sustenance. In his studies on the *maquis,* Kedward has pointed out that under-pinning the *maquis* was an 'outlaw society' of villages and communities which supported armed groups in the mountains and the woods.[6] The individual outlaw or the rebel group was only sustained by a larger counter-society of safe houses, couriers, suppliers and the rest, which existed within, but opposed to the regimes of the northern and southern zones. It was small and precarious in such a hostile atmosphere, but this was the home front created by the Resistance during the war and one whose worth is increasingly valued by historians.

In the larger society of France, women played major roles during the war and in the counter-society of the Resistance they occupied similarly crucial positions. What happened during the period of the occupation was that the Resistance slowly built up a home front of supply. intelligence, shelter and safety; in the apartments, houses, farms, and workplaces of supporters and sympathisers. Within this context the position of women was vital to the continuance of safe houses, supply and the rest. They also played a vital part in the liaison and communications between resisters, in servicing letter drops and maintaining contact within disparate locations. Furthermore, they were widely involved in the production and distribution of tracts and journals, hiding materials, and passing information.[7]

Until relatively recently historians have shown little interest in this 'home front of the counter-society'. Indeed the general approach to women's participation in the Resistance tended for a long time to relegate women to the fleeting footnote or cramped appendix. Even the pages devoted to undoubted 'heroines' of the Resistance, like Lucie Aubrac, Bertie Albrecht or Marie-Madeleine Fourcade, underlined the exceptional nature of women's participation in the Resistance, emphasising the fact that Resistance, like war, was, by definition, male. More recent historians, notably Paula Schwartz, have sought to extend the definition of Resistance, pointing out that the Resistance was 'a system of action supported by many', and that in this context women comprised 'the ground floor of the French underground'.[8] It is in this sense that one can realistically describe the support structure of the Resistance, largely female, as the home front of the resistance counter-society. Like all home fronts it needed to be mobilised in order to serve the cause. French women thus found themselves addressed by two competing sides, each regarding them as their own legitimate 'home front'. For the Vichy regime, the home front was of course perceived in the most traditional way, and as an integral part of paternalist rhetoric. Women were urged to procreate, stay in the home, bring up their children and tend their families; this was a message which was mediated through a series of restrictive legislative measures which both continued and extended the Third Republic's natalist obsessions.

One might have expected the opposing Resistance to have conveyed a rather different message, if only in order to point up the differences between the hated Vichy regime and the hoped-for Resistance-led future. The evidence produced up till now suggests that this is far from being the case. Marie-France Brive's study of the image of women in the clandestine press at the Liberation concluded that women's status and, for example, the question of votes for women, were accorded little attention by the Resistance press.[9] The appeal to the home front was, on the whole, couched in terms as traditional and paternalistic as those of the enemy, whether the Resistance appeal came from the Communist Left, the non-Communist left, the Gaullists or the right.

'L'Humanité' and the French Communist Party

In the early days of the occupation and defeat the role alotted women by the PCF (Parti Communiste Français) was very much in keeping with its Popular Front activities and the traditionally subordinate place they occupied in French Marxist thinking as members of an exploited working class rather than a group for themselves.[10] The first references to women in the Communist press during and after the defeat of France were the classic ones of women as suffering mothers. Even in the infamous 'Il faut mâter les bandits impérialistes' ['The imperialist bandits must be put down'] article of 15 May 1940, women were mentioned briefly as a backdrop; 'Tandis que des milliers de femmes de France attendent avec angoisse des nouvelles du fils ou du mari ...' ['Whilst thousands of French women wait anguishedly for news of sons or husbands'][11] This ritualisation of women as the symbol of a suffering French nation made a regular appearance in the Communist press throughout the war: at the time of the Service du Travail Obligatoire (STO) (Forced Labour) in early 1942, the occupation of the south and during the last winter of the war.[12] The only common feature of these articles was that the women in them generally suffered because their husbands were dead or imprisoned, their sons taken for forced labour or their children starving. They rarely suffered because they themselves were alone and hungry.

The second immediate theme of *L'Humanité* was to promote the kind of women's protest about food and fuel which had been common in the Popular Front and traditional in France since the time of the women's march to Versailles in 1789. It also involved the age-old image of women as guardians of the family and protectors of children. The paper noted a particularly vigorous action against the Vichy authorities in Marseilles in November 1940 by women demanding potatoes. It went on to analyse the action as: 'Les femmes du peuple son bien decidées à ne pas laisser affamer leur famille par les profiteurs de la guerre et de la défaite.' ['The women of the people are resolute in their refusal to let their families be starved to death by those who have profited from war and defeat.'][13]

A similar theme can be found in the article 'Femmes de France, Arrachez vos Enfants à la Mort' ['Women of France, snatch your children from the jaws of death']:

> Mères de famille angoisse qui voyez dépérir vos petits enfants, il faut sauver le fruit de vos entrailles. Il faut aller chercher ce qui leur manque là où les profiteurs de la misère se vautrent dans l'orgie. [Mothers, anguished as you are, you see your little ones wasting away. You must save the children of your womb. Go and find what they need where the profiteers of misery are wallowing in an orgy of eating.][14]

With so many of the male members of the Communist Party either jailed by Daladier, rounded up by the occupier, in prisoner-of-war camps or on the run, the party was obliged to rely more on its women supporters to provide a class-based response to the suffering of defeat. The party had taken up a predominantly internationalist, class-struggle rhetoric after its suppression in late 1939 and the women were a manifestation of that: not women with a particular role, but women as part of an oppressed class. The PCF does have some justification in claiming that it began to resist the occupier from a fairly early period in the war and some of the propaganda surrounding the early women's actions had a mixture of patriotic and class struggle themes. The phrase 'women of France' became far more common than the labels of class identification, but neither of these sobriquets mobilized women as a social group with their own set of grievances and potentialities. By 1941 the PCF had turned to predominantly Resistance themes – even before the German invasion of the Soviet Union – but women served typical Communist Party ends.

The idea of a 'presence on the streets' has always been the PCF's interpretation of class struggle or mass mobilization policies and in the strange half-life of 1940, when the clandestine party leadership in France thought it might exist legally again, women were urged onto the streets to provide that presence. These demonstrations at town halls and prefectures became a common element of PCF protest during the war, because although illegal they were less likely to draw reprisals from the authorities. But unlike the days of the Popular Front these actions could lead to death and imprisonment. Most of these demonstrations were organised with the secondary purpose of gathering recruits for the reformed women's committees in neighbourhoods and communities. The surprise in this respect was that many of the early women's committees were in German-occupied Paris where the conditions of occupation were difficult from the very beginning. Thus the clandestine PCF journal of the 20th arrondissement noted large demonstrations by its Women's Committee, which at the time seemed to represent the only organised Communist presence in the neighbourhood.[15] There were women's actions within the workplace, particularly when they were sacked under Vichy employment legislation, and they were occasionally encouraged through the citation of 'good examples' to protest in their factories,[16] but demonstrations for sustenance were more often seen as the normal activity of Communist women's groups.

The 'Edition Féminine' of *L'Humanité* (edited mainly by women during its wartime run) was obviously more concerned with women as a group than the regular numbers, and somewhat more expansive in its ambitions for women. By 1943, a special number of the 'Edition Féminine' followed other Party journals in devoting many valuable column inches to the Red Army's victories and especially to Russian women fighting in uniform. They were praised but never held up as a model for French women to follow, as if the latter were culturally unsuited to what the former were doing with such conspicuous bravery. At least the variety of the messages to women had moved on from the early days of defeat. The paper urged them to persuade their menfolk to join the Resistance, more or less on the theme of 'Women of France say "Go" ', but it also suggested practical action. The defence of the family had become 'protéger l'enfance; c'est préparer l'insurrection nationale' ['Protecting the children is preparing for the national insurrection']; they were encouraged to hide 'réfractaires', to aid resisters arrested by Vichy and the Gestapo, uncover traitors, feed the *Milice Patriotique* and stop food going to Germany. The paper declared that:

> Dans la France rénovée qui naîtra de la victoire, les femmes auront enfin droit de cité. Elles seront appelées à connaître des affaires de la nation et à donner leur avis. [In the renewed France which will come out of victory, women will at last become full citizens. They will be called to understand something of what is happening in the nation and give their opinions of it.]

> Françaises, nous sommes les filles d'un peuple qui fut au long des siècles prodigue en vaillance. Mais nous voulons être plus que les mères ou les épouses d'hommes libres et forts. [French women, we are the daughters of a people who were down the centuries lavish in valour. *We* want to be more than just the mothers or wives of strong free men.][17]

The 'Edition Féminine' also reported numerous women's demonstrations, against STO in Arras, Montluçon and Nantes, and demanding food, clothing and fuel in many parts of the country. This listing of actions was, and is, typical of Communist propaganda demonstrating that the Party is leading a huge tide of popular feeling, but it also demonstrated to even the most casual reader that women were vigorously active in the Resistance movement across the country. Whilst the special numbers for women clearly had great ambitions for them at the Liberation, they were infrequently expressed, whilst the listing of home front actions (often in, or for the family home) delimited a much smaller role for them in the Resistance.

Towards the period of the Liberation, as German round-ups and atrocities began to increase, the paper went further in its calls for women's resistance and towards the uncharted territory of armed action. There had already been examples of women taking armed action in the *Groupes Francs* of the M.U.R. [Mouvements Unis de la Résistance] (Aubrac and Baudouin for example), but it was a distinct change for a Communist publication to write:

Il s'agit donc de ne plus attendre que l'on vienne piller, brûler nos maisons, fusiller nos maris et nos fils, mais de comprendre qu'il faut apprendre à résister et nous le pouvons en contribuant au développement de la lutte armée et en participant nous-mêmes à cette lutte. [So we must stop waiting for them to come and pillage and burn our houses, and shoot our husbands and sons. We must realise that we have to learn to resist and we *can* do so by helping the armed struggle to develop and taking part in it ourselves.]

In practice this turned out to be somewhat limited:

Que peuvent faire les femmes pour contribuer à la lutte armée? Aider ceux qui se battent déjà; devenir marraines de guerre des vaillants FTPF [Franc-Tireurs et Partisans Français]. [What can women do to help the armed struggle? Help those already fighting – be *marraines* [godmothers] for the valiant FTPF.]

And somewhat reluctantly the paper noted that:

Les femmes doivent participer elles-mêmes à la Lutte armée et a son développement ... de toutes le femmes entraînées dans les actions préliminaries surgiront certainement des femmes courageuses physiquement et moralement fortes, capables de faire le coup de feu, qui constitueront des groupes de partisanes. [Women too must participate in the armed struggle and its development ... from all those women trained in the preparatory actions we will definitely find that physically courageous, morally strong women will emerge who are capable of shooting and who will form groups of women fighters.]

The rather under-whelming tribute to women who had died during the occupation saluted

Les femmes patriotes qui sont tombées dans la lutte, ou su résister à toutes les tortures et accepter la mort sans faiblir comme les plus grands de nos héros [by implication, men like Péri and Sampaix?] [Patriotic women who have fallen in the struggle or were able to resist every torture inflicted on them and accept death without flinching like our greatest heroes.][18]

The main theme of an article entitled 'L'Insurrection Nationale et les Femmes Françaises', in the 'Edition Féminine' for June 1944, was the need for women to join the *Milice Patriotique,* so that, in conjunction with the peasantry, they could organise the distribution of potatoes at the Liberation. The article did note that: 'Vous pouvez devenir, vous aussi, des soldats capables de se battre avec des armes contre l'envahisseur' ['You too can become soldiers, capable of fighting in the armed struggle against the invader'] and, in a rather back-handed compliment, they saw this as a graduation from the role of *marraines*:

Aujourd'hui nombreuses sont les femmes qui aident déjà les francs-tireurs et partisans français à mener à bien leur tâche de soldats. Dans les services auxiliaires, elles ont su mériter la confiance de leurs compagnons [the men of the *FTPF*].' [Today there are many women who already helping the French *francs tireurs* and fighters in their job as soldiers. In the auxiliary services, women have earned the confidence of their companions.][19]

Whilst this may suggest that the central organisation of the clandestine party through its main organ *L'Humanité* had graduated from lauding the feats of arms carried out by Soviet women, to encouraging armed resistance by French women, this was not quite the case. In the 14 July issue of the 'Edition Féminine', which was full of exhortations to direct action for the FTPF, women were told, rather vaguely, that 'La place de chaque femme communiste est au milieu des innombrables femmes dont elles partagent soucis et espoirs' ['The place of every Communist woman is among the countless other women whose fears and hopes they share'][20], whatever this meant. The French Communist Party displayed a nervously confused attitude to women towards the end of the war and the Resistance experience. They lauded the fighting prowess of Soviet women but were reluctant to suggest the same course of action for French women. When they did so, it was with a welter of special pleading and hedged round with qualifications, often to be later contradicted.

Other central organs of the PCF such as *L'Avant Garde* of the *Jeunesse Communiste*, which carried the masthead of a young man and young woman in equal prominence, tended to follow the exact *L'Humanité* line. Its concerns with women started with warnings not to join a Vichy association with a similar name to the Communist *Jeunes Filles de France* [21] and went on to call for them to demonstrate for food and to protest against wage cuts and lay offs.[22] Unfortunately, this was not as a class position, but because young women naturally want to create 'un foyer heureux'! Typical of the limited view of women's part in society were the various editions of *L'Avant Garde* for 14 July 1942. One urged mothers to parade with their children dressed in tricoleur colours,[23] another urged them to unite because of their generous dispositions, their love of life, of singing and dancing, and because the Germans thwarted their 'plus doux et chers projêts'. It ended with the stirring call;

Unissez-vous dans le Front Patriotique de la Jeunesse; n'acceptez pas la servitude et l'esclavage dans lesquels veulent vous plonger les boches et les traîtres, et bientôt vous pourriez chantez à pleins poumons. Vive la vie, vive la joie et l'amour. [Join together in the *Front Patriotique de la Jeunesse*, don't accept the slavery that the boches and the traitors are forcing on you. And then you will soon be able to sing at the top of your voices, "vive la vie, vive la joie et l'amour".][24]

The other number for July did not mention women at all.[25] By 1944, *L'Avant Garde* had reported the exploits of Soviet women soldiers several times and approvingly noted that young women in areas like the Dordogne had demanded guns as vociferously as the men. But there was never any call for female Communist youth to arm themselves as there were for the young men.

The *Jeunes Filles de France* section of the Communist youth movement, as seen through its paper, was even more restrained. This carried endless articles on how girls could help the men of the Resistance with food, clothes and shelter, but it never suggested a more active role. Even in 1944, while every journal and tract was debating the future, it rarely even hinted at the role women might expect to play in the political life of France after the Liberation.[26] Perhaps the limited ambitions of the female Communist youth movement can best be seen in the tract written by Communist women teachers at the Lycée de Jeunes Filles in Auxerre. Just after the Liberation of their town in September 1944, under the title 'Rôle des Jeunes Patriotes', they wrote:

> Toutes les jeunes Françaises ont leur place à la résurrection de notre pays. L'Union des Jeunes Filles Patriotiques a choisi pour elles les tâches les plus délicates: création des pouponnières, jardins d'enfants, aide aux veillards. [All young French women have their place in bringing the resurrection of our country. The *Union des Jeunes Filles Patriotiques* has chosen the most sensitive tasks: creating crèches, kindergartens, helping the old.][27]

This from an organisation, two of whose founding leadership in 1935 - Danielle Casanova and Marie-Claude Vaillant-Couturier - became heroines of the Communist Resistance for their activities and the sacrifice of their lives.

Though it was quite reasonable for the Communist Party's aid committees for prisoners' families to concentrate entirely on social welfare as a woman's role, (although the mothers of such families often took on many new tasks), most of the PCF's smaller or local groups who produced journals either ignored women or gave them an even more limited role than the national Communist press. *L'Enchaîné* of the PCF Nord/Pas de Calais Federations was typical of local Communist journals. In October 1940, their appeal to women was simply to join the Communist Party and 'struggle for milk, bread and work'.[28] In 1941 it encouraged the petitioning of mayors and the emulation of the Soviet Union, 'where no child goes hungry'.[29] Their special women's edition in 1943 was full of calls for women to defend their children and of salutes to the memory of Danielle Casanova and other heroines, but nothing on action outside traditional demonstrations, which had been shown to be very dangerous in this German-occupied and administered part of France.[30]

The Local Women's Committees

The two types of organisation that the PCF consistently urged its female supporters to join were the Women's Local Committees and the support groups for the FTPF, the *Marraines*. Here one might expect to find a more agressive and ambitious attitude to the work of women in the Resistance and beyond. The idea that women might be part of the fighting front was possible at this level, but the tracts and journals of these groups only reinforced the home front role of women. The tone was set by the national *Comité Féminin du Front National* in its tracts which constantly urged the familiar protests for food to save starving children, but nothing more.[31] In Marseilles, Villejuif and Tarbes, as in many other towns, the work of the committees was devoted to drawing up lists of demands, making small demonstrations, editing tracts and petitioning the mayors and prefects: the very stuff of 1930's left-wing politics.[32] Women in Montceau-les-Mines remembered Yvonne Emorine, the wife of a local Communist miners' leader who died in deportation, for her efforts in unifying the working women of the community, but the connection between her quite moderate activity and her death was not made.[33] Indeed the Parisian journal of the *Union des Femmes pour la Famille et la Libération de la France* asserted that the successful 14 July celebrations of 1943 proved that the faint-hearted could go onto the streets and take action without being arrested.[34]

In this, as in many other women's committee tracts and journals, there was a mixing of the martyrdom of the local activists with famous names in the movement, but more to celebrate the famous names rather than the local heroines. The 'normality' of Communist women's committee actions is remarkably consistent. The *Cri d'Alarme* of the *Union des Femmes Françaises* in Paris carried a long article on education in the spring of 1944, which was a somewhat irrelevant attack on the failures of Vichy. The citation of a good example of a women's protest against the inadequate school canteens of Vincennes hardly seems the sort of stirring example needed to rouse the female population in advance of the Liberation.[35] In this, as in other publications devoted to the activities of women, there seemed to be almost an under-playing of their role in the lead up to Liberation, as if they were being reduced to the most mundane domestic concerns of the home front, ready for a more subordinate position after the Liberation.

The organisations which brought women closest to the fighting front of the Resistance were the *Marraines* of the FTPF. The journals of the FTPF rarely mentioned women and then only to cast them in a sedentary role. Their most active task was to encourage their menfolk to join the fighting:

Les Femmes de Paris protestent énergiquement contre les mesures édictés par les négriers PETAIN, LAVAL ... elles viennent de conseiller a leur fils de s'enrôler dans les unités de Francs Tireurs et Partisans... Hourra pour les mamans de France. [The women of Paris protest vehemently against the edicts of the slave-drivers, Pétain and Laval... They have just advised their sons to enrol in FTP units... Well done the Mums of France!][36]

Their task was to sustain the men of the fighting Resistance, but this work was rarely described in the language of the fighting front. Typical of the way in which their work was characterised was an article in *Les Marraines*:

Françaises, nos soldats traqués par l'enemi manquent de tout; ils ont besoin de vêtments, de chaussures, de vivres. Ils ont besoin de sentir autour d'eux votre sollicitude et votre affection. [Women of France, our soldiers, hounded by the enemy, need clothes, shoes, food. They need to feel your concern and affection for them.]

Françaises, vous accomplirez votre devoir patriotique en devennant marraines de nos glorieux FTP... Vous acquitterex ainsi votre dette envers ceux qui souffrent et meurent pour la France. [Women of France, you will fulfill your patriotic duty by becoming *Marraines* for our glorious FTP... In this way you'll pay your debt towards those who are suffering and dying for France.][37]

The *Commune de Paris* group of the FTP *Marraines* in Paris with their revolutionary name was typical of many groups on a related theme. In February 1944 they called for 'intensification of action' as the Liberation approached, but this 'intensification' consisted of the familiar call for the support of resisters' wives and children, not direct action on the fighting front. Finally in 1944, some of the *Marraines* began to advise closer contact with the fighting front in May and June 1944. After a eulogy of Russian women fighters, *La Patriote*, the main journal of the national *Marraines* group, called on women: 'Femmes, engagez-vous dans les Partisans, comme agent de liaison et transmission, dans les groupes de combat, les services de renseignments, de propagande et sanitaire.' ['Women, join the Partisans, as liaison agents or couriers, in fighting groups, the intelligence service or propaganda and health services.'][38]

In July 1944 the *Marraines* in the Nord and Pas de Calais urged women to join the *Milice Patriotique*, because if they had committed themselves earlier, the massacre of Ascq might have been avoided: 'Il y a des choses que les femmes peuvent réaliser plus facilement que les hommes: désagrégation des forces policières pour les appeler à la fraternisation.' ['There are some things women can do more easily than men: breaking up the police force to get them to fraternise.'][39]

But the PCF was trying to expand the *Milice Patriotique* very rapidly at the moment of the Liberation and their policy for their new creation was that they should maintain order, round up traitors, distribute sustenance and give the PCF a presence at the local level in post-Liberation administration. The nearest the *Marraines* came to admitting the concept of armed women resisters was in Alsace Lorraine, where their exploits were seen as mirroring the patriotic efforts of Russian women.

> Déjà les femmes ont demandé à rejoindre les FTP pour combattre avec eux, ou pour servir dans leurs organisations auxiliaires. Les meilleures parmi les Marraines voudront avoir l'honneur d'être devenues des partisanes comme les femmes Russes qui luttant pour libérer leur pays. Allons chères amies, courage. Nous avons déjà fait beaucoup. Nous ferons plus. Renseignez-vous auprès de celles qui vous remettent le journal, sachez òu vous pourrez servir et engagez-vous pour que la France soit libre. [Women have already asked to join the FTP to fight with men or to serve in their auxiliary organisation. The best of the *Marraines* will want the honour of having been partisans like the women of Russia who are fighting to liberate their country. Come friends, Courage! We've done much already. We'll do more. Ask the women who give you this paper to let you know where you can serve and enrol to liberate France.][40]

Once again there was a grudging tone and only vague directives to action. The journal was responding to a growing demand, early in the year of Liberation (which was not to come until September/October for the region) by women who wanted to join the FTP and wanted to take direct action. But there was prevarication and generality, instead of calls to action. No women are recorded in the histories of the FTP and those who come close to it are still in their 'home front' homes, acting as safe houses or restaurants. Here, in an organisation where the roles of women might have most easily developed and ambitions for them expanded towards the time of Liberation and the new Republic, there seems to be the same strict delineation of the home and fighting front, with the women firmly restricted to the home front. Admiration of Russian women fighters was clearly no reason for the Resistance to expand their perceived role of women in the French struggle.

The Non-Communist Left

What is most noticeable about all the non-communist Resistance is that it generally ignored women and the roles that women might play in the fight against the Germans. It is not that they saw the development of a home front with women in their homes or their neighbourhoods leading non-violent protest, but that for a large percentage of their publication they simply omitted to mention women in their journals and tracts. *Le Populaire* included women in their descriptions of the havoc and suffering wrought by the Germans, but special numbers or substantial mentions of women were rare. In one such, *La Femme dans la Cité*, the Socialist paper recounted the history of women in France since the First World War, making the point that the war had brought women into the workplace and that this had continued into the 1930's. Vichy was sending them back 'behind their casseroles'. In the Second World War the same thing happened; men disappeared and the women took up their jobs only to suffer defeat, occupation and unemployment at the hands of the Germans. The Socialists declared that they would encourage women to 'come out into the real world',[41] but they made no firm proposals.

Although women – particularly Susanne Buisson – played a crucial part in the restoration of the SFIO (Section Française de l'Internationale Ouvrière) after its fission and collapse in 1940, they did not appear as a major concern of Socialist policy in 1944. Histories of the Socialist movement also note the activity of women in the rebuilding of the party at all levels, but there are few references to them in the literature of the movement and few mentions of their activity outside that of liaison work within the party.

On the left of the Resistance, even those with a class struggle policy, such as the extremist *L'Insurgé*, called on women to play very traditional roles:

> Menagères, mamans, vos maris, vos enfants ont faim. Suivez l'example de celles qui n'ont pas hésité à manifester devant les maries at les préfectures. Faites-le calmement avec un seul mot d'ordre du Pain... du Pain. ['Housewives and Mothers! Your husbands and children are starving. Follow the example of those women who have gone right out to demonstrate at town halls and prefectures. Do so calmly. Your one watchword should be Bread, Bread.][42]

The Trotskyite *La Verité* is typical of this strict adherence to the idea of women as part of the working class. The first two numbers in September and October 1940 called for the formation of housewives' committees, but the 'woman in the home' was roundly condemned in November. In later attacking the former CGT leader Rene Bélin for passing a decree against women's work, they declared: 'La verité c'est que Mr. Bélin, suivant les voeux des réactionnaires et des jésuites, veut réduire la femme au rôle d'esclave doméstique, de bonne a tout faire, dont le travail principal sera de faire la soupe...' ['The truth is that Mr Bélin, acceding to the wishes of reactionaries and jesuits, wants to reduce the role of women to that of a domestic slave, a maid of all work, confined to doing the cooking.'][43]

But this was not so much in order to liberate women from the home, rather it was to ensure that women took their place in the proletarian struggle which would begin in the factories after the Liberation. *La Verité* wanted women already in factories to slow down their work to fit the overall call for less work for the Germans; yet it recognised that many women were desperately in need of their salaries and suggested that they slow down their work in such a way as to avoid the sack. This was a step forward from food protesting, but calls for women's action on supplies continued in the Trotskyite press right through to the Liberation. In the February 1944 manifesto of the European Fourth International conference there was no place for women.[44]

The left-leaning southern Resistance group *Libération* included numerous small references to women's activities in their journal, but nearly always as illustrations of suffering or as records of social protest against Vichy and the German occupier. In its rare special articles for women the message was very much in favour of women taking their places exclusively on the home front. After the implementation of the forced labour decrees in the southern zone (16 February 1943) *Libération* was one of the southern journals which led the way in demanding civil disobedience, including human barriers on railway lines. But in its first real appeal to women in August 1943, they took a moderate line.

Appel aux Jeunes Filles et aux Jeunes Femmes
Depuis plus de trois mois chaque jour des jeunes gens son déportés en Allemagne. Tous ne peuvent se dérober, mais tous ceux qui en ont la possibilité, prennent le maquis. Bientôt jeunes Françaises vous resterez seules dans le villes avec les gens âgés, les malades. C'est pourquoi il faut montrer que vous êtes dignes de tous les absents, de tous les réfractaires. C'est pourquoi il vous faut prendre la place de vos fréres, de vos fiancés, de vos maris dans l'armée de la Résistance. [For three months now, young people are being deported to Germany each day. They can't all hide, but all those who can are joining the *maquis*. Soon, young women of France, you will be the only people left in the towns, alongside the old and sick. That is why you must show yourselves to be worthy of all those who have gone, the *réfractaires*. That's why you must take over the places of your brothers, fiancés and husbands in the army of the Resistance.][45]

But whilst this appears to be a call to arms, the article goes on to say that the job of women is to keep up morale among the affected communities, support the families of the absent, maintain supplies to the maquis and to the political prisoners: 'C'est vous surtout qui deviendrez l'âme de la Résistance.' ['You above all will be the soul of the Resistance.']

The Montbeliard version of *Libération* warned women to be careful 'in the home': 'en l'absence du mari, c'est elle qui va assurer la continuité du foyer, on sait le prix de quels sacrifices, de quelle magnifique abnégation.' ['with the husband gone, the woman will be carrying on the home. We know what magnificent self-sacrifices that will need.'][46] Once again the suffering woman, but this time at least suffering for herself rather than for the problems of her menfolk.

Even *Franc d'Abord*, a normally direct and hard-hitting paper, was not immune to mawkish sentimentality when dealing with the subject of women and the Resistance: 'Pour que tous ensemble, nous retrouvions la liberté d'aimer, de créer un foyer sans crainte et de chérir nos vieux parents dans la paix reconquise.' ['So that together we can all win back the freedom to love, set up a home without fear and look after our aged parents when peace is won.']⁴⁷

In its journal for women, *Femmes Françaises*, *France d'Abord* was just as predictable. They lauded the great heroines of the Resistance in a hagiographic way, and urged 'ordinary women', as their act of resistance, to create a climate of confidence, rather than defeatism, in the home. The idea that this creation of a home front mentality was secondary to other resistance is seen in their declaration: 'Que vos pères, vos maris, vos frères soient sûrs d'y trouver toujour une collaboratrice fidéle, une femme qui connait leurs besoins et ne s'en écarte pas.' ['Your fathers, husbands and brothers must be sure they can always find a faithful helpmate, a woman who knows their needs and doesn't run away.']⁴⁸

At the local level, women's committees with left leanings were no more ambitious than the national organisations and the non-feminist atmosphere of the times which hindered such ambition can be seen in the journal of *La Femme Comtoise*: 'Il faut que nos enfants deviennent des hommes (sic!) forts et instruits.' ['Our children must become strong, educated men (sic!).']⁴⁹

The Centrist and Conservative Resistance Groups and Women

The centrist but Gaullist organisation, *Combat,* was at the origin of the *Groupes Francs*, where women took part in the armed resistance and whose leader Frenay relied vitally on his woman assistant, Bertie Albrecht. But the movement's news-paper, frequently published and widely distributed, had very few references to women. Typical of these omissions were three from the central and regional press of the movement in 1943. Late in that year *Combat* ran a series of articles entitled 'Le Front Interieur', 'Sur le Front de la Résistance' and so on, but there was not a single mention of women in them. Even in those that specifically described the home front, the subject matter was sabotage, armed attack, the *maquis* and other direct action undertaken by the male military wing of the organisation; nothing on their women supporters. The supplements for Lyon and the Languedoc, however, both demanded that women collaborators should be denounced (by women) and executed: 'Il faut mettre un terme à ces "flirts nazis", et c'est aux filles indignes que nous nous en prendrons.' ['We must end these nazi flirts. It's the unworthy girls we shall be settling up with.']⁵⁰

These papers gave the names and addresses of women collaborators in long lists and exhorted women to take their scissors and cut off the collaborators' hair, a pastime which became very popular with men at the Liberation. This example of early denunciation campaigns seemed to imply that women were responsible for the 'horizontal collaboration' of their sisters and clearly expected that it was the Resistance women's responsibility to denounce and settle scores with women collaborators.

The Catholic Resistance movement was clear in its conservative view of the place of women in both the opposition to Germans and the future society of France. The Catholic student movement, which might have been expected to have the most liberal views amongst its co-religionists, was strongly in favour of large families, of women in the home and of less divorce in the new France. The main movement, *Témoignage Chrétien*, in its *Cahiers* and *Courriers* took much the same line. In attacking the Vichy law of 2 February 1944, which allowed for the requisitioning of female labour for work in Germany, they phrased their opposition in the following way: 'Notre Christianisme á toujours denoncé toutes formes d'ésclavage et proclamé la grandeur, la dignité, mais aussi la délicatesse de la vocation féminine... qui est incompatible avec ces mesures de guerre totale.' ['Our Christianity has always denounced all forms of slavery and proclaimed the greatness and dignity, but also the sensitivity of the female vocation... which is not compatible with these measures of total war.'][51]

In the next issue on 25 April, 1944, the paper quoted Mgr Saliège, the archbishop of Toulouse and a notable opponent of the Germans and the Vichy government. In a rejection of the occupiers' plans to round up women for work in the factories Saliège declared that liberal capitalism had turned women into workers, debasing and devaluing them: 'L'état a le devoir de maintenir, de favoriser, de défendre, comme le plus precieux des patrimoines, le sens chevaleresque du respect de la dignité de la jeune fille et de la femme.' ['The State has the duty to maintain, encourage and defend as one of its most precious heritages, the sense of chivalry and respect for young girls and women.'][52]

As might be expected, publications of the conservative groups tended to conceive of women's roles in the Resistance within very traditional frameworks. *La Voix du Nord* called upon women not to take up employment in factories, when most other journals had been decrying the lack of women's employment on the very sensible grounds that the Germans had ordered enterprises to employ women as a means of releasing men for work in Germany. The paper assumed that women were the natural guardians of the household and used this to ask: 'Femmes de France que pensez-vous mainenant de Vichy qui avait juré de sauvegarder la famille française et qui peu de temps après avoir enlevé les ouvriers songe déjà a vous arracher de vos voyers.' ['Women of France, what do you think now of Vichy? Vichy swore to safeuard and protect the French family. Now, but a short time after, taking the workers away, it's thinking of tearing you away from your homes.'][53]

Ceux de la Résistance started a rubric 'Sur le front intérieur' in its internal bulletin, but this concentrated exclusively on the fighting Resistance in France, did not mention the home front and thus ignored women entirely.[54] The *Cahiers de Défense de la France* ignored women in its wartime publications, but in its proposal for a post-war constitution it had a small article, number 188: 'A travail égal doît correspondre un salaire égal sans distinction de sexe où de nationalité.' ['For equal work there must be equal pay without any discrimination on the grounds of sex or nationality.'][55]

The Free French in London and then in Algiers produced a large number of journals, tracts and propaganda material. Most of them, particularly the poster and art work propaganda, portrayed a traditional home front and a traditional role for women in that home front. In *La France Interieur*, a bulletin specifically published to disseminate information about the domestic fighting Resistance and the home front in France, women were mentioned very little. In the March issue of 1944, under the rubric 'Idées' there was an article entitled 'L'Opinion d'une Femme de la Résistance'. This was mainly a very bathetic description of one woman's experience of the defeat and exodus of 1940, followed by a declaration that listening to the Free French broadcasts from London had inspired her, de Gaulle's message given her hope and, finally, the idea of resisting given life a meaning. The whole thing was a eulogy of de Gaulle and carried no information on the home front or this individual woman's role in it. So what appeared to be a genuine promotion of women's part in the Resistance turned out to be a laudatory self-congratulation by the editors of the *Bulletin Interieur*.[56]

The Role of Women in the Resistance Home Front and at the Liberation

The home front created by the Resistance to support the 'fighting front' of armed action, sabotage, espionage and propaganda, relied very greatly on the determination and sacrifice of women. Resistance ideas on their home front, however, were either full of traditional and stereotypical female roles, or tended to reinforce and sustain those roles. Some of the more extreme left-wing organisations saw women primarily as members of the working class, rather than housewives, but the generality of the left, including the Communist Party, emphasised their subordinate roles as providers of food and shelter. Recent literature dealing with the debate on the Manouchian Group has unwittingly produced evidence that this direct action unit was maintained and organised through a group of women liaison agents and messengers who were vital to its survival.[57] Yet the material of the clandestine French Communist Party hardly mentions this vital work and did nothing to encourage women to become involved with such units. Indeed, it would appear that the Resistance – Communist, left wing or other – was unified in seeing women's role as the guardian of the children and menfolk in the home. The main thrust of Resistance propaganda was that woman were most useful in the home, rather than outside its confines, apart from the occasional demonstration for food or against deportations. In one sense then, the Resistance narrowed the horizons of women, particularly those who had thought that the appearance of women ministers in the Popular Front government was more of a beginning than a token gesture.

This limitation of women's roles in the Resistance made the heroism of the few well-known female leaders or martyrs stand out in even sharper relief at the end of the war. Thus it was possible for historians to categorise them as heroines because they were exceptional and unique women within their gender. In fact the courage, mental and physical strength of a woman resister who hid escapees, radio sets or resisters for three or four years was probably equal to, if not greater, than one of the 'heroines'. But because the thousands of women who had opposed the occupier and Vichy were seen as having undertaken lesser actions, confined to the home *and* because heroines were unusual, it was easier to ignore the political, social, economic and personal needs of women at the Liberation. Noguérès has argued that there was an equality of effort by men and women in the Resistance, which made their contributions equal.[58] Plissonier, a loyal long-term Communist Party leader, made the same argument[59] and Houssin and Estrada went as far as to declare that in the literature of the Resistance: 'La première fois, la femme n'apparait ni comme un personnage sécondaire, ni comme un être inutile, mais comme une individualité ayant conquis son autonomie propre dans la société des hommes.' ['For the first time, women appear not as useless secondary characters, but as individuals who have achieved their own independence in men's society.'][60]

The facts of the Liberation tell a different story. There were no women Regional Commmissioners, no women prefects or sub-prefects and no women presidents of Departmental Liberation Committees or Local Liberation Committees. One or two were secretaries, or special delegates of these committees, with little influence or power. Of the 1653 members of Departmental Liberation Committees, Foulon notes only 125 women, half of whom were from the *Union des Femmes Française* and mainly sat on Communist-dominated committees.[61]

In a radio broadcast of the BBC's French service from London, Maurice Schumann – one of the its most well-known commentators – declared that 'La délivrance de la patrie entraînera l'émancipation de la française.' ['The deliverance of France will lead to the emancipation of French women.']62 But there was little recognition of this statement in later Free French and Provisional Government statements. The Communist Party also made several grandiose promises to women at the time of the Liberation, but in their programmes for a post-war France there was hardly a mention of women's issues and concerns. The Socialist Party had urged women to come out of their homes into the 'real world'(!) and had promised them 'egalité complète'; not just the vote, but 'droit à la culture, à l'indépendance, à la profession' and 'justice égale pour tous'.63 These were sweeping statements, but in their proposals for a new constitution and a new France, only the vote for women appeared as a firm item. This was supported by the Communists, Radicals and Christian Democrats. The latter even went so far as to support the Gouin 1943 proposal of a 'family vote' for the parents of large families.64 But there was no mention of women in the Liberation programmes and documents of the conservative groups or the Catholic movements. The women of France found themselves once again, in the hard winters of 1944-5 and 1945-6, asked to agitate for more food, defend their children and provide for the family. The continuity of limited perspectives, limited recognition and limited social and political action for women had been preserved from the 1930's through the war and into the Liberation. Breton has suggested that the Resistance was an important step in 'l'évolution de la condition féminine', which was not successfully completed 65 and Noguères has said:

> Toutes choses accomplies comme s'il allait de soi qu'elles le fussent, toutes tâches "accessoires" que les femmes de la Résistance, lorsqu'elles ont surveçu à l'épreuve, ont retournées (parfois sans les avoir jamais abandonnées) au lendemain d'une "libération" qui, s'il y avait eu une justice, aurait dû aussi être la leur. [Everything happened as if it was inevitable. "Secondary" tasks which the women of the Resistance – when they managed to survive – had put off (often without ever abandoning them) to the aftermath of a "Liberation" which, had there been any justice at all, should also have brought their own liberation.]66

But it was not their liberation.

NOTES

References to archival material at Anglis Polytechnic consist either of a number beginning with 'A' for paper documents, or a reel number for those in the collection *Périodiques Clandestins 1939-1945* (ACRPP) on microfilm.

1. Typical of many historians on the period is J. Williams, *The Ides of May: The Defeat of France, May-June 1940* (London, 1968), p. 93: 'Neither the military nor civil leaders were giving the country any moral preparation for the trials to come. Apart from the disappearance of most able-bodied males, civilian France retained an almost peace-time atmosphere in these waiting months.'
2. H. Michel, *La Drôle de Guerre* (Paris, 1971).
3. H. Shamir, 'The "drôle de guerre" and French Public Opinion', *Journal of Contemporary History*, 11 (1976) and S. Hoffman, 'Le désastre de 1940' in M. Agulhon and A. Nouschi (ed.), *La France de 1940 à nos Jours* (Paris, 1988).
4. F. Bedarida and Nemoz (ed.), *Témoignage Chrétien* (Paris, 1980).
5. C. Bourdet, *L'Aventure Incertaine* (Paris, 1986).
6. R. Kedward, 'The Maquis and the Culture of the Outlaw' in R. Kedward and R. Austin (ed.), *Vichy France and the Resistance* (London, 1985), pp. 232-52.
7. Margaret Rossiter has detailed the immense effort of women in Resistance organisations, particularly in escape chains, where she notes that 40% of the *reseaux* were led by women: *Women in the Resistance* (New York, 1986) and 'Le role des femmes dans la Resistance en France', *Guerres Mondiales et Conflits Contemporaines*, 155 (July 1990).
8. P. Schwartz, 'Redefining Resistance: Women's Activism in Wartime France' in J.R. Higonnet and J. Jenson (ed.), *Behind the Lines: Gender and the Two World Wars* (Yale, 1987), pp. 141-53.
9. M-F. Brive, 'L'Image des femmes à la Libération' in *La Libération dans le Midi de la France* (Toulouse, 1986), pp. 387-98.
10. F. Delpha, 'Les Communistes Français et la sexualité 1932-1938', *Le Movement Sociale*, 91 (1975); J. Kergoat, *La France du Front Populaire* (Paris, 1986). See especially propaganda from the newly-founded *Union des Jeunes Femmes Françaises* in 1935 and the PCF Congress of Villurbanne (1936) for the scope and the limitations of the policy and cf. R. Rousseau, *Les Femmes Rouges: Chronique des Années Vermeersh* (Paris, 1983).
11. *L'Humanité Clandestine*, 15 May 1940, reel 18.
12. See for example, *L'Humanité*, March 1943 and March 1944.

13. Ibid., 25 November 1940, For a typical 1789 reference see *L'Appel des Femmes*, Comité Féminin de Toulouse, September 1943, A.1184.
14. *L'Humanité*, 'Péri-Sampaix Special', January 1942, A.0775.
15. *L'Eveil de XXème* (PCF 20th Arrondissement), 27 December 1944. See also, *Le Prolétaire Drancienne*, 16 September 1940, A.1719 and *L'Humanité*, 9 March 1942, A.0773.
16. *L'Humanité* (ed. féminine), special number for 1943, A.1224.
17. Ibid., March 1943, A.1225.
18. Ibid., May, 1944, A.1228.
19. Ibid., June 1944, A.1229.
20. Ibid., July 1944, A.1230.
21. *L'Avant Garde* (Zone Sud), October 1940, reel 1.
22. Ibid., November 1940 and February/March 1941.
23. Ibid., (Zone Nord), 14 July 1942.
24. Ibid., (Zone Nord), July 1942.
25. Ibid., (Zone Sud), July 1942.
26. *Jeunes Filles de France* (special number), March 1941, A.1252.
27. *L'Espoir* (FUJP) Lycée des Jeunes Filles, Auxerre, A.1258.
28. *L'Enchainé*, October 1940, A.1073.
29. Ibid., 23 February 1941, A.1079.
30. Ibid., September 1943, A.1089.
31. For example the *Comité Feminin du Front National* (nd) 1941, reel 16.
32. *Le Comité Populaire des Femmes de Marseilles*, 1941, A.0306; *La Managère de Villejuif*, no.1, February 1943, A.1275 and *L'Echo des Femmes*, Tarbes, 1 July 1944, reel 16.
33. *Les Comités Féminins de Montceau-les-Mines*, March 1942, A.0305.
34. *Parisienne Patriote*, September 1943, A.1301.
35. *Cri d'Alarme*, no.3, March 1944, A.1055.
36. *Francs-Tireur Parisien*, 10 June 1943, A.1178.
37. *Les Marraines* (Femmes Patriotes du Nord et du Pas de Calais), May 1944, A.1270.
38. *La Patriote* (Organe des Femmes dans la Lutte Armée), [1944], A.1289.
39. *Les Louises de Bettigrues* (Femmes Partisans du Nord et du Pas de Calais), July 1944, A.1269.
40. *Jeanne de Lorraine* (Marraines des Groupes FTP 'La Lorraine'), January 1944, A.1191.
41. *Le Populaire* (Zone Sud), October 1943, reel 11.
42. *L'Insurgé*, no.17, 2ème Année.

43. *La Verité* (facsimile), (études: documentations internationales, Paris, 1978).
44. Ibid., no.69, 15 July 1944.
45. *Libération*, August 1943, reel 10.
46. Ibid., (Montbeilard), 20 August 1944, cited in F. Marcot, *Les Voix de la Résistance* (Besançon, 1989).
47. *France d'Abord*, January 1942, reel 9.
48. *Femmes Françaises* (edité per *France d'Abord*), January 1944, A.0708.
49. *La Femme Comtoise*, August 1943, A.1179.
50. *Combat*, Supplement Lyonnais, June 1943, A.0688; see also reel 7.
51. *Témoignage Chrétien*, no.10 in Bedarida and Nemoz (eds.) (above, note 4); see also R. and F. Bedarida, *Témoignage Chrétien, 1941-1944, Les Armes de L'Esprit* (Paris, 1977).
52. *Témoignage Chrétien*, no.10 in Bedarida and Nemoz (ed.) (above, note 4).
53. *La Voix de Nord*, 15 November 1942, A.1002.
54. *Ceux de la Résistance* (Bulletin Interieure), 20 May 1944, reel 6.
55. *Cahiers de Défence de la France* 'la Cité Libre', 1944, reel 6.
56. *La France Interieur*, 15 March 1944, reel 1.
57. S. Courtois *et al.*, *Le Sang de l'Etranger* (Paris, 1989) and also C. Ouzoulias-Romagon, *J'Etais Agent de Liaison FTPF* (Paris, 1986).
58. H. Noguères, 'Egalité de participation des femmes et des hommes dans le Résistance' in *Les Femmes dans la Résistance* (Paris, 1977).
59. G. Plissonier 'Portée et caracteristique de la participation des femmes Communistes à la Résistance en Zone Sud' in ibid.
60. M. Houssain and J.T. Estada, 'Image(s) de femmes dans la litterature crée pendant la Résistance de 1940 à 1945' in ibid.
61. C. Foulon, *Le pouvoir en province à la Libération* (Paris, 1975).
62. M. Schumann, cited in Noguères (above, note 58) and also *Ici Londres* (Paris, 1982).
63. *Le Populaire* (Zone Sud), 1943, reel 11. See also D. Mayer, *Les Socialistes dans la Résistance* (Paris, 1968) and Leon Blum's letter to Gouin (15 March 1943) in ibid., p. 211.
64. *Témoignage Chrétien* (above, note 4); see also Gouin's report to the Consultative Assembly in H. Michel and B. Mirkine-Guezevitch, *Les idées politiques et sociales de la Résistance* (Paris, 1954).
65. D. Breton, 'La Résistance, étape importante dans l'évolution de la condition féminine' in *Les Femmes dans la Résistance* (above, note 58).
66. H. Noguères, *Le Vie quotidienne de Résistants de L'Armistice à la Libération*, (Paris, 1984), p.148.

Further Reading

General

C. Emsley *et.al., World War II and its Consequences.* Book IV of *War, Peace and Social Change: Europe 1900-1955* (Buckingham, 1990).

P. Fussell, *Wartime. Understanding and Behaviour in the Second World War* (Oxford, 1989).

M. Howard, 'Total War in the Twentieth Century: Participation and Consensus in the Second World War' in B. Bond and I. Roy (eds), *War and Society. A Yearbook of Military History* (London, 1976).

A. Marwick, *War and Social Change in the Twentieth Century* (London, 1974).

A. Marwick (ed.), *Total War and Social Change* (London, 1988).

A. Milward, *War, Economy and Society, 1939-1945* (London, 1977).

N. Rich, *Hitler's War Aims. The Establishment of the New Order* (London, 1974).

A. Toynbee and V. Toynbee, *Hitler's Europe* (Survey of International Affairs, London, 1954).

G. Wright, *The Ordeal of Total War* (New York, 1968).

Britain

P. Addison, *The Road to 1945: British Politics and the Second World War* (London, 1975).

A. Calder, *The People's War: Britain 1939-1945* (London, 1971).

A. Calder and D. Sheridan, *Speak for Yourself: A Mass-Observation Anthology 1937-1949* (London, 1984).

T. Harrison, *Living through the Blitz* (London, 1976).

I. McLaine, *Ministry of Morale: Home Front Morale and the Ministry of Information in World War II* (London, 1979).

A. Marwick, *Britain in the Century of Total War* (London, 1968)

T.H. O'Brien, *Civil Defence* (London, 1955).

H. Pelling, *Britain and the Second World War* (London, 1970).

H.L. Smith (ed.), *War and Social Change: British Society in the Second World War* (Manchester, 1986).

R. Titmuss, *Problems of Social Policy* (London, 1950).

Germany

J.W. Baird, *The Mythical World of Nazi War Propaganda 1939-1945* (Minneapolis, 1974).

M. Balfour, *Propaganda in War 1939-1945. Organisations, Policies and Publics in Britain and Germany* (London, 1979).

E.R. Beck, *Under the Bombs. The German Home Front 1942-1945* (Lexington, 1986)

C. Bielenberg, *The Past is Myself* (London, 1968).

L. Burchardt, 'The Impact of the War Economy on the Civilian Population of Germany during the First and Second World Wars' in W. Deist (ed.), *The German Military in the Age of Total War* (Leamington Spa, 1985).

R. Grunberger, *A Social History of the Third Reich* (London, 1971).

E.L. Homze, *Foreign Labour in Nazi Germany* (Princeton, 1967).

I. Kershaw, *Popular Opinion and Political Dissent in the Third Reich* (Oxford ,1983).
   The Hitler Myth. Image and Reality in the Third Reich (Oxford, 1987).

B.R. Kroener, 'Squaring the Circle. Blitzkrieg Strategy and Manpower Shortage, 1939-1942' in W. Deist (ed.), *The German Military in the Age of Total War* (Leamington Spa, 1985).

A. Milward, *The German War Economy* (Oxford, 1965).

R. Overy, 'Mobilisation for Total War in Germany, 1939-41' *English Historical Review*, 103 (1988).

M. Roseman, 'World War II and Social Change in Germany' in A. Marwick (ed.), *Total War and Social Change* (London, 1988).

L. Rupp, *Mobilizing Women for War. German and American Propaganda 1939-1945* (Princeton, 1978).

S. Salter, 'Structures of Consensus and Coercion: Workers' Morale and the Maintenance of Work Discipline, 1939-1945' in D. Welch (ed.), *Nazi Propaganda. The Power and the Limitations* (London, 1983).

M. Steinert, *Hitler's War and the Germans* (Athens, Ohio, 1977).

The Soviet Union

J. Barber and M. Harrison, *The Soviet Home Front, 1941-1945: A Social and Economic History of the USSR in World War II* (London, 1991).

S. Bialer, *Stalin and His Generals: Soviet Military Memoirs of World War II* (London, 1970).

Further Reading

197

R. Bidlack, *Workers at War: Factory Workers and Labor Policy in the Siege of Leningrad* (The Carl Beck Papers in Russian and East European Studies No. 902, University of Pittsburgh, 1991).

A. Dallin, *German Rule in Russia, 1941-1945: A Study of Occupation Policies* (London, 1957).

R.W. Davies, *Soviet History in the Gorbachev Revolution* (London, 1989).

K.S. Karol, *Solik: Life in the Soviet Union, 1939-1946* (London, 1986).

S.J. Linz (ed.), *The Impact of World War II on the Soviet Union* (Totowa, N.J, 1985).

W. Moskoff, *The Bread of Affliction: The Food Supply in the USSR During World War II* (Cambridge, 1990).

H.E. Salisbury, *The 900 Days: The Siege of Leningrad* (London, 1971).

N.A. Voznesensky, *War Economy of the USSR in the Period of the Patriotic War* (Moscow, 1948).

A. Werth, *Russia at War* (London, 1964).

The United States

J.M. Blum, *V was Victory: Politics and American Culture During World War II* (Englewood Cliffs, N. J, 1968).

D. Campbell, *Women at War with America: Private Lives in a Patriotic Era* (Cambridge, Mass. & London, 1984).

A. Clive, *State of War: Michigan in Wartime* (Ann Arbor, 1979).

S.B. Gluck, *Rosie the Riveter: Women, The War, and Social Change* (New York, 1987).

P. Irons, *Justice at War: The Story of the Japanese Internment Cases* (New York, 1982).

N. Lichtenstein, *Labor's War at Home: The CIO in World War II* (Cambridge & New York, 1982).

R. Polenberg, *War and Society: The United States 1941-1945* (New York, 1972).

L. Rupp, *Mobilizing Women for War. German and American Propaganda 1939-1945* (Princeton, 1978).

S. Terkel, *"The Good War": An Oral History of World War II* (London, 1985).

N.A, Wynn, *The Afro-American and the Second World War* (New York & London, 1976).

Japan

J.B. Cohen, *Japan's Economy in War and Reconstruction* (Minneapolis, 1949).

A. Coox, *Japan: The Final Agony* (New York, 1970).
    Chapter in P. Duus (ed), *The Cambridge History of Japan*, vol. 6, *The Twentieth Century*, (Cambridge, 1989).

G. Daniels, 'The Great Tokyo Air Raid, 9-10 March 1945' in W.G. Beasley, (ed.), *Modern Japan* (London, 1975).

R. Guillain, *Le peuple Japonais et la Geurre* (Paris, 1947).

T.R.H. Havens, *Valley of Darkness: The Japanese People and World War II* (New York, 1978).

T. Iritani, *Group Psychology of the Japanese in Wartime* (London, 1989).

T. Marks, 'Life in Wartime Japan' in I.H. Nish (ed), *Japan and the Second World War* (ST/ICERD Pamphlet, IS/89/1970, 1989),
    'Children's Life in Wartime Japan' in *Proceedings of the Japan Society* [of London], 112 (1989).

I. Nish, 'The Greater East Asian Co-Prosperity Sphere' in K. Neilson and R.Prete (eds), *Coalition Warfare: An Uneasy Accord* (Montreal, 1983).
    'Japan and the Outbreak of War in 1941' in A. Sked and C. Cook (eds), *Crisis and Controversy. Essays in Honour of A.J.P. Taylor* (London, 1976).

I. Saburo, *The Pacific War* (Oxford, 1978).

B-A. Shillony, *Politics and Culture in Wartime Japan* (Oxford, 1981).

T. Shunsuke, *An Intellectual History of Wartime Japan* (London, 1989).

R.L. Sims, 'National Elections and Electioneering in Akita, 1930-42', in W.G. Beasley (ed.), *Modern Japan* (London, 1975).

D. Storry, *Second Country* (Norbury, 1986).

Italy

D. Ellwood, *Italy 1943-1945* (Leicester, 1985).

P. Ginsborg, *A History of Contemporary Italy* (Harmondsworth, 1990).

S. Hood, *Carlino* (Manchester, 1985).

M. Knox, *Mussolini Unleashed 1939-1941: Politics and Strategy in Fascist Italy's Last War* (Cambridge, 1985).

M. Michaelis, *Mussolini and the Jews: German Italian Relations and the Jewish Question in Italy 1922-1945* (Oxford, 1978).

E. Newby, *Love and War in the Appennines* (London, 1971).

J. Steinberg, *All or Nothing: The Axis and the Holocaust* (London, 1990).

The Netherlands

J.C.H. Blom, 'The Second World War and Dutch Society: Continuity and Change', in A.C. Duke and C.A. Tamse (eds), *Britain and the Netherlands*, vol. VI *War and Society* (The Hague, 1977).

E. Groenevelt, 'Dutch Historiography and the Second World War, 1945-75' in *La Seconda Guerra Mondiale Nella Prospettiva Storica a Trent Anni Dall' Epilogo* (Como, 1977).

G. Hirschfeld, *Nazi Rule and Dutch Collaboration: The Netherlands under German Occupation 1940-1945* (Oxford, 1988).

W. Warmbrunn, *The Dutch under German Occupation* (Stanford, 1963).

Poland

N. Davies, *God's Playground: A History of Poland.* Vol. 2, *1785 to the Present* (London, 1982).

J. Garlinski, "The Polish Underground State" *Journal of Contemporary History*, 10 (1975).

The German New Order in Poland (London, n.d.).

J.T. Gross, *Polish Society under German Occupation* (Princeton, 1979).

J. Hanson, *The Civilian Population and the Warsaw Uprising of 1944* (London, 1982).

J.Karski, *Story of a Secret State* (Boston, 1944).

S. Korbonski, *Fighting Warsaw: The Story of the Polish Underground State 1939-1945* (New York, 1968).

R.C. Lukas, *The Forgotten Holocaust. The Poles under German Occupation* (Lexington, 1986).

France

D. Breton, 'La Résistance, étape importante dans l'évolution de la condition féminine' in *Les Femmes dans la Résistance* (Colloque UFF, Paris, 1977).

M-F. Brive, 'L'image des femmes à la Libération' in *La Libération dans le Midi de la France* (Toulouse, 1986).

M. Houssain and J.T. Estada, 'Image(s) de femmes dans la littérature créé pendant la Résistance de 1940 à 1945' in *Les Femmes dans la Résistance* (Colloque UFF, Paris, 1977).

R. Kedward, 'The Maquis and the Culture of the Outlaw' in R. Kedward and R. Austin (eds), *Vichy France and the Resistance* (London, 1985).

H. Noguères, 'Egalité de participation des femmes et des hommes dans la Résistance' in *Les Femmes dans la Résistance* (Colloque UFF, Paris, 1977).

R. Paxton, *Vichy France* (New York, 1972)

G. Plissonier, 'Portée et characteristique de la participation des femmes Communistes à la Résistance en Zone Sud' in *Les Femmes dans la Résistance* (Colloque UFF, Paris, 1977).

M. Rossiter, *Women in the Resistance* (New York, 1986)

P. Schwartz, 'Redefining Resistance: Women's Activism in Wartime France', in M.R. Higgonet and J. Jenson (eds), *Behind the Lines: Gender and the Two World Wars* (New Haven, 1987).

D. Veillon, 'Régister au feminin', *Pénélope*, no. 12 (Spring 1985).